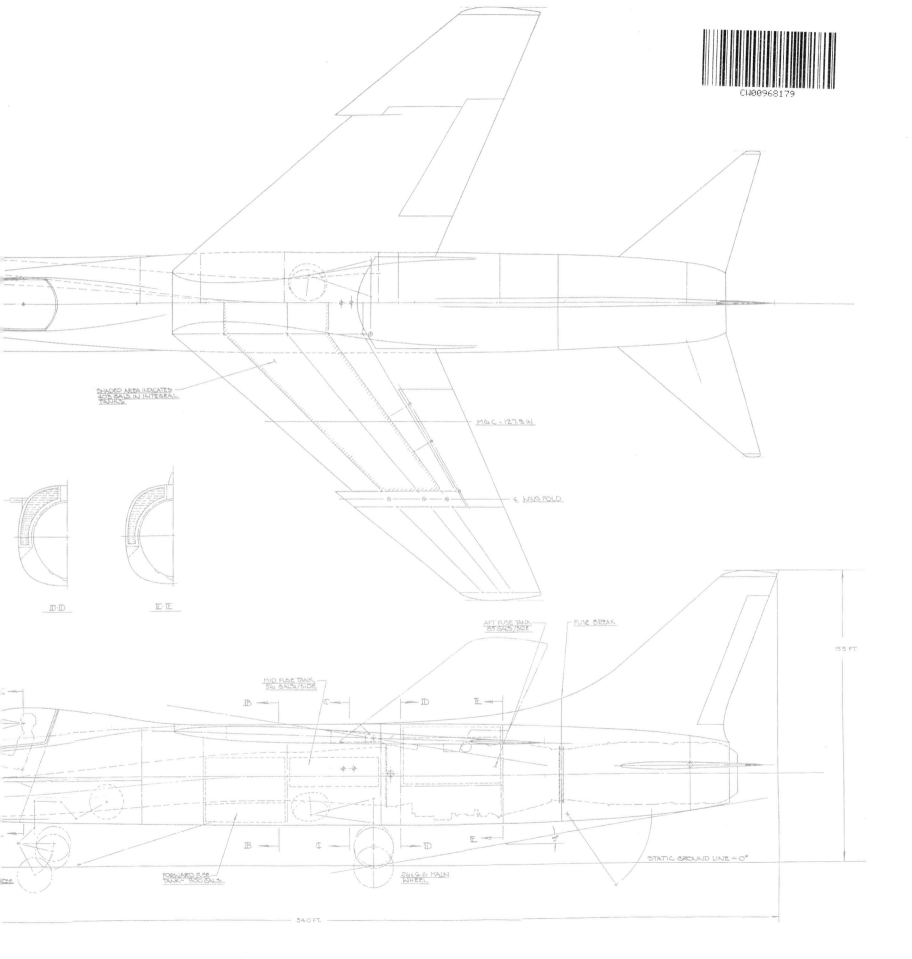

SHADED AREA INDICATES
403 GALS IN INTEGRAL
TANKS

MGC – 127.3 IN

℄ WING FOLD

D·D   E·E

AFT FUSE TANK
35 GALS/SIDE   FUSE BREAK

155 FT

MID FUSE TANK
56 GALS/SIDE

B   C   D   E

B   C   D   E   9°

STATIC GROUND LINE ~ 0°

FORWARD FUSE
TANK ~ 900 GALS.   29 x 6.6 MAIN
WHEEL

34.0 FT

specialtypress

Vought F-8 Crusader

William D. Spidle

Development of the Navy's First Supersonic Jet Fighter

Specialty Press

Specialty Press
838 Lake Street South
Forest Lake, MN 55025
Phone: 651-277-1400 or 800-895-4585
Fax: 651-277-1203
www.specialtypress.com

Edit by Mike Machat
Layout by Monica Seiberlich

ISBN 978-1-58007-242-7
Item No. SP242

Library of Congress Cataloging-in-Publication Data
Names: Spidle, Bill, author.
Title: Vought F-8 Crusader : development of the Navy's first supersonic jet fighter / Bill Spidle.
Description: Forest Lake, MN : Specialty Press, [2017] | Includes bibliographical references and index.
Identifiers: LCCN 2017003284 | ISBN 9781580072427
Subjects: LCSH: Crusader (Jet fighter plane)–History. | Crusader (Jet fighter plane)–Design and construction.
Classification: LCC UG1242.F5 S645 2017 | DDC 623.74/644–dc23
LC record available at https://lccn.loc.gov/2017003284

Written, edited, and designed in the U.S.A.
Printed in China
10 9 8 7 6 5 4 3 2 1

Front Cover: *When Marine aviator John Glenn made the first supersonic U.S. coast-to-coast flight in July 1957, he flew an F8U-1P photo-recon version of the Crusader, seen here on approach to a carrier.*

Front Flap: *This view of the larger radome on the F8U-2NE with its gaping chin-mounted air intake shows why the Crusader was nicknamed "Gator" by its pilots.*

Front End Paper: *Tech art from December 1952 shows a general arrangement drawing of the V-380 concept with a Pratt & Whitney J57 engine and two-position wing.*

Title Page: *Navy Commander Duke Windsor posing on the steps of a factory-fresh Crusader parked on the Oklahoma City ramp during the 1956 National Air Show.*

Table of Contents Page: *Vought's stunning F8U-2NE demonstrator (147036) was the second F8U-2N airframe modified to serve in the "2NE" flight test program.*

Rear End Paper: *A three-view drawing from Vought's technical illustration group shows a proposal for the V-456 Attack Variant of the F8U-2N Crusader.*

Rear Flap: *Author Bill Spidle hails from Frisco, Texas, and has served in the commercial aviation industry and on museum staffs as an A&P mechanic and manager.*

Back Cover Photos

Top: *Shown here painted in its distinctive flight test color scheme, the F8U-1P aerodynamic demonstrator (141363) was eventually delivered to the fleet.*

Bottom: *During NATC operations the unique two-seat F8U-1T is shown spotting on the starboard bow catapult of the aircraft carrier USS* Independence *(CVA-62).*

DISTRIBUTION BY:

UK and Europe
Crécy Publishing Ltd
1a Ringway Trading Estate
Shadowmoss Road
Manchester M22 5LH England
Phone: 44 161 499 0024
Fax : 44 161 499 0298
www.crecy.co.uk
enquiries@crecy.co.uk

Canada
Login Canada
300 Saulteaux Crescent
Winnipeg, MB, R3J-3T2 Canada
Phone: 800 665 1148
Fax: 800 665 0103
www.lb.ca

TABLE OF CONTENTS

ACKNOWLEDGMENTS

I have a small list of thanks and will get on with the writing. I thank Specialty Press for taking a chance on an unknown writer. Acquisitions Editor Mike Machat, for putting up with my questions and schedule bumps; I hope the final effort is worth your patience. Thank you to my friend Tommy Thomason, an expert on naval aviation. I thank Dick Atkins and all the people at the Vought Aircraft Heritage Foundation (VAHF) for opening their arms and files to me. Unless otherwise noted, all photos are from the VAHF or the authors collection. I am truly blessed by knowing all the retirees and being able to help them with their aircraft restoration projects. I also wish to honor all those who have developed, built, flown, and maintained the F8U Crusader. I need to take a moment also to honor the memories of all those who died in all aspects of F8U operations.

Thanks to my wife and daughters, Lorene, Holly, and Cara, for putting up with my airplane obsession. Their love and support is essential in a project of this magnitude. And finally, a special shout out to Craig Wall. The name might not be familiar, but if you follow F8Us his work certainly should be. Craig was a major driver behind getting 1X restored at the Seattle Museum of Flight. That historic aircraft has recently graced the cover of many aviation magazines showing off her freshly restored look. Thank you, Craig!

— Bill Spidle

Brilliant in bare metal, an early-model FBU-1 takes off into a cloud-filled Texas sky, wheels coming into the wells.

PREFACE

The rumble of four Pratt & Whitney R-4360 radial engines disturbed the late-morning quiet at Hensley Field, Texas. It was 11:25 am on 3 March 1955 and the first XF8U-1 Crusader was, in a manner of speaking, airborne at last. While it may have been just another routine flight for a workhorse of the Cold War, the Douglas C-124C Globemaster II, to the employees of Chance Vought Aircraft (CVA) Corporation this flight was very different. The future of the company hinged on what was contained in the cargo hold of that trusty Douglas transport. As the Globemaster roared past the Chance Vought factory in Grand Prairie, Texas, new F7U-3 Cutlasses were on the flight line, while the F7U-3P and -3M were yet to roll off of the production line. The last of the famed F4U Corsair line, an F4U-7, had been delivered just one month prior.

The F4U had been surpassed by jet-powered airplanes in the fighter role. During the Korean War, Corsairs were slugging it out in strike and close-air support roles. F7U-3 Cutlass aircraft were stored around the facility awaiting engines. Sixteen Regulus I missiles rolled off the line in 1953, and Regulus production lasted another five years, with a total of 514 being built. The supersonic Regulus II was still three years away from first flight and not generating any significant factory work yet.

"Beginning in 1950, when the F7U-3 airplane was being put together on paper after the F7U-2 project was cancelled, we have had a hard time keeping the F7U-3 configuration firm. At that time we had virtually no prospective business and we were in a mood to try anything the Navy suggested with the Cutlass in order to sell it. We accepted pretty severe requirements for the airplane along with a very difficult production schedule. We tried to swallow our own design troubles without letting them affect the schedule," wrote Fredrick Detweiler, Chairman of United Aircraft Corporation, in a 19 March 1953 letter to the Leadership Team at the Chance Vought Division of United Aircraft.[1]

Chance Vought needed new business as the F7U-3 production was winding down and was going to suffer another setback in January 1954 with another order cancellation due to slow delivery of Westinghouse J46 engines. This book is the compelling story of how Chance Vought Aircraft fought back from the brink of disaster and created one of the most successful jet fighters in the history of naval aviation.

Rows of F7U-3 aircraft waiting for engines to be delivered for the empty engine bays.

Publisher's Note: In reporting history, the images required to tell the tale will vary greatly in quality, especially by modern photographic standards. While some images in this volume are not up to those digital standards, we have included them, as we feel they are an important element in telling the story.

INTRODUCTION

Welcome to the development world of the Chance Vought Aircraft (CVA) Navy Day Fighter, the F8U Crusader. In writing this book, I am not presenting a rehash of the F-8's combat or service history, nor will I extensively cover the loss of the F8U-3 contract or other naval aviation developments outside of the F8U, as Tommy Thomason has written extensively on these subjects. I suggest you locate his other extensive and outstanding works by Specialty Press. My goal is to share insights into what it took to get the airplane from its BuAer Operational Specification into an operational weapon system. I had the great fortune of having access to the archives of the Vought Aircraft Historical Foundation for several years. This collection existed due to the "rat packing" of a number of individuals including Dick Atkins and Jesse Santamaria.

These records offered a substantial view into the decision making and process that CVA used to develop the Crusader. Through Dick Atkins' and VAHF's vision these records have been saved at the University of Texas at Dallas (UTD), Eugene McDermott Library in the History of Aviation Collection. Bobbye Jo Crouch was hired by the foundation to curate the VAHF materials into the UTD History of Aviation Collection. She did an outstanding job of getting as much of this rich material into the collection as possible without duplication. Thank you, Bobbye Jo! If you find yourself in the Richardson, Texas, area, drop by UTD and visit Paul Oelknug and Patrizia Nava at the History of Aviation Collection.

Chapter 1

WINS, BUT LOSSES

A factory-fresh F8U-1 sits on the Vought ramp as AU-1 129379 assigned to MCAS Quantico taxis for takeoff at NAS Dallas.

The Chance Vought Division of United Aircraft Corporation had long been known for creating innovative high-performance designs that were truly cutting edge. From the experimental flying saucer–like V-173 and XF5U-1 "Flying Flapjack" to the classic and legendary F4U Corsair series, Vought aircraft was known for being both distinctive and operationally effective. Although the company's first turbojet-powered airplanes, the F6U Pirate and F7U Cutlass, were not considered stellar successes, they kept Vought in the aircraft manufacturing game well into the beginning of the Jet Age.

F4U Corsair

In 1935 the first drawings for the V-166 (Vought's in-house numbering system) were being developed. The V-166 evolved into the XF4U-1 Corsair. An example of Vought's innovation was the F4U Corsair, the first American fighter to top 400 mph in level flight taking advantage of the 18-cylinder 2,000-hp Pratt & Whitney R-2800 Double Wasp radial engine spinning a large 13-foot 4-inch propeller. The F4U gave the Navy a fighter that met or exceeded the performance of contemporary land-based fighters even with the penalty of the structure and equipment necessary for aircraft carrier operation.

During World War II the F4U Corsair evolved into a fighter bomber, at first with primitive field-produced bomb suspension pylons that led to later factory-produced rocket rails and multiple bomb pylons. This versatility and heavy-load-carrying capability proved to be important in keeping the F4U in service longer than her World War II contemporaries. The AU-1, a ground attack specific variant, continued in service until 1957 with the U.S. Navy/Marine Corps and September 1964 with the French Navy. The final F4U Corsair combat action came in 1969 during the "Football War" between El Salvador and Honduras. From 1940 until 1953 a total of 12,571 Corsairs were produced by Chance Vought with wartime production supplemented by Goodyear and Brewster Aircraft Companies.

TBU Sea Wolf

Another forgotten stablemate of the F4U was the TBU Sea Wolf. The TBU was Vought-Sikorsky's entry into the Navy's 1939 VTB (heavier than air, torpedo, bomber) competition to replace the Douglas TBD Devastator. Grumman's XTBF-1 Avenger won the competition with the TBU selected for the building of a prototype because of the design's potential. The TBU proved to be sleeker and possessed better top-speed performance than Grumman's TBF. A contract for 1,000 aircraft was awarded as a backup to the TBF. Unfortunately, Chance Vought did not possess sufficient production capacity to support the F4U, OS2U, and TBU production. Vultee was chosen by the Navy to build the production aircraft for the fleet as TBYs. An existing truck manufacturing plant in Allentown, Pennsylvania, was converted to house production of TBY Sea Wolf aircraft. Development problems with the tailhook and rear fuselage led to a redesign capable of bearing arrested landing loads.

Consolidated Aircraft merged with Vultee in early 1943. Because of workforce and plant conversion delays in Allentown, the first production contract was canceled. The eventual production aircraft were designated TBY-2 with an uprated Pratt & Whitney R-2800 engine. The first production TBY-2 aircraft were delivered in late 1944. By that time the Grumman TBF/General Motors TBM was firmly in place in large numbers on the Navy's carrier decks. Production of the TBY-2 continued until 1945, when it was canceled in anticipation of the end of the Pacific War with 180 aircraft eventually delivered. The aircraft served the Navy until 1947, when the entire TBY-2 fleet was scrapped.

A French Navy F4U-7 awaiting delivery.

One of the last Corsairs destined for U.S. military service, the AU-1 at Vought's Grand Prairie factory.

A TBY-2 shows off its Vought heritage with the gull wing. (VS2-701001)

The XF6U-1 33532 Pirate during a test flight. This was before the afterburner and tail modifications had been incorporated.

F7U-1 124419 in formation with a F6U-1 over NAS Patuxent River. (USN)

F6U Pirate

In December 1944 Chance Vought was awarded a contract to build three V-340 (F6U) jet fighters using the Westinghouse 24C (J34) axial flow turbojet engine. The aircraft built upon the use of Vought's Metalite skin, which saw limited use on the F4U and extensive use on the XF5U. Chance Vought Metalite is a sandwich material with balsa wood core and aluminum faces that has exceptional strength and stiffness qualities in large sheets and is especially well adapted to use as wing and fuselage skin because of the smoothness and regularity of the resulting surface.

A typical Metalite panel was .391 inch thick. That typical panel was constructed of a .350-inch balsa wood core with a .016-inch aluminum skin bonded to the bottom and a .012-inch aluminum skin

bonded to the top. Along the edges of the panel and in areas where fasteners were located the core wood was spruce and a .032-inch doubler was added at the bottom along with a .025-inch aluminum doubler added to the top surface. The additional doublers increased the panel thickness at the edges and fastener areas to .427 inch, providing the necessary strength for panel attachment.

The F6U Pirate was underpowered with inadequate directional stability. One claim to fame for the short-lived F6U series, however, was that it was the first production aircraft in the United States to incorporate an afterburner. The Solar Model A-103B provided approximately a 30-percent increase in thrust, but that was not enough to create a production contract for more than 30 aircraft. Ultimately, stability and thrust problems delayed the F6U long enough that other jet fighter designs surpassed it.

A front view of F6U-1 122483 with wingtip fuel tanks and the Solar afterburner installed. (CVA-1548, 24 October 1949)

A rear view of F6U-1 122483 showing the extensive modifications to the rear fuselage for incorporation of the afterburner. (CVA-1161, 3 August 1949)

F7U-3 129588 D-407 of VF-124 prepares to launch from USS Hancock during catapult trials. (USN)

VF-124 Cutlass being towed over the barrier straps on USS Hancock. This photo of a folded up F7U-3 gives an idea of the size of the aircraft both in deck handling and cockpit access. (USN)

An early F7U-3 128463 shows off the belly-mounted rocket pack, the secondary armament of the type until the advent of the F7U-3M with the Sparrow I guided missile. (CVPR-43)

F7U Cutlass

The F7U Cutlass was the Chance Vought Aircraft (CVA) entry into the 1945 Navy Day Fighter Program. The Cutlass was a cutting-edge answer to the problem of combining high speed and high performance into a carrier-based aircraft. The airplane pushed the state of the art for controls, hydraulics, aerodynamics, and power plants. As a result, it had development challenges in all those same areas. The one challenge that was never fully overcome was the low thrust capability of the early Westinghouse jet engines. In June 1946, CVA received a contract for three XF7U-1 aircraft with four 20mm cannons and two afterburning Westinghouse J34 engines. The Pirate had been the first with afterburning included in the production model; the F7U was the first with afterburning incorporated into the design. With approach visibility and continued thrust problems, the design progressed to the F7U-3. The F7U-3 had a radically redesigned cockpit for pilot visibility during aircraft carrier operations and a newer Westinghouse J46 engine. The F7U-3 program was continually beset with engines having down-rated thrust, never good when more is needed.

A factory shot of the F7U-3 rocket pack with the front door open to expose the rocket tubes. This system was a developmental challenge for the F7U that only got more difficult with the F8U design. (CVPR-47)

Chapter 2

NAVY DAY FIGHTER PROGRAM

Created in the classic genre of aviation art during the Fabulous Fifties, this artist concept of the V-383 firing unguided aerial rockets from the fuselage rocket pack illustrates the basic attributes of Vought's new fighter without revealing too many details of the design.

In July 1952, through its Washington office, Chance Vought Aircraft leadership learned of a forthcoming competition for a simple, lightweight, low-cost day fighter with a maximum speed of Mach 1.0 (670 mph). With the Korean War raging on, the skies over the Yalu River were dominated by such transonic aircraft as the North American F-86 and Soviet MiG-15. The thought of a supersonic jet

fighter (much less one that could operate routinely from the deck of a U.S. Navy aircraft carrier) was tantamount to science fiction.

In an attempt to keep the BuAer from pursuing an aircraft with inferior performance to land-based fighters, CVA made a sales presentation protesting that there was no substitute for the highest possible performance in the airplane. Fredrick Detweiler, Chance

Vought general manager, visited Captain Jim Russell in the Chief of Naval Operations section during the first week of September 1952 to discuss the day fighter specifications.

In the discussions, Captain Russell explained the current concept of carrier fighter mission assignments. Writing a 16 September 1952, letter to H. M. "Jack" Horner, president of United Aircraft Corporation, Fred Detweiler shared what had been gleaned from the visit. The fighter assignments fell into three distinct groups: Interceptor, Day Superiority Fighter, and General Purpose Fighter. The first category that Russell detailed was the Interceptor; Detweiler wrote:

"The interceptor has limited range and endurance but an extremely high rate of climb and speed with latch-on fire control and armed to destroy enemy aircraft in the air. Because of the short endurance of these interceptors, the canted carrier deck and a third catapult amidships is required to be available to launch interceptors at all times regardless of whether or not the carrier is recovering or launching other aircraft. It was expected that interceptor type aircraft would only operate with about 20 minutes warning from the time enemy attack is detected. It was expected that each carrier will only have four to eight of these special purpose aircraft. Currently, the F4D is the Navy's interceptor type."[2]

Russell went on to describe the Day Superiority Fighter about which Detweiler wrote:

"The Day Superiority Fighter will be the work horse of the VF (Heavier than Air Fighter) squadrons and will be the preponderant aircraft with the Fleet. This fighter is expected to combat in good weather with sufficient performance, endurance, and armament to destroy opposing fighters in the air or on the ground. The Navy is currently moving on from the F9F straight wing and F2H fighters to the next generation of swept wing, which includes the F7U-3, F9F-6, and FJ-2. However, the life span of this generation is considered short and a new design competition for a Day Superiority Fighter has been announced calling for design proposals in January 1953 and production airplanes for the new type at the end of 1956."[3]

The mission requirements then focused on the General Purpose Fighter, of which Detweiler wrote:

"General Purpose Fighter to be equipped for night and foul weather operation. Each carrier shall have no more than a squadron of General Purpose Fighters. The Navy's operational types, if any, in this category are the F4U-5N, F2H-3, and a very few F9Fs and F2Hs which are partially equipped for this mission. Coming along in development, however, are the F10F and F3H General Purpose Fighter models. Both of these models have a take-off weight in excess of 30,000 pounds. The F10F, at this stage, is not particularly attractive to the Navy and it appears that the F3H mission is being changed from a General Purpose Fighter to a Day Fighter by a program to eliminate airborne radar gear and airplane weight similar to the weight reduction program accomplished for the F7U-3. It is likely that a new design completion for improved General Purpose Fighter will be held by the Navy in fiscal 1954."[4]

Detweiler went on to write about the forthcoming Day Fighter specification:

"Much emphasis is being placed on getting a small fighter. There is a great desire to keep the fighter simple and to give the contractor an opportunity to design and package the electronic equipment to provide ease of maintenance. Unofficially twin engines are preferred and (RADM) Combs told me that BuAer is prepared to go ahead with a light weight refinement of the J46 (Westinghouse J-46 jet engine). Unofficially, also, afterburners are taboo." In closing, Detweiler wrote: "Combs told me that CVA was the logical contractor to get this award from the industrial planning and workload point of view but that we must beat the competition which he knew would be exceedingly tough. Combs said that what the Navy really needs from Vought are some new ideas in this Day Fighter."[5]

Outline Specification 130 (OS-130) Released

The Bureau of Aeronautics (BuAer) invited CVA (and others) to submit proposals for a new Navy day fighter on 16 September 1952, with special emphasis placed on simplicity, small size, low cost, and a maximum speed of Mach 1. The request for proposals was based on Outline Specification 130 (OS-130). An outline specification is a brief, concise list of statements that describe the characteristics of an aircraft the Navy is looking to procure. The specification gives enough information to the contractors (bidders) to formulate their proposal aircraft to pitch to the Navy. OS-130 was dated 2 September 1952. The specification was written for a VF day fighter airplane (V: heavier than air; F: fighter).

The highlight requirement of the specification was for a single-seat, high-performance, carrier-based day fighter airplane. "The primary mission of the airplane shall be to maintain air superiority in daylight fair weather, both over friendly task forces and over hostile target areas, during the period of task force strikes when the enemy will mount large numbers of aircraft." The basic features requested were described in this sentence: "While speed, rate of climb, and combat ceiling are important features of this airplane, the basic features desired are those which will allow adequate numbers of the aircraft to be operated by carrier task forces to ensure successful fulfillment of the mission. . . ."[6]

The OS-130 detailed a little more framework for the design: "Minimum size, maximum carrier spottability (number of aircraft and use of the limited aircraft carrier deck space), low gross weight, low initial cost, simplicity of concept, ease of maintenance, reliability, and versatility in the air-to-air combat role. It encouraged the use of new techniques, materials, and ideas that would contribute to the quality of the fighter, ease of manufacture, and ensure high in-service reliability."

Gross weight was defined in an interesting way: "The gross weight shall be the minimum weight attainable which will meet the requirements of this specification." The empty weight was to be determined by the contractor. OS-130 specified a maximum speed at 35,000 feet, in level flight, at combat weight, of at least Mach 1. The combat radius (distance from the ship) was to be not less than 300 nautical miles. An altitude of 52,000 feet was the specified combat ceiling at maximum power with a combat load (fuel and weapons).[7]

"Performance calculations shall be in accordance with the requirements of Spec. MIL-C-5011A for General Purpose and Escort Fighters, except that combat time shall be made up as follows:

- First Period: Combat for 10 minutes at Vmax (Speed Maximum) in level flight with maximum power at combat ceiling (52,000 feet).
- Second Period: Combat for 5 minutes at 15,000 feet at maximum Mach number."

An interesting note was in the specification: "The Bureau of Aeronautics anticipates that the airplane procured as a result of this competition may at some future time during its operational life, need to be capable of increased performance. Therefore consideration shall be given to the design of the basic configuration such that a significant increase in level flight, high speed will be provided by improvement of thrust output. It is acknowledged that the combat radius specified herein may not be met with the increased performance."[8]

The aircraft size was limited by the requirement to permit spotting of at least 25 airplanes in a spotting area 200 by 96 feet; wing folding was allowed in the design to increase the number of airplanes in the spotting area. OS-130 specified the following limitations on spotting:

- The aircraft shall be spotted in the wings folded (as applicable) static ground attitude, with tip or wing tanks installed.
- A minimum clearance of 1 foot shall be maintained between adjacent aircraft.
- A minimum clearance of 1 foot shall be maintained between the landing gear wheels and the edges of the spotting area.
- The study shall approximate a three-dimensional aircraft spot, i.e., one aircraft overlap another where minimum clearances permit.
- All airplanes shall be pointed essentially in the forward direction or not more than 30 degrees from dead ahead.
- The airplane shall be sized so that fore and aft spotting on an aircraft carrier elevator 58 feet long by 48 feet wide, with 6-foot corner radius with a minimum clearance of 1 foot between the edge of the elevator and any part of the airplane.

If the proposal had non-folding wings, the maximum wing span was limited to 27 feet 6 inches to permit passing of other airplanes on the carrier deck.

OS-130 specified that the maximum practical all-around vision shall be provided for the pilot particularly in the carrier approach atti-tude. This was important to get right on Chance Vought's day fighter design as the carrier approach visibility on both the F4U and F7U in landing configuration had been the subject of concern of both designs.

The North American FJ-4 and the Grumman F11F (as the F9F-8 and then F9F-9) programs were initiated by the BuAer in 1953 without a formal competition using budget designated for product improvement of a production airplane, the FJ-3 and F9F-6/7 respectively. (Before McNamara, the services had a lot more flexibility in funding airplane development programs.) The FJ-4 and the F11F were what the BuAer fighter class-desk officer at the time believed to be most appropriate for a day fighter: light, small, simple (inexpensive), maneuverable. Both were powered by the Wright J65, which had only about 75 percent of the dry (non-afterburning) thrust of the P&W J57. The FJ-4 didn't even have an afterburner, although Grumman had the foresight to add one to its little F11F. Both had first flights in 1954, several months before the XF8U-1 first flew.

In effect, the FJ-4 and F11F were designed substantially in accordance with the original OS-130 requirement. As a result, the F8U, which was designed to the revised OS-130 that emphasized speed, almost literally blew them away. The FJ-4 could not maintain a supersonic speed in level flight; the F11F was just barely supersonic in level flight. FJ-4 fighter production was therefore assigned to the Marine Corps (the Navy subsequently bought a variant, the FJ-4B, as a carrier-based attack airplane to give Ed Heinemann something to think about during early A4D development and production when it felt that Douglas wasn't being responsive to its concerns). The F11F made only a few deployments before it was relegated to service as an advanced trainer for fighter pilots and assigned to the Navy's Blue Angels flight demonstration team.

Chance Vought Aircraft Develops a Proposal Aircraft

The Navy's outline specification (OS-130) for the day fighter contained several significant technical challenges in such a simply written document. Management and engineering were confident Chance Vought Aircraft could build an airplane that would exceed the OS-130 specifications. The same group also felt the Navy was selling itself short with the specifications. During 1952 several meetings took place between Navy and Vought officials concerning the day fighter specification. The performance concern showed up in discussions with the Navy as illustrated in a letter to Chairman Fredrick Rentschler of United Aircraft Corporation (Chance Vought Aircraft's parent company) on 1 October 1952.

H. M. Horner wrote: "I was able to get in to see Admiral Combs [RADM Thomas S. Combs] yesterday afternoon. While the subject of my visit was to further discuss the matter of releasing product for export [F4Us], he brought up the matter of the Navy fighter competition and his hope that Vought would come in with a really good proposal. I told him, of course, Vought was going to make a tremendous effort on this particular competition but that preliminary information indicated to us that possibly Navy was driving for an aircraft which would not be competitive with land-based aircraft. The Admiral said this was just not an acceptable situation to Navy."[9]

A couple of other points of interest came up in the conversation. The first from the CVA viewpoint was Horner informing RADM Combs that in order to have decent range and be competitive with land-based airplanes, the fighter's weight would have to increase 6,000 pounds above the specification to around a total of 22,000 pounds. The Admiral's reaction was "rather startled and interested." The second interesting point was the revelation that the Admiral was convinced that "two small engines would do a better job for a Navy fighter than one large one."[10]

In the same letter Hobbs went on to ask if the research department of Chance Vought could make a quick study comparing the Navy specification to the Air Force fighters currently being developed, including the F-100 and F-102. The thought was that if the Navy specification was inferior to those airplanes currently under contract it might help convince the Navy that they are asking for a second-rate airplane.[11]

Day Fighter Course Set

On 6 October 1952, a pivotal sales-engineering meeting was held at Vought. Discussion of the day fighter proposal was on the top of the list of topics discussed. In attendance were Fred Detweiler (general manager), H. B. Sallada (assistant general manager), Paul Baker, Fred Dickerman (chief engineer), R. C. Blaylock (assistant chief engineer), John Clark (assistant chief engineer aircraft development), H. B. Gibbons (chief of development), William Schoolfield (chief of aerodynamics), A. L. Jerrett, Paul Thayer (sales and service manager) and F. Mann (chief of military sales). The minutes of the sales-engineering meeting on 6 October 1952 (SM-28) give insight into the conversations in the meeting. In the day fighter discussion, Horner agreed that the proposal needed to deviate from the specification to give the company the best chance to win the day fighter competition and every effort needed to be made to win this competition. Hobbs made a suggestion to study three different airplanes to meet the Navy requirement. One would have maximum possible performance, the second would be an absolute minimum airplane to meet the letter of the specification, and a compromise airplane taking the minimum airplane and mixing in all the maximum performance possible.[12]

During the meeting, further summation of the discussions with RADM Thomas Combs, chief of the BuAer, captured these subtle changes in the Navy position (No. 2 and No. 3):

- Simplicity and minimum airplane size were important.
- Any performance over Mach 1 would be very attractive.
- Performance would rate very high in any airplane meeting the specification.
- Twin engines were preferred.

In the meeting with the admiral, he had also asked that two proposals be submitted, one single-engine and the other with twin engines. The admiral said that the engine list would be modified to add additional Westinghouse engines.[13]

The current engine list comprises eight engine models: General Electric J47 and J73; Pratt & Whitney J57; Westinghouse J34, J40, J46, and J65; and Wright J65. Given the ongoing concerns about Westinghouse engines and the F7U-3 Cutlass, that manufacture was not seriously considered. It also helps that Pratt & Whitney was under the same corporate umbrella with Vought when the project first started.

Also included in discussion at the sales meeting was the news that Captain Sosnoski, deputy director of the Aircraft Division of the BuAer, who worked on the OS-130, had been replaced by Captain Gibbons. With the personnel change came a different consideration of the performance requirements in the specification. Captain Gibbons considered the specification as being minimum requirements rather than optimum requirements. He also indicated that all the airplane proposals would be at a 13,000- to 19,000-pound take-off weight. Captain Gibbons felt that the airplane that met the basic requirements with the highest performance would win. During the meeting it was decided to meet back with Horner by the end of October 1952 to review the possible submissions to the day fighter competition.[14]

In response to Horner's previous request, the research department at Vought returned with an analysis of the OS-130 specification compared with current and future USAF fighter (land-based) aircraft. The research department's conclusion was not clear cut, but indicated that in the high-speed category, the Navy Day Fighter would be outclassed.[15]

In a 31 October 1952 letter to Fred Detweiler, Paul Baker strongly suggested that they should continue working on an airplane that met the BuAer specifications and rules "with no regard for future performance growth, a J65 single-engine airplane. Strictly adhering to the principles of making a simple, minimum-sized airplane."[16]

He went on to recommend development of the J57-powered aircraft featuring the variable incidence swept wing with a tail configuration, of which three were being considered. The three J57 designs under consideration were a minimum airplane without afterburner to meet the OS-130 specifications, a heavier airplane with afterburning and fuel to meet the radius of action with strength to allow future improvements, and an afterburning airplane that met the minimum requirements of the specification. These were the finalists in a major Vought effort to consider the various configuration options.

Design Considerations Affecting Selection of the Proposal Airplane

The requirements of OS-130 and the ongoing discussions within CVA helped shape the various configurations considered for the proposal airplanes. The following wing and tail configurations were extensively studied for the day fighter airplane:

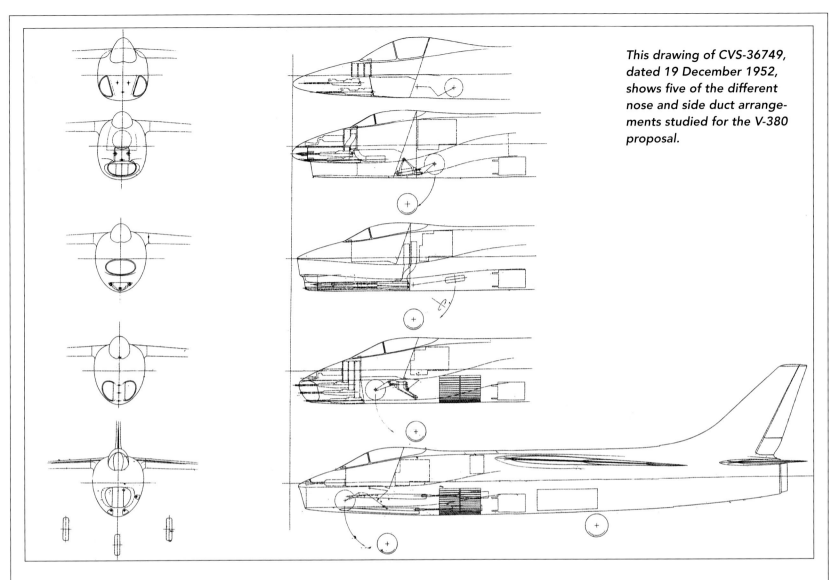

This drawing of CVS-36749, dated 19 December 1952, shows five of the different nose and side duct arrangements studied for the V-380 proposal.

- A thin straight wing with a conventional horizontal tail
- A swept wing with a conventional horizontal tail
- A delta wing without a horizontal tail
- A delta wing with a horizontal tail
- A swept wing without a horizontal tail
- A swept wing with a horizontal tail and two-position wing tips

Each of the six basic configurations was studied with and without a variable incidence feature on the wing, resulting in a total of 12 configurations. In detailed study of the various possible configurations and the requirements of the day fighter, several objectives stood out as defining the requirement in performance terms. Having this list enabled CVA to determine the configuration of the proposal aircraft. Those design objectives of most influence on the proposal airplanes were:

- Combat ceiling with thrust augmentation (afterburning) inoperative of at least 48,000 feet

- Longitudinal acceleration in level flight at 35,000 feet of about .1 g at Mach 1.2
- Gun platform limit maneuvering gs at 35,000 feet of about 4.5 g
- Approach speed to carrier of less than 130 knots, or not exceeding 5.5 g during arrested landing
- Excellent vision on approach to the aircraft carrier

After initial analysis of the preliminary design data concerning the 12 design configurations, 3 basic configurations were eliminated from further detailed study:

1. The delta wing with a horizontal tail was eliminated because of the difficulty in attaining satisfactory flying qualities for equivalent performance with the other designs.
2. The swept wing without a horizontal tail was eliminated because of lower performance at high supersonic speeds compared to the other designs.

3. The swept wing with a horizontal tail and two-position wing tips was eliminated because of the specification requiring a 300-nautical-mile normal load radius of action and does not gain enough performance to include this novel concept.

The three remaining configurations: thin straight wing with a conventional horizontal tail, swept wing with a conventional horizontal tail, and a delta wing without a horizontal tail were studied in detail to determine the proper configuration for the day fighter proposals. Each was to be evaluated with and without a variable-incidence wing.

The straight wing with conventional horizontal tail airplane was eliminated due to a lack of longitudinal acceleration and poor flying qualities in the transonic speed range, both important in the evaluation of the combat effectiveness of the day fighter.

In comparing the swept wing tailed and delta wing tailless, the requirements of the military power (no thrust augmentation) ceiling of 48,000 feet and high-speed maneuverability in combat helped to separate the two basic design concepts. Between the two designs the swept wing tailed airplane had a faster rate of climb to obtain the 48,000-foot combat ceiling and had greater maneuverability in combat. For a tailless delta to meet the altitude requirement it took a larger wing area than would be needed for the shipboard landing requirement.

Having a larger wing area on the tailless delta airplane caused higher trim drag, decreasing the speed of the aircraft compared to the swept wing tailed airplane. The tailless delta's maneuverability was not as good as the swept tailed airplane because its available trimmed lift without a tail was relatively low compared to the swept wing tailed design. The tailless delta airplane was also thought to have poorer longitudinal damping qualities. Considering these factors aerodynamically, the tailless delta airplane was ruled out in favor of the swept wing tailed design.

The final comparison was between a delta wing tailed airplane and swept wing tailed airplane. In order to meet the ceiling objectives, a wing sweep of approximately 42 degrees was chosen for the swept wing tailed airplane. The delta wing tailed airplane had a sweep of about 44 degrees to meet the same ceiling objective.

An important difference between the two wing designs involved the taper ratios. A taper ratio is the ratio of the wing's chord (width) at the tip compared to the center of the wing root chord, measuring how much the width changes over that distance. The swept wing airplane had a taper ratio of .25 and the delta wing had a zero taper ratio. The available wind tunnel test data at the time showed that the

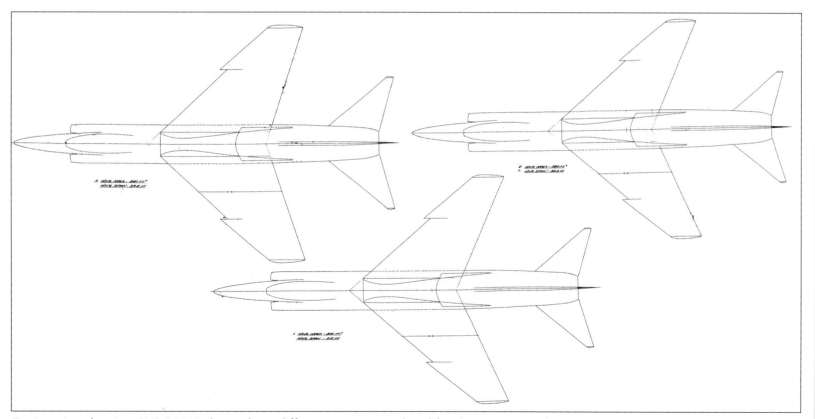

Engineering drawing CVS-36747 shows three different wings considered for the V-380. Number 1 (lower) with a wing area of 300 square feet and a span of 31.5 feet. Number 2 (top right) shows a wing area of 280 square feet and a wing span of 30.3 feet. Number 3 (top left) shows a wing area of 340 square feet with a wing span of 32.8 feet.

stability characteristics and lower maximum lift coefficient of a zero taper ratio wing with a 42- to 44-degree sweep was not as desirable.

Due to the length restrictions of OS-130, a delta wing tailed airplane would have a shorter distance to the horizontal tail from the wing, which would reduce the dampening qualities of such a tail. Reduced longitudinal and directional damping qualities would have a negative effect on the gun platform aspects of the design. A shorter length to the tail also results in the need for a larger horizontal tail to be effective, which adds to the weight and structural challenges of the design. Due to the disadvantages of the tailed delta wing configuration as tested it was not chosen for the day fighter submission. It should be noted that the Douglas A4D had this configuration and was very successful.

In working their way through the 12 design configurations considered to meet or exceed the OS-130 specifications, the engineers concluded that from an aerodynamic point of view, the swept wing tailed airplane was the best configuration to use for the proposal airplanes.

It was felt to remain competitive into the late 1950s an airplane would need to have a maximum speed of at least Mach 1.2 or higher. The continued problem facing the engineers was that the Navy had informally advised them that submissions with excess space and strength reserved for the later addition of afterburning engines would be penalized in the competition.

Russell Clark of CVA had a further visit to the BuAer on 6 November 1952, in which he visited with Ivan Driggs, Bill Frisbie, Sid Sherby, and Ralph Weymouth in separate meetings. Topics included that a twin-engined airplane would not meet the specifications and Admiral Combs' desire for a twin-engined fighter. Clark and Driggs both agreed that the Westinghouse engines now on the list would not meet the specified thrust targets. In his discussions with Bill Frisbie, Clark learned that all the contractors were talking about submitting two airplanes for the competition, one minimum and one stretch. Frisbie expressed his unhappiness that under the rules of OS-130 he could only evaluate the minimum airplane. He was pushing Sid Sherby to clarify OS-130 to allow the evaluation of all airplanes submitted. Clark was surprised by a change in viewpoint from Sherby during their discussions:

"Sid said he had the spec written the way it is so he hoped the contractors would 'read between the lines' and submit at least two airplanes, a minimum and a growth airplane, so that BuAer could have a look at both and choose what they wished!" Clark went on to write "I think this is new rationalizing on his part due to pressure from Frisbie, and the contractors."[17]

In a 7 November letter to L. S. Hobbs (vice president of engineering), H. M. Horner wrote, "I think your suggestion that Vought consider indicating in their Navy fighter bid its growth potential is a "must," at least if we choose the larger J57 job."[18]

Jack Horner then wrote a letter to Fred Rentschler about the day fighter competition. He wrote, "Vought's problem in connection with this very important Navy day fighter design competition continues to be most difficult to outguess. One of the main reasons for our quandary is the divergence of opinion within the Navy itself on what is really needed."[19]

He went on to describe Vought's design studies would be limited to one type in two configurations, "The basic type chosen was an orthodox looking swept wing aircraft with both horizontal and vertical tails. The only really unorthodox feature is that it is a high wing design with variable incident to provide a nearly horizontal fuselage in landing and takeoff. With a fixed incidence wing the awkward extreme nose high attitude is necessary."[20] He also went on to describe the two configurations as a minimum aircraft with the J65 engine and a larger, high-performance airplane with the J57 engine.

Fred Rentschler, chairman and president of United Aircraft Corporation, wrote to Horace "Jack" Horner, president of United Aircraft Corporation, on 10 November 1952, describing his concerns about the Navy's requirements being too low: "I have read through all the various comments by yourself, (Luke) Hobbs, (Charles) McCarthy, and others on the Navy's new fighter project. It seems to me that the Navy are keeping their sights too low. One of the Navy officers, I noticed, indicated that he felt a new smaller fighter would outperform the MiG and he believed it would be a long, long while before the Russians would have in production anything better that the MiG."[21]

"I still believe that Navy's prime requirement is a shipboard fighter which will most nearly approach or if possible, be the equivalent of, land-based fighters. The Air Force are pinning all their hopes on more and more thrust. The Navy seems to be moving in exactly the opposite direction."[22]

"I realize that Leonard is suggesting that we possibly could undertake two proposals. If this is reasonable, then we might not be thrown out for not performing to Navy desires but, of course, it will be delaying and expensive. I noticed in your memorandum to Hobbs you raise the question of indicating future ratings up to 1960 on the J57 development. Such a study might have a great influence on Navy thinking. All I can suggest is we continue: to follow closely Navy's thinking and maybe a little later on we can make a better evaluation of it all."[23]

Changes to OS-130

In mid-November, CVA was informally informed that the Navy was seriously considering amendments to the original OS-130 requirements. This information was quickly followed by an official amendment to OS-130.

This change coincided with the departure of the fighter class desk officer who had insisted that the day fighter be inexpensive, which meant among other things, no afterburner. His emphasis on affordability at the expense of performance was not widely held at the BuAer.

On 18 November 1952, the BuAer issued amendments to OS-130 Day Fighter Specification. The revisions placed emphasis on speed, rate of climb, maneuverability, and combat ceiling with less emphasis on size and weight. The revised specifications increased the maximum speed from Mach 1 to Mach 1.2 at an altitude of 35,000 feet with thrust augmentation. The non-augmented maximum speed was Mach .97 at the same altitude. The radius of action and combat problems were adjusted to be more favorable to the use of thrust augmentation. They directed the CVA group to the J57-P-7 as the only engine that could deliver an airplane to meet or exceed all requirements. In their minds, twin-engined airplanes based on the J46 engine would no longer meet the requirements.

The other available engines considered for a twin-engined configuration would create larger airplanes. Using the amended data, the CVA design had evolved into an airplane with attractive performance but approach speeds that were estimated to be higher than those of the F7U-3's 115 knots. Speeds of 145 to 160 knots, depending on the wing area of the design, were higher than the specification, which was limited by the load limits of a straight-deck short–run out arresting gear system.

On 29 December 1952, the BuAer released Amendment 3 to the OS-130 specification with restricted catapulting and arresting accelerations to 5.5 Gs in response to the increasing approach speeds. (The acceleration limits were imposed until the canted deck carriers with longer arresting runout were declared satisfactory by service trials then underway.) An additional change in the amendment: The thrust augmented J65 engine was added to the approved engine list.

Having advanced knowledge of Amendment 3, changes were made to the wind tunnel model for the proposal airplane. Changes made to meet the new requirements were greater wing area, lower drag fuselage, refined intake duct, high lift devices (drooped ailerons used as flaps), boundary layer suction, and an arresting gear device to relieve peak deceleration forces. With the incorporation of these changes and the results of wind tunnel testing, CVA finally had a configuration for their day fighter proposal, the V-380.

Right before the release of the V-380 information, H. M. Horner wrote to Fred Rentschler on 9 January 1953, offering a few thoughts on the day fighter proposal from Vought that had been presented to leadership the day before. He reviewed the proposal airplanes for Rentschler and in closing added, "We feel that Vought has come up with a sound proposal; we cannot by any means say we feel they are in the driver's seat to win this competition. As stated above, the competition is going to be terrific."

He also spent a paragraph discussing the possibilities from the other manufacturers, "Also we can be sure that North American will come up with a very excellent design. In addition, we face Douglas and their Ed Heinemann, who has been a prime advocate of the small light airplane which is so dear to the hearts of many in the Navy, especially the all-important Driggs. Douglas not only has the opportunity to come up with a brand-new trick design, but a

modification of their present production F4D will probably closely approach the specifications for this Navy fighter and if chosen would offer tremendous cost savings to the Navy. Lockheed and McDonnell will also be in there pitching for all they are worth as will Martin and probably others.

"It can therefore be seen that Vought's chances are only so-so to win the competition although I am sure that Vought is in a very much higher regard with the Navy at the present time than they were a year or two ago."[24]

The V-380

On 5 January 1953, CVA published Engineering Report 8697 V-380 Navy Day Fighter Proposal to the BuAer. The reported noted: "The basic design objectives are to obtain an airplane entirely suitable for carrier operations with maximum performance and maneuverability; satisfactory flying qualities; minimum size and weight; superior potential for stretch in performance, versatility, and load carrying ability; simplicity in concept and detail design; reliable; serviceable; incorporating new, saleable ideas; and an attractive arrangement."[25]

Comments were added to the report to explain those items that might be considered complex in the proposal airplanes. Those items included variable incidence wing, wing leading edge droop, trailing edge flap/aileron, unit horizontal tails, power control system for flight controls, boundary layer suction system, arresting hook g-reducing device, wing folding, and wing fuel. The variable incidence wing, wing leading edge droop, trailing edge flap/aileron, unit horizontal tails, and boundary layer suction system were incorporated to reduce approach speeds and maintain pilot vision to enable acceptable characteristics approaching the aircraft carrier. To address limitations placed on g-forces for carrier landings, the engineers came up with a unique solution, the arresting hook g-reducing device. This device was a liquid spring strut installed in the arresting hook assembly. It was 15 inches long and 4 inches in diameter and worked in a similar fashion to an airplane landing gear shock strut.

The report also discussed a possible contender airplane, the Douglas F4D. The F-100 and F3H were also mentioned as contenders. In the discussion of the three designs the F4D and F-100 were the only designs considered to approximate the requirements of the day fighter specification without major configuration changes. The designs included the necessary power plant, equipment, and fuel. The Douglas F4D was considered the closest to meeting OS-130. It had the J57-P-7 engine with 14,800 pounds of thrust that enabled it to almost meet the speed and ceiling requirements. Speed requirements could be met at the expense of maneuverability, fuel capacity, and maximum altitude by reducing wing thickness or wing area, the report noted. The F4D was considered to have outstanding maneuverability, most likely the best of any design in the competition.[26]

CVA proposed two aircraft: one maximum performance with the J57 and one minimum performance with the J65 engine, both with

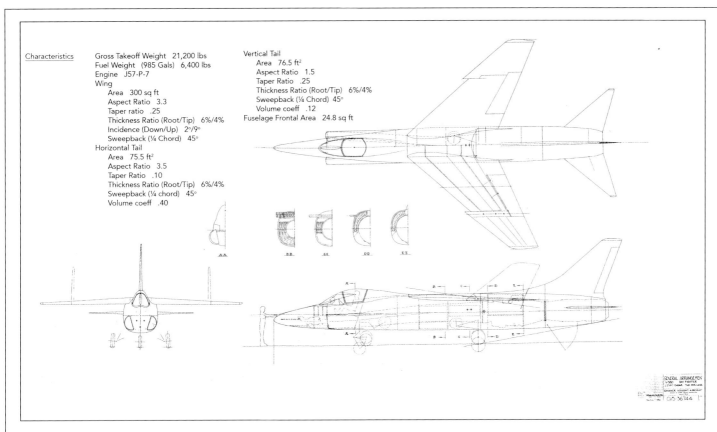

Characteristics

Gross Takeoff Weight 21,200 lbs
Fuel Weight (985 Gals) 6,400 lbs
Engine J57-P-7
Wing
  Area 300 sq ft
  Aspect Ratio 3.3
  Taper ratio .25
  Thickness Ratio (Root/Tip) 6%/4%
  Incidence (Down/Up) 2°/9°
  Sweepback (¼ Chord) 45°
Horizontal Tail
  Area 75.5 ft²
  Aspect Ratio 3.5
  Taper Ratio .10
  Thickness Ratio (Root/Tip) 6%/4%
  Sweepback (¼ chord) 45°
  Volume coeff .40

Vertical Tail
  Area 76.5 ft²
  Aspect Ratio 1.5
  Taper Ratio .25
  Thickness Ratio (Root/Tip) 6%/4%
  Sweepback (¼ Chord) 45°
  Volume coeff .12
Fuselage Frontal Area 24.8 sq ft

CVS-36744 dated 19 December 1952 is a general arrangement drawing of the V-380 with the J57-P-7 engine and a two-position wing. It features the smaller wing along with side intakes and an F7U-3–looking canopy.

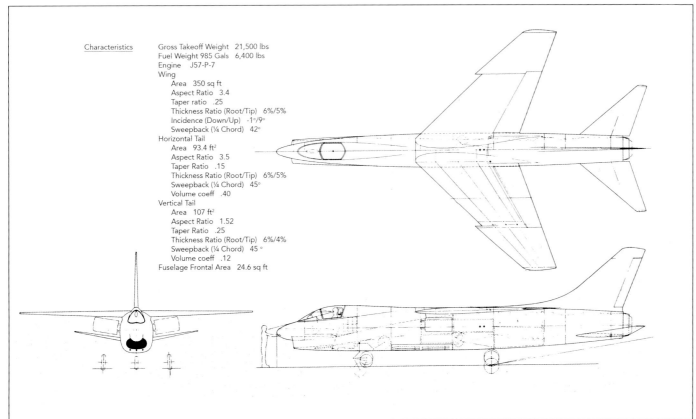

Characteristics

Gross Takeoff Weight 21,500 lbs
Fuel Weight 985 Gals 6,400 lbs
Engine J57-P-7
Wing
  Area 350 sq ft
  Aspect Ratio 3.4
  Taper ratio .25
  Thickness Ratio (Root/Tip) 6%/5%
  Incidence (Down/Up) -1°/9°
  Sweepback (¼ Chord) 42°
Horizontal Tail
  Area 93.4 ft²
  Aspect Ratio 3.5
  Taper Ratio .15
  Thickness Ratio (Root/Tip) 6%/5%
  Sweepback (¼ Chord) 45°
  Volume coeff .40
Vertical Tail
  Area 107 ft²
  Aspect Ratio 1.52
  Taper Ratio .25
  Thickness Ratio (Root/Tip) 6%/4%
  Sweepback (¼ Chord) 45 °
  Volume coeff .12
Fuselage Frontal Area 24.6 sq ft

CVS-37300 is a general arrangement drawing of the V-380 in its final form with speed brakes mounted under the wing and a straight wing with no anhedral.

Comparison of OS-130 and CVA Specifications

The following table compares the OS-130 and OS-130 amended specifications with the CVA specifications for the day fighter. This gives a clearer picture of what CVA is proposing to the Navy.

Item	CVA Specification	Navy OS-130 Specification	Navy OS-130 Specification Amendment 2 and 3
Mission	Destroy Enemy Aircraft on Ground and in Air	Maintaining Air Superiority in Daylight Fair Weather during Strikes when Enemy will Mount Large Numbers of Aircraft	
Performance Vmax at 35,000 Ft	Mach 1.3	Mach 1.0	Mach 1.2 Combat Mach .97 at Military Power
Combat Ceiling	55,000 Ft	52,000 Ft	48,000 Ft
Maneuverability	2.5g at 35,000 Ft	High	High
Take-off	C-11 No Wind	C-11 10 Kts Wind	C-11 10 Kts Wind
Landing	MK7 1.1 Stall Speed No Wind 40% Fuel Capacity of Gear	MK7 1.2 Stall speed 25 Kts 20% Fuel Capacity of Gear	MK7 1.2 Stall speed 25 Kts 20% Fuel
G for Arresting and Catapult			g
Radius	400	300 (400 Overload)	300 (400 Overload)
Warm-up, Takeoff	5 Min Normal Power +1 Min Max Power	5 Min Normal Power +1 Min Max Power	5 Min Normal Power +1 Min Max Power
Combat	10 Min at Mach 1.1 at Max Power at 35,000 Ft	10 Min at Max Power at Ceiling + 5 Min Max Power at 35,000 Ft 5% Total Fuel + 20 Min at Speed for Max Endurance at Sea Level	5 Min at Max Power at Ceiling + 5 Min Max Power at 35,000 Ft 5% Total Fuel + 20 Min at Speed for Max Endurance at Sea Level
Reserve	20 Min at Speed for Max Endurance at Sea Level or Total Flight Time 2 hours, whichever is greater		
Climb Rate at Takeoff	1,000 Ft/Min	No Specification	No Specification
General Folded Span Max	25 Ft 4 In	27 Ft 6 In	27 Ft 6 In
Spotting	16 in Rectangular Boxes	25	25
Folded Height Max	17 Ft	17 Ft	17 Ft
Vision	Same as F7U-3 MCR-8	Maximum Practical	Maximum Practical
Aerodynamics	Unrestricted Mach No.	Unrestricted to as great a degree a consistent with lightness and simplicity	
Structural Design	7g	6g	6g
Speed Brakes	At least as good as F7U-3 (.68 deceleration at 500 Knots)	Decelerate from Maximum Speed to best Climb Speed or Minimum Speed for Fighting in not more than 16 seconds	
Engines	Afterburning Engines and JP-4 Fuel	Non-Afterburning Engines and JP-4 Fuel	Afterburning Engines and JP-4 Fuel
Fuel System	Bladder Cells Plus Inerting for Combat	Bladder Cells	Bladder Cells
Instruments	Turn and Bank Rate of Climb Gyro Horizon Altimeter Airspeed Accelerometer Magnetic Compass Tachometer Tailpipe Temperature Fuel Quantity Oil Pressure	Turn and Bank Gyro Horizon Altimeter Airspeed Accelerometer G-2 Compass Tachometer Tailpipe Temperature Fuel Quantity Cabin Altimeter Speed Brake Indicator Wheel & Flap Indicator	Turn and Bank Rate of Climb Gyro Horizon Altimeter Airspeed Accelerometer S-2 Compass Tachometer Tailpipe Temperature Fuel Quantity Cabin Altimeter Speed Brake Indicator Wheel & Flap Indicator
Electronics	ARC-34 UHF APX-6 IFF ARN-21 NAV APG-30	ARC-27A UHF APX-6B IFF ARN-21 NAV APG-34	
Armament	4 MK 12 600 Rounds 20mm MK 6 sight Space Provisions for MK 16 sight No Bulletproof Glass Armor Protection	4 MK 12 or 3 T-160 500 Rounds 20mm MK 16-2 sight No Bulletproof Glass No Armor Protection	
Alternate Armament	2.75-In FFAR at weight not greater than gun and ammo	2-In FFAR at weight not greater than guns and ammo. Strong Points for four "Sparrows"	
Furnishings	Single ejection seat, oxygen, cabin pressurization and air conditioning required	Single ejection seat, oxygen, cabin pressurization and air conditioning required	

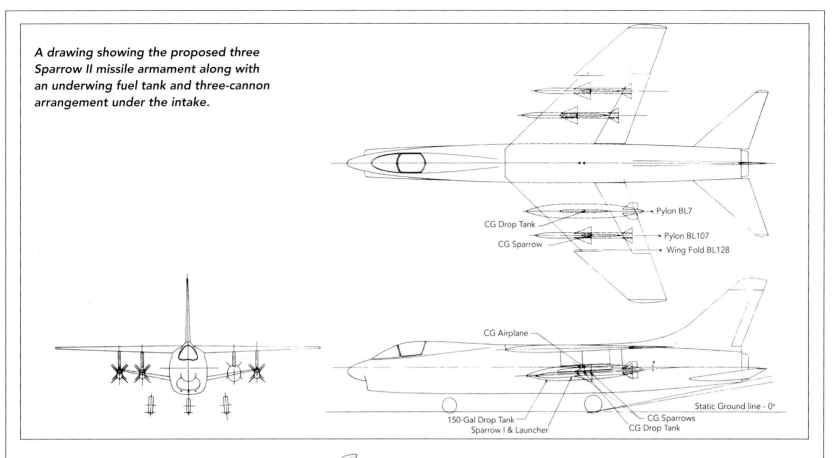

A drawing showing the proposed three Sparrow II missile armament along with an underwing fuel tank and three-cannon arrangement under the intake.

Pylon BL7
CG Drop Tank
CG Sparrow
Pylon BL107
Wing Fold BL128

CG Airplane
CG Sparrows
Static Ground line - 0°
150-Gal Drop Tank
Sparrow I & Launcher
CG Drop Tank

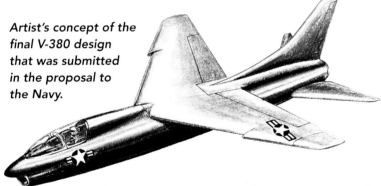

Artist's concept of the final V-380 design that was submitted in the proposal to the Navy.

afterburners. The V-380 design would be divided into two design numbers, the V-383 and the V-384, respectively, for the detailed submissions for the Day Fighter competition.

Description of the Proposal Airplanes V-383 and V-384

Vought Engineering Report 8699 "Design Philosophy Navy Day Fighter" dated 21 February 1953 provides a number of insights into the V-383 and V-384 design proposals. The design objectives established by Chance Vought for a new carrier-based day fighter are based on meeting, and exceeding in some cases, the requirements of Navy Specification OS-130.

Two possible approaches were taken to meet the OS-130 design objectives:

1. The V-383 design utilizing the smallest possible airplane with the maximum thrust engine (J57) available that will meet, and in most cases exceed, the design objectives
2. The V-384 design utilizing the smallest possible airplane with the lowest thrust engine (J65) that will meet the design objectives

Chance Vought gave equal emphasis to both possible approaches and submitted both airplanes for consideration by the BuAer.

The Chance Vought V-383 proposal airplane was designed around the Pratt & Whitney J57 afterburning engine. The J57 was the most powerful engine available for consideration during the Day Fighter competition. Unlike the company's F7U-3 Cutlass, a tailless aircraft, the V-383 airplane was a more conventional arrangement consisting of a high-mounted swept wing positioned on the mid-fuselage and a unit horizontal tail (UHT) mounted low on the aft fuselage. The airplane was 54 feet long with a wing span of 35.6 feet. Takeoff weight was 22,600 pounds. Sixty 2-inch Rockets and three 20mm cannons could be carried separately or simultaneously.

Both the V-383 and V-384 were offered with the provision to mount four Sparrow missiles under the wings. This provision was

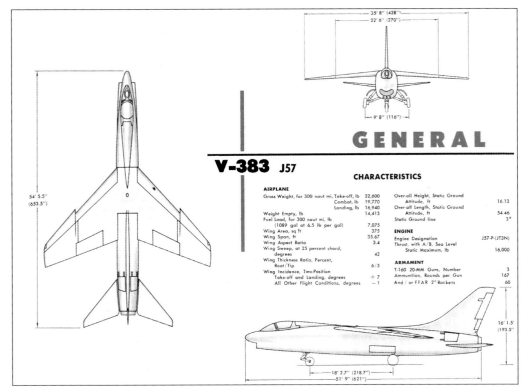

GENERAL

V-383 J57

CHARACTERISTICS

AIRPLANE

Gross Weight, for 300 naut mi, Take-off, lb	22,600
Combat, lb	19,770
Landing, lb	16,940
Weight Empty, lb	14,413
Fuel Load, for 300 naut mi, lb (1089 gal at 6.5 lb per gal)	7,075
Wing Area, sq ft	375
Wing Span, ft	35.67
Wing Aspect Ratio	3.4
Wing Sweep, at 25 percent chord, degrees	42
Wing Thickness Ratio, Percent, Root/Tip	6/5
Wing Incidence, Two-Position	
Take-off and Landing, degrees	+ 7
All Other Flight Conditions, degrees	— 1

Over-all Height, Static Ground Attitude, ft	16.13
Over-all Length, Static Ground Attitude, ft	54.46
Static Ground line	3°

ENGINE

Engine Designation	J57-P-(JT3N)
Thrust, with A/B, Sea Level Static Maximum, lb	16,000

ARMAMENT

T-160 20-MM Guns, Number	3
Ammunition, Rounds per Gun	167
And / or FFAR 2" Rockets	60

General arrangement of the V-383 Day Fighter with the powerful J57 engine.

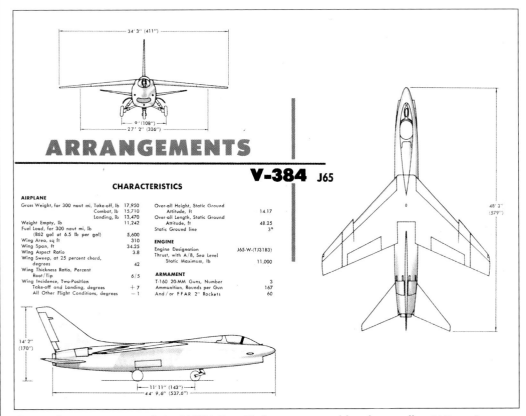

ARRANGEMENTS

V-384 J65

CHARACTERISTICS

AIRPLANE

Gross Weight, for 300 naut mi, Take-off, lb	17,950
Combat, lb	15,710
Landing, lb	13,470
Weight Empty, lb	11,242
Fuel Load, for 300 naut mi, lb (862 gal at 6.5 lb per gal)	5,600
Wing Area, sq ft	310
Wing Span, ft	34.25
Wing Aspect Ratio	3.8
Wing Sweep, at 25 percent chord, degrees	42
Wing Thickness Ratio, Percent Root/Tip	6/5
Wing Incidence, Two-Position	
Take-off and Landing, degrees	+ 7
All Other Flight Conditions, degrees	— 1

Over-all Height, Static Ground Attitude, ft	14.17
Over-all Length, Static Ground Attitude, ft	48.25
Static Ground line	3°

ENGINE

Engine Designation	J65-W-(TJ31B3)
Thrust, with A/B, Sea Level Static Maximum, lb	11,000

ARMAMENT

T-160 20-MM Guns, Number	3
Ammunition, Rounds per Gun	167
And / or FFAR 2" Rockets	60

General arrangement of the V-384 Day Fighter powered by the smaller J65 engine.

never used. The three proposed T-160 guns were installed under the cockpit below the air intake duct. Enough internal fuel was provided for 300 and 400 nautical miles radius of action with cannons *and* rockets, or 500 nautical miles with guns *or* rockets. The V-383 airplane featured power wing folding with the outboard sections folding up. Twenty-five V-383 airplanes could be spotted in a straightforward manner on 200 feet of aircraft carrier deck.

The V-384 airplane that Chance Vought proposed utilized the Wright J65 afterburning engine. At 7,220 pounds of thrust this engine was the lowest-powered engine available to meet the requirements for the day fighter. Again, CVA went with a conventional aircraft arrangement nearly identical to the V-383, only varying in length and wing span. The V-384 airplane had a length of 48 feet and a wing span of 34.2 feet. It weighed 17,950 pounds at take-off. As with the V-383, 60 2-inch rockets and three 20mm cannons can be carried separately or simultaneously. The 3 T-160 20mm guns on the V-384 were mounted differently than the V-383, all under the air intake duct method.

On the V-384 the three cannons were mounted one on each lower side of the cockpit and one centerline on the bottom of the fuselage under the cockpit. Internal fuel was again provided for 300 and 400 nautical miles radius of action with guns *and* rockets or 500 nautical miles with guns *or* rockets. Unlike the V-383, the V-384 had manual wing folding to save weight and complexity. The outer wing panels on the V-384 folded downward to allow for manual folding without ladders or special equipment. Twenty-seven V-384 airplanes could be spotted in a straightforward manner on the specified 200 feet of aircraft carrier deck.

Variable-Incidence Wing

The V-383 and V-384 shared several significant design elements, such as the wing. The day fighter proposals included a variable-incidence wing. The wing had two fixed incidence positions relative to the fuselage, a low position (retracted wing actuator) at -1 degrees for all flight conditions except landing and take-off, and a high position (fully extended wing

Comparison of Design Objectives and Characteristics of the Two Proposal Airplanes

Design Objective	V-383 Airplane	V-384 Airplane
Maximum speed utilizing military power Mach 1.0 at 35,000 ft	Mach 1.0	Mach .98
Development potential maximum speed using combat power Mach 1.3 to 1.5 at 35,000 ft	Mach 1.50	Mach 1.25
Military power ceiling greater than 48,000 ft	49,800 ft	48,700 ft
Climb to 35,000 ft in less than 2 min	1.7 min	2.1 min
Overload radius 500 nm internal fuel	Yes	Yes
Gun platform maximum g greater than 4.5 g at 35,000 ft and Mach .9	5.1	5.5
Acceleration at Mach 1.2 of .1 g level flight at 35,999 ft	.086	.016
Take off, land, wave off on military power	Yes	Yes
Approach speed less than 130 kts	125 kts	123 kts
Spotting 25 airplanes straightforward	25 straightforward	27 straightforward
Sit close to deck for servicing and handling	Yes	Yes
Adaptable to new carrier techniques, such as flex deck and canted deck	Yes	Yes
Simple catapulting; no ramps or sink off the bow of the ship	Yes	Yes
Excellent vision in carrier approach	Yes	Yes
Simplicity and reliability; simple reliable structure and systems	Yes	Yes
Producibility and maintenance, easy to assemble and low cost	Yes	Yes
Vulnerability; protection of pilot and major systems	Satisfactory	Satisfactory
Mission flexibility; able to adapt to short or long missions, new weapons, able to carry rockets and guns simultaneously	Yes	Yes
Development potential	Mach 1.7 with 18,000-lbs thrust	Mach 2.0 with XJ79 engine

Upper view of the variable wing actuator on a production F8U. A single bolt attaches the actuator to the wing and takes the flight loads. This view also shows how high the wing extends from the fuselage. The curved top of the inlet duct is visible.

An underside view of the variable-incidence wing in the raised position. The wing center section is fairly smooth on the underside with a minimum of wires and tubes attached to it.

actuator) at +7 degrees for landing and takeoff. A single, rugged hydraulic actuator with mechanical linkage to lock in both up and down positions was used for wing incidence changes. The actuator attached at the right front of the wing center section and the wing assembly hinged at the aft portion of the center section.

The low incidence position (wing retracted) of -1 degrees for climb, cruising, and combat met the lateral-directional stability requirements of Navy Specification SR-119B at high altitude without the use of a lateral stabilization system.

The high incidence position (wing extended) for takeoff and landing permitted excellent carrier suitability as follows:

- Excellent vision for the pilot in takeoff and carrier approach conditions.
- Permitted a well-faired windshield and canopy, which contribute to high performance.
- A performance gain of 100 knots at 35,000 feet by using a small canopy and good fair in line with the fuselage instead of a more conventional large-size canopy that did not fair in well with the fuselage.
- For catapult takeoffs the fuselage was parallel to the deck without the use of complex devices such as ramps and dynamic rotation, which were excluded by OS-130.
- The landing gear were as short as possible, allowing the fuselage to sit close to and nearly parallel to the deck. This provides ease of deck handling, pilot access, maintenance, and servicing.
- It was anticipated that placing the fuselage attitude small relative to the deck, about 6 to 8 degrees during carrier landing, loads on the nose gear structure would be considerably lower than on other aircraft.
- As configured the airplane was adaptable to use on flexible-deck aircraft carriers since the airplane lands with a small fuselage angle relative to the deck. This should lessen the risk of bouncing or porpoising on a flexible deck. At the time, flex-deck aircraft carriers were under consideration as a way to save aircraft weight by not having landing gear installed. Onboard ship a deck cart would be used to handle aircraft.
- The high incidence wing position also provided high lift at low speeds, reducing takeoff runs on conventional runways.

The swept wing mounted on top of the fuselage permitted a simple wing structure with a continuous center section and a three-point attachment to the fuselage to enable the variable incidence system. The high wing also allowed ample clearance for any future stores that potentially could be attached to the wing. The wing height also aided in adaptation to flex-deck aircraft carrier operations by having to strengthen only the bottom of the fuselage.

The wing planform was determined by the OS-130 ceiling requirements. A wing sweep of 42 degrees was chosen for its good longitudinal stability characteristics and low gross weight impact

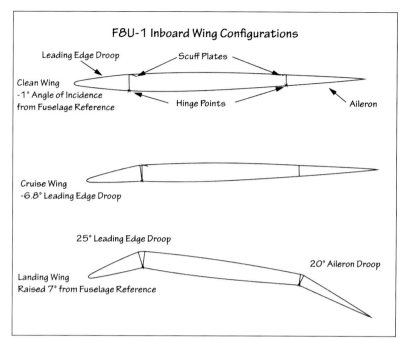

This drawing courtesy of Tommy Thomason illustrates the three positions of the leading edge droops. The top position is with the wing in the down position and the droops retracted; the second drawing illustrates the leading edge droops in the cruise droop position. With the leading edge slightly drooped, it changes the airfoil of the wing to give the F8U a better cruise performance. The lower illustration shows both the leading edge droops and trailing edge flaps in the extended position as would be used during takeoff and landing to increase lift to enable the aircraft to fly at lower speeds.

to the airplane. A lightweight wing was enabled with a taper ratio of .25. Wind tunnel test data indicated this was an optimum taper ratio for this particular wing, having good stability characteristics and developing the lift necessary for the OS-130 48,000-foot ceiling requirement.

The wing leading edge on the outboard panels had a "saw tooth" extension for aerodynamic reasons. During wind tunnel testing at NACA and United Aircraft's wind tunnels, the saw tooth extension gave significant improvement in longitudinal stability at high speeds. Test data indicated reduced pitch up, improved directional stability at low speeds, and increased buffet onset g during maneuvering of about 25 percent over a plain wing design.

When the wing actuator unlocked and the wing moved toward the up position, the leading edge droop actuators extended the droops down 25 (center section) and 27 degrees (outer panels) to the land position. As the wing continued to move through its 7 degrees of arc, a mechanical linkage repositioned the trailing edge flaps and ailerons down 20 degrees. The lift of the wing was significantly increased with the combination of the extended leading edge droops and the drooped flaps and ailerons. As the wing moved through its

7 degrees of travel, the unit horizontal tails (UHTs) moved 5 degrees nose down to balance out the changes in pitching moment from the leading edge droop and trailing edges extending. Last, the surface travel of the ailerons and rudder were limited to prevent over-control at the slower landing speeds. The important result of the wing repositioning was to provide excellent visibility for the pilot during his approach to landing without the need for a raised cockpit.

On the production F8U-1, the droops also had a cruise position that could be used in flight regimes other than takeoffs and landings. The cruise droops lower the leading edges -1 degree. The cruise droop position is noticeable in photographs if the leading edge of the wing is compared with where it meets the fuselage. With the leading edge droops in the cruise position, drag was reduced during climb and maximum cruise flight. The droops also decreased the stall and buffet speeds in low-speed flight and in subsonic turning flight above 30,000 feet of altitude. The major performance penalty of cruise droops in operation was a loss of maximum speed.

Unit Horizontal Tail

The Unit Horizontal Tail (UHT) or flying tail is not a novel concept. The design has been used on the F-100 and other contemporary aircraft. Unit horizontal tail is the name for the all-moving horizontal stabilizers. This terminology continued into the Ling-Temco-Vought (LTV) A-7 Corsair II aircraft as well. The flying tail can pivot to about +10 degrees nose up, and to about -30 degrees nose down. The advantage over a conventional fixed stabilizer and elevator system is that it maintains satisfactory longitudinal control for the high-speed range of the V-383/384 airplane at speeds from 100 knots to 900 knots.

The UHT is mounted in a low position on the aft fuselage of the airplane. This position allows the airplane to have satisfactory longitudinal stability characteristics throughout a wide speed range. Wind tunnel data from tests at NACA and United Aircraft wind tunnels has shown it necessary to place the UHT below the plane of the wing. This is particularly helpful to avoid pitch-up and a lack of positive longitudinal control in the transonic Mach number range of .95 to 1.05.

Pitch-up was a problem experienced with some other high-performance airplanes at the time. There was no carry through connection between the left and right UHT surfaces. A system of pushrods took the control stick movement and moved slider valves on the left and right UHT power control packages. The slider valves ported hydraulic fluid to the elevator power control cylinders to move the surfaces for the desired unit horizontal tail surface movement. The two unit horizontal tails' surfaces were synchronized by adjusting the input rods. Rigging the UHTs was exacting work; the input rods were adjusted in 1/2-turn increments until the surfaces were within 12 minutes (1/5) of a degree apart according to the Chance Vought Aircraft F8U-1 Surface Control Training Manual.

Drag Considerations

To obtain the maximum speeds and acceleration targets of OS-130, considerable attention had to be paid to drag producing items such as the fuselage, canopy, wing, and intake duct. To reduce drag, a high fuselage fineness ratio of about 11 was used. Fineness ratio is the length of the fuselage divided by the diameter of the fuselage. The larger the number (higher fineness ratio) the less drag of the design. The frontal area, windshield/canopy, wing fuselage joint, fuselage stations, and tail were all carefully reviewed to reduce drag.

Speed Brakes

The speed brakes for the proposed V-383 and V-384 airplanes were located on the aft fuselage between the vertical and horizontal tails. The design was subject to refinement by continued wind tunnel testing. Preliminary wind tunnel test data indicated that the speed brakes would perform satisfactorily in this location.

Hydraulic System

The hydraulic systems for the V-383/384 consisted of two power control systems, PC-1 and PC-2, and a utility system. Each system was pressurized to 3,000 psi by a dedicated pump that was mounted on an engine-driven gearbox. New, lightweight, hydraulic pumps were used to power the supply and distribution systems throughout the airplane. The systems were entirely separate, each a closed system (pressure and return) with a reservoir to store hydraulic fluid. The two PC systems powered all of the flight control surfaces, ailerons, and horizontal tails. Unit horizontal tail and ailerons were positioned by tandem irreversible hydraulic actuators.

Tandem actuators are essentially two cylinders in one unit, one driven by PC-1 and the other by PC-2. Pilot input by stick was mechanically transmitted to a slider valve attached to the actuator. The slider valve piston was positioned in accordance with pilot input to allow fluid flow into the cylinders to extend or retract the piston attached to the surface. In the event of the loss of one system or the other, the actuator would still have sufficient hydraulic power to maintain control of the airplane. The rudder was mechanically operated by the pilot through a conventional cable and pulley system.

A Marquardt ram air turbine (RAT) was installed in the lower right side of the fuselage. In the event of a dual PC system failure, the RAT could be deployed into the airstream. The RAT would drive its own hydraulic pump to pressurize the PC-1 system to give limited control of the aircraft. This procedure was usable only if the PC-1 system was intact (i.e., the system had not lost its fluid). During the life of the Crusader this system was used several times to land a disabled aircraft.

The Utility Hydraulic System, pressurized by a pump on the engine-driven gearbox, was separate from the PC-1/2 systems with its own reservoir and was also pressurized to 3,000 psi. The utility system operated all other airplane systems except the primary flight controls The landing gear, arresting gear, wing incidence with leading edge droops, speed brake, wheel brakes, nose gear steering, and outer panel wing fold (V-383 only) were all utility system powered. A back-up pneumatic system was provided in case of utility system failure. The backup allowed one-time operation of critical systems for emergencies.

For emergency landing gear, the nose gear was powered to the down-and-locked position. The main landing gears were unlocked, which allowed gravity and ram air pressure to force it to the down-and-locked position. The pneumatic system allowed for extending the arresting gear. The landing position of the wing incidence and leading edge droops was also possible with the pneumatic backup system. A limited number of brake applications were available during landing rollout.

The tricycle landing gear was housed within the fuselage. The nose gear was mounted just aft of the cockpit in the lower forward fuselage. The nose gear retracted aft, powered by a utility system hydraulic actuator. It was covered by two landing gear doors. The main landing gear was located on the lower center fuselage section. The gears consisted of a tension strut and an oleo shock strut, with a utility hydraulic actuator for retraction. The main landing gear retracted forward into a separate gear well on each side of the fuselage. As with the nose gear the main landing gear was completely enclosed by doors when retracted, reducing drag.

The fuel system was made up of three subsystems: the main, fuselage transfer, and wing transfer systems. The total fuel capacity was 1,188 U.S. gallons (8,033 pounds) of JP-5 jet fuel. All fuel supplied to the engine passed through the main fuel tank. The main tank, located in the fuselage forward of the main landing gear, was a bladder tank wrapped around the engine inlet duct. The fuel system had six electric pumps. Four of the pumps supplied fuel during normal flight with the other two pumps dedicated to inverted flight. The inverted-flight pumps operated when a mercury attitude switch turned on the pumps at a nose-up attitude exceeding 90 degrees, nose-down attitude exceeding 45 degrees, or a roll attitude of 90 degrees or more.

The fuselage transfer system was pressurized by ram air to 1.0 psi at all times to prevent fuel from boiling at altitude and to protect the bladders from collapsing during maneuvering. The fuselage transfer system had four cells, two mid-fuselage and two aft near the fuselage break point. The fuselage transfer system supplied fuel to the main tank through a pump located in the lower left fuel cell. The cells were shielded with double-walled titanium panels that were air cooled. Fuel in the wing was pressurized by engine bleed air and transferred to the main tank without the need for pumps.

Electrical System

Vought proposed an alternating current (AC) for the prime electrical power source, which enabled savings of almost 100 pounds compared to a similar direct current (DC) system. A heavy aircraft battery was not required and lighter-weight electrical wiring was possible. A transformer rectifier converted AC power to DC for those systems that required direct current power. The V-383/384 propos-

als utilized an engine bleed air driven turbine drive for primary AC power generation to provide additional weight minimization, since the bleed air turbine generator was lighter than an equivalent engine driven generator.

In the event of a generator failure, the Marquardt RAT (ram air turbine) could also be deployed to obtain 9kva of electrical power for a return to base.

Power Plants and Intake Ducting

The selection of a power plant and ducting is critical to the success of a jet aircraft. The wrong sized duct can choke off an engine in certain flight regimes and allow too much air in others. Either of those events can greatly reduce the thrust available to the airplane, which ultimately reduces the performance.

Power plant selection for a new airplane is primarily dependent upon the military characteristics required by specification. Navy Specification OS-130 included a list of approved engines for use in the airplane design proposals. Considerations in choosing an engine include the following: thrust, both augmented (afterburner) and unaugmented; fuel consumption, which relates to the fuel capacity necessary to deliver the radius of action specified; performance of the engine at various altitudes, especially the military power ceiling; and finally, the combat power rating and resulting maximum speed. Approved engines were evaluated on these characteristics for use in the day fighter proposals.

A lesson learned in the Pirate and Cutlass programs was that turbojet engine technology was still developing and challenges could arise that might prevent delivery of the promised performance. One important consideration was alternate engines under development or available in case of difficulties with the engine chosen for the airplane design proposal. In the case of the Navy Day Fighter, engines on the approved list but not selected were evaluated for suitability as replacements in the airframes. That way, if the primary engines failed to deliver specified performance after the airplanes had been built, an option was available.

The Pratt & Whitney J57 engine was used in the V-383 design. Two alternate engines of similar size and availability were the Allison J71-A-7 and the General Electric YJ73-GE-5. The alternates could each be fitted to the V-383 airframe without substantial rework. The downside of the two alternates would be the reduced thrust compared to the J57, which would in turn reduce the performance of the V-383. The J57 engine proved to be the best engine choice to power the V-383. It was the first American jet engine to reach 10,000 pounds of thrust.

The engine was a twin-spool, 16-stage compressor axial flow design. Unlike CVA's previous experience with early jet engines that limited the potential of the F6U and F7U programs, the J57 delivered the predicted thrust values. The PT4 turboprop was intended to power the XB-52 Stratofortress; however, more thrust was needed and the engine evolved from turboprop to turbojet. The North American F-100 and Convair F-102 both used afterburning versions of the engine. The F-100 became the first production airplane to exceed Mach 1 in level flight on its maiden flight, a fact not lost on CVA management.

Connie Lau wrote to J. R. Clark and William. C. Schoolfield that "if the reported maximum speed of 1.34 of the F-100A is correct, the corresponding speed for the XF8U-1 is 1.46." This conclusion was based on an evaluation of the differences in propulsive force due to the different inlet ducts of the two designs along with a look at the aircrafts and all drag producing items such as canopies, wing folds, wings, and fuselages.[27]

The V-384 was designed around the Wright J65 engine with no alternate engine available for the day fighter. At the time, it was felt that the General Electric XJ79-GE-5 engine could be in the airplane's future, giving it much greater performance. It would have, however, required a larger air intake duct with an increased fuel consumption requiring more fuel capacity. The XJ79-GE-5 was expected to complete its 150 hours qualification testing by the end of 1956.

Both the V-383 and V-384 airplanes featured an underslung nose scoop inlet and duct. This design evolved from extensive research studies on airplane induction systems. Several design studies were conducted on various duct configurations, including side mounted intakes and pitot openings with split ducts (like the Regulus I). Visits were made to the three NACA laboratories at Ames, Cleveland, Langley Field, and the United Aircraft Research Department to discuss intake configuration.

The design of an engine air intake involves competing elements: the amount of air delivered to the engine, duct drag, airplane frontal area, boundary layer air, length of the duct, and shock wave effects, to name a few.

The underslung nose scoop was the compromise reached from the competing factors of duct losses, airplane drag, and design arrangement. The design eliminates the need for variable ramps to obtain shock recovery by using the pre-compression field behind the bow shock wave to obtain shock recovery at the inlet.

This design allows for low frontal area while still providing for nose-mounted equipment. Also, the inlet is easier to change in this configuration should flight testing show the need for modifications to meet performance objectives or future larger engine installations. The longer duct of the underslung nose scoop design had the disadvantages of greater weight and higher internal pressure losses. It was decided, however, that the "improved shock recovery due to the forward underslung location more than compensates for the somewhat higher internal pressure losses due to the long duct."[28]

Carrier Suitability

Numerous ideas were tried to overcome the problem of pilot visibility during approach to the aircraft carrier for landing. Increas-

This approach shot gives an idea of the challenges while flying the F7U-3M. The visibility on approach to the carrier was the reason for the seat and canopy being raised in the design.

ing pilot visibility meant major design changes from the XF7U-1 to the F7U-3 airplane during its development. Swept wings, mission requirements for higher speeds (cleaner designs), and the need for increased angles of attack to reduce approach speeds led to further design changes. Because the techniques in place for meeting these objectives were losing effectiveness, several new strategies were investigated during development of the day fighter.

Among the potential solutions evaluated were a drooping nose section hinged behind the pilot; a very heavily flapped airplane; a variable-incidence wing with two incidence positions using high incidence for takeoff and landing, low incidence for all other flight conditions; an "elevator" cockpit that moved the cockpit, pilot, canopy, and windshield several inches above the normal flight position; and a "hinged" cockpit, hinged at the front end to rotate the cockpit, canopy, and windshield to raise the pilot several inches above his normal position.[29]

In studying potential solutions to the approach vision problem it became clear that the variable-incidence wing arrangement met all requirements without the weight and complexity of the other designs. The variable-incidence wing also contributed to other OS-130 objectives, such as providing an airplane that would catapult off the deck without dynamic rotation, ramps, or other trick devices and without sink off the bow, and an airplane that would sit as close to the deck as practical with wheeled landing gear. The shorter landing gear saved weight and allowed for easy deck handling, servicing, and maintenance, along with cockpit access.

The airplane landed with a small fuselage angle relative to the deck, reducing the chances of the airplane porpoising on any possible flexible deck, should it be needed in future operations. The height that the nose gear had to drop to the deck during arrested landing was reduced by the fuselage angle at arrestment. This reduced nose gear loads on landing, which in turn saved weight in the design of the nose gear. The variable-incidence wing permitted the wing to be mounted high on the fuselage, which also aided carrier suitability by providing ample deck clearance for (potential) wing-mounted stores.

Design Selection

Chance Vought Aircraft was notified by BuAer TWX (teletypewriter) exchange on 19 May that the V-383 had been selected and that a contract would be awarded. The message specifically stated that this was "for information only and should not be considered as an advance notice of award or authority to proceed with the work." An interesting way to tell but not tell of a pending contract award. However, based upon this notification the CVA engineering department was authorized to proceed with design operations. Postponed wind tunnel tests were now rescheduled and design engineering work resumed.

The official "go-ahead" for the XF8U-1 was received in a Letter of Intent NOa(s) 53-1075 on 30 June 1953. This letter authorized the design and fabrication of three airplanes plus a static test article. With the letter of intent in hand the pace of the program quickened; schedules for testing, flight testing objectives, and detail specifications were among the many documents created during the month. At this same time, the BuAer and CVA began to discuss how to move the program from test to production in an orderly manner.

CVA Reputation Concerns and Schedule

Continuing delays in the F7U program caused a deterioration in the standing of CVA with the Navy. It was felt the Navy considered CVA "a high-cost, slow delivery company." The pressure was expressed and felt within the Operating Plans and Coordination (OP&C) group during development of the XF8U-1 master schedule. Delivery and cost would be under scrutiny by the BuAer, and CVA needed to deliver an on-schedule, highly successful program.

An analysis of the Master Schedule No. 2 by OP&C caused a few cautionary items to be raised:

- The F7U-1 had taken 27 months to first flight (4 months behind first estimates) and the F8U-1 program was promised as a 22-month program.
- Of the 22 months, 10 had already been used and the program was averaging two weeks behind schedule.
- The production design concept had to be preserved to accomplish production follow-on promptly.
- The airplane had to be fully instrumented prior to first flight, something the F7U-1 was not.
- No short cuts involving omission of parts and equipment could be taken prior to first flight.
- No padding was provided in the schedule for future redesigns that were likely to occur.
- The Regulus II program (behind schedule) was competing with

the XF8U-1, and the possibility of further competition from the A2U-3 (a follow-on to the A2U-1 getting ready to start production and at risk of cancellation) and the V-382 (a design that CVA felt won the F-105 competition for the USAF, but was never built) was a matter of concern.

- Because of the above factors, the first flight date might slip by three or more months, endangering production start in 1956.[30]

It was recommended to give the XF8U-1 priority over the Regulus II and emphasize the importance of better planning and coordination to meet the timelines and objectives.

Detail Specification

During May and June 1953, the BuAer and CVA negotiated the detail specification for the XF8U-1. The goal was to have a signed detail specification agreed to by 10 July 1953.

Chance Vought Engineering Report 8978 was released as a first draft of the proposed detail specification on 3 June 1954. This engineering report formed the basis for the BuAer SD-500 Preliminary Detail Specification for the XF8U-1 airplane. The detail specification is exactly what the title suggests. It takes the beautiful flying machine and breaks it down into all the expectations and deliverables agreed upon by the contractor and the BuAer. The detail specification is where the Navy's previous experiences with aircraft procurement and operations are mixed into the new design. Standard specifications are called out for various aircraft systems and parts installations.

Without including the entirety of the XF8U-1 detail specifications, here are a few sections to give a flavor of the document. Every model of the Crusader would have a detail specification related to it, including some of the special test aircraft that were built during the program.

The detail specification SD-500 for the XF8U-1 was signed on 2 July 1953. From this information the production plan was started. The basis for the production plan was a run of 316 aircraft to be completed by May 1957. From this work the F8U-1 Program Plan proposal would be created to be presented to the BuAer in mid-August 1953. The proposal contained details of assignments to the first 12 aircraft for testing, operational development, and demonstration with an additional 5 aircraft being proposed for further demonstration and testing.

In anticipation of the detail specification agreement and signing, CVA engineering started preparing the design schedule plan in June 1953.

NACA Testing

The National Advisory Committee for Aeronautics (NACA), the BuAer, and CVA agreed on 29 June 1952 to test the XF8U-1 design using rocket models for drag and flutter characteristics. Stability, spin, inlet and duct investigations, and high speed with and without

Sparrow missile installations were to be tested in NACA's high-speed wind tunnel. At NACA Ames the variable stability F6F-3 Hellcat aircraft would be used for flight simulation testing. The heavily modified Hellcat was fitted with servo equipment to vary the lateral and directional stability and handling characteristics to simulate the characteristics of other aircraft. Results of testing with the variable stability aircraft were used to refine the design of the flight control system of the XF8U-1.

The F6F-3 revealed an undesirable lateral damping and roll-coupling characteristics in the landing configuration. These same characteristics were experienced during the early test flights of the XF8U-1.

Another discovery was a lateral acceleration following abrupt aileron movement at high speed without coordinated rudder input. The solution to this condition was an aileron-rudder interconnect system. The NACA variable stability simulator F-86A was used to test this configuration. The aileron-rudder interconnect was proven to solve the problem with a side effect of improving the air-to-air tracking capabilities of the aircraft.

High-speed wind tunnel testing revealed another set of problems for the fledgling design: aerodynamic center, directional stability in the clean condition, maximum lift in landing configuration, and the rear-fuselage-mounted speed brakes causing too much trim change. To correct the speed brake problem several different configurations were tried, including speed brakes mounted on the sides of the mid-fuselage, over the gun compartment, and final configuration under the fuselage center section. To fix the aerodynamic center problem the wing moved aft 9 inches and the engine moved forward. Non-aerodynamic changes included fixes to nose gear interference with the structure, increasing the engine inlet duct by 10 percent, and decreasing the fuselage fuel tanks from nine to five to reduce center of gravity changes caused by fuel burn. The NACA rocket flutter tests showed a need to stiffen the wing and unit horizontal tail (UHT) trailing edges due to the destructive onset of flutter. By August the fuselage design was a month behind schedule with more changes to come.

Wind tunnel results in October 1953 indicated the V-383's drag was higher than anticipated. The maximum speed with the J57-P-4 engine was expected to be only about Mach 1.3. The guaranteed maximum speed for the V-383 was Mach 1.45. Further results from the Langley tunnel in November indicated that the drag was even higher than previously predicted. The top speed now was down to Mach 1.22 with the J57-P-4 and Mach 1.13 with the J57-P-2 engine. The J57-P-4 engine developed 10,200 pounds of thrust dry and 16,000 pounds of thrust in afterburner compared to 13,700 pounds of thrust for an afterburning J57-P-2.

A crash program was started to reduce aerodynamic drag. Several design changes combined to reduce drag and increase speed. The changes started with a more slender nose; then a thinner wing and tail were successfully incorporated. The horizontal tail was moved forward 6 inches and the area reduced by 7 square feet. The BuAer also pushed for fuselage changes in accordance with the area rule, or "coking," since the result was similar to the shape of the Coca Cola bottle of the time. CVA resisted coking due to the amount of change it would require. Confidence was growing that the design would meet specifications without coking. The incorporation of the slender nose and duct design with improved "boat-tail" angle improved the Mach number by .19, which resulted in a calculated estimate of Mach 1.41.

The revised aerodynamic design models entered wind tunnel and rocket testing in mid-December 1953. NACA's tests utilized .11-scale rocket-powered models of the XF8U-1. The configurations tested were the original nose and forward fuselage, the modified nose and a

NACA photo of the variable stability F6F-3 that was used to test the proposed control system for the V383.

Supersonic wind tunnel model of the F8U in the hands of R. C. McWherter. (CVPR-2250)

Historical factory photo of the F8U-1 mock-up with the early speed brake position and guns still mounted forward on the fuselage sides.

more difficult to recover from a spin than the F7U Cutlass. A 24-foot spin recovery parachute was considered for successful recovery, as well as a rocket recovery system. Rockets mounted on the wing tips and in the nose of the fuselage proved unsatisfactory for spin recovery. By the time spin tunnel testing had been completed, fuselage canards and a 28-foot-diameter parachute were considered necessary for spin recovery. For spin testing, a special aft section would be manufactured with the spin chute installation.

Mock-Up

slimmer canopy, and a slimmer nose and sharper inlet duct. The rockets boosted the scale XF8U-1 models to supersonic speeds. The purpose of the testing was to measure drag at transonic and low supersonic speeds. Radar data was collected during the deceleration phase of the models' flight once it had separated from the booster. The models were visually tracked using an internal smoke system. Drag numbers were calculated from the radar tracking data. The modified nose showed a drag reduction between the speeds of Mach 1.1 and Mach 1.28. During December, the design changes incorporated were sharp lips on the engine air inlet, tilting the nose cone up 5 degrees to reduce drag at high Mach numbers and provide higher duct recovery.

The last major external design changes came during April/May 1954. The aileron span was lengthened and the flap area increased to support a higher lift coefficient, and a 22-inch extension was added to the tail cone on the No. 1 XF8U-1. The basic design was at 95-percent release point on 27 May 1954, about three weeks ahead of schedule.

Spin tests were the last of this series of wind tunnel test to be accomplished. In May through December 1954 the spin tests were performed. Preliminary information showed the V-383 would be

The construction of the XF8U-1 mock-up began the week of 22 May 1953. The aircraft mock-up was completed on 22 August. The mock-up was subjected to an in-house evaluation by CVA on 26 August. Several recommendations from that review resulted in substantial changes. Relocation of the speed brakes and of the cannons from under the fuselage to the sides of the inlet was accomplished prior to the Navy's inspection of the mock-up. The mock-up was moved to the production hangar prior to a pre-inspection on 11 September. Several recommendations arose from the evaluation that were incorporated prior to the official Navy review of the mock-up.

The Navy Formal Mock-up Board reviewed the XF8U-1 mock-up during 16–18 September 1953. The inspection was satisfactory with a number of minor changes recommended by the board. The recommendations were to improve rear vision without changing the existing canopy lines, create a provision for dumping fuel from the wing tanks to lighten the airplane in the event of an emergency, and make the circuit breaker location inaccessible to the pilot. This last change also deleted "self-resetting" circuit breakers, which presented a fire hazard because the remote location would prevent the pilot from stopping the reset.

Side view of the F8U-1 mock-up taken 29 August, with the squashed, fat-lipped inlet and blunt nose. An interesting boarding ladder is attached for access. The outboard under-inlet cannon is visible along with the extended tailhook. (CVA-17239)

Another side view of the F8U mock-up, this time in the clean configuration. Wing is down, gear retracted, canopy closed, and tailhook raised. CVA-17226 taken on 23 August 1953.

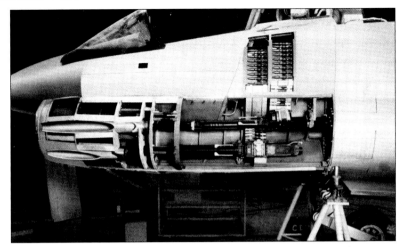

Low-resolution, but important photograph of initial gun configuration in F8U mock-up.

By September 1953 the guns had moved twice and now did not even show on the mock-up, although evidence of the move from the bottom of the inlet to the sides is still visible in this view. The intake lip has sharpened, as has the nose. (CVA-387)

Items CVA had to study and address included rearward vision, fuel dumping, and canopy jettison clearance over the tail at slow speeds.

Additional Mock-Ups

In addition to the XF8U-1 airplane mock-up, functional parts of aircraft systems were created with mock-ups. These additional mock-ups included power plant, power control with flight simulator, fuel system, electrical and electronic, integral wing tank, antenna design, and stabilization and trim system. In addition to that extensive list of mock-ups, ejection seat tests, horizontal tail support bearing, and armament test rigs were added to the list of systems to be mocked up and tested.

Cockpit lighting and vision mock-ups were completed and successfully evaluated by the Navy and CVA in November 1953 and February 1954, respectively.

Using the cockpit mock-up, the ability to reach controls and switches in a full pressure suit was demonstrated. This one is using a USN full-pressure suit.

Essential in the list of activities important to be able to perform in a fully inflated pressure suit is ejection from a stricken aircraft. Here, the pilot is pulling down on the face curtain while engineers observe.

The same testing in the cockpit mock-up that was performed in a USN full-pressure suit was also accomplished in the stylish USAF partial-pressure suit. Here, the pilot models the suit prior to cockpit entry.

Here, the USAF partial-pressure suit is used for control reach checks in the cockpit mock-up.

A nice from-the-rafters view of the F8U control system "iron bird." This rig was used to test the flight control components and tied to a rudimentary cockpit simulator for testing.

CVA proposed that a Pratt & Whitney be authorized by the BuAer to fabricate a mock-up of the J57-P-2 engine, due to the popularity of the Pratt & Whitney J57 for mock-up in various aircraft programs. A mock-up engine was delivered in February 1954 and the installation mock-up satisfactorily completed in May. The installation mock-up involved separating the aft section of the airplane and removal and installation of the J57 engine as would be done on production airplanes.

One of the most challenging mock-ups was the power control system. Delays were encountered with drawings and because of the addition of a powered rudder system (the original proposal was not power assisted). An iron bird control system simulator was built to attach all the components of the flight control system. The simulator was completed by mid-September 1954 and testing began about two weeks behind schedule.

A REAC (Reeves Electronic Analog Computer) was connected to the simulator in November and tests of the lateral-directional control system started. An instability in the yaw stabilization system was discovered at high angles of attack that needed to be resolved. The problem was resolved with larger motors and a counter balance to cancel out axial g loading on the actuator, and the flight control system was considered flight ready by the end of December 1954.

The electrical and electronic systems were successfully bread boarded and those mock-ups tested without delay. A fuel system

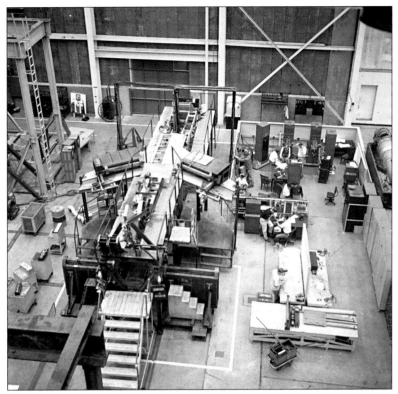

The fuel system simulator for the F8U. All the connections and simulated tanks were in place to test flows, pumps, tanks, and the workings of the fuel system.

In the background, the "cockpit" for the iron bird can be seen along with the various machines used to measure and record movements in the flight control system.

A peek into the inner workings of the iron bird. Here, a technician is working on the linkage to the simulated right-hand UHT. In the case of the UHTs, the surface was simulated by the weight of the surface without having to complicate and create a hazard on the iron bird with a surface flapping around.

mock-up was under construction during late summer 1954 and was completed in late October 1954, almost a month late, because of a shortage of vendor components. Testing of the fuel system started in early November and was completed in February 1955 to qualify the system for flight.

The final mock-ups of note were the armament test rigs at NOTS (Naval Ordnance Test Station) Inyokern and CVA. During the mock-up and detail specification process the three under-fuselage-mounted T-160 cannons had been revised to four Mk12 cannons mounted on the fuselage sides. Tests of the Mk12 20mm cannons were performed at CVA's Dallas facility. Originally a simple fixture was to be used for cannon testing; however, a simulated nose and front section was available and utilized. Gun firing in February 1955 showed that the fuses that prevented backflow through the gun charging valves were not up to the task. An alternate system was developed to not slow the testing until the fuses could be properly replaced. The blast port castings became the next weak part of the system. Magnesium castings failed after 200 rounds, and high-purity aluminum castings failed after 300 rounds. Steel weldment pieces were finally used acceptably in the testing and would be incorporated into the first 12 airplanes with stainless-steel castings to follow.

Tooling for Production

Discussions took place between the BuAer and CVA about the transition from experimental phase to production for the F8U-1 in June 1953. The need for additional airplanes to support the development of the type was incorporated into contract discussions.

The XF8U-1 was divided up as follows: nose section, front section, mid-section, aft section, center wing section, and outer wing sections to facilitate fabrication and assembly of the aircraft.

Planning and design of the basic tooling mock-ups started in October 1953 and was completed the following February. For each of the major sections, fixtures were built to support the fabrication of that particular assembly. The reason for constructing production-type fixtures rather than hand building each aircraft was the anticipated receipt of additional follow up orders for production of the F8U-1 aircraft. Time spent now would speed the service introduction of the production aircraft. A 1/96-scale model of the production line was built to help with tool design, shop layout and production flow. The detail of the model extended down to time clocks on the walls. The time spent on modeling would pay off with a smoother transition from experimental to the production airplanes.

The basic mock-up tool design was completed in February 1954. Fabrication, planning, detail tool design and fabrication, along with subsequent and major tool assembly design all started in February. By November all the basic tooling required for producing the XF8U-1 was completed. While this was happening, the fabrication of XF8U-1 detail parts had already started. In June 1954, the master tooling fabrication was completed. The mock-up was completed and major assembly tool designs were completed as well. In August, the major fixtures for the wing center section, front fuselage, nose section, and ailerons were completed.

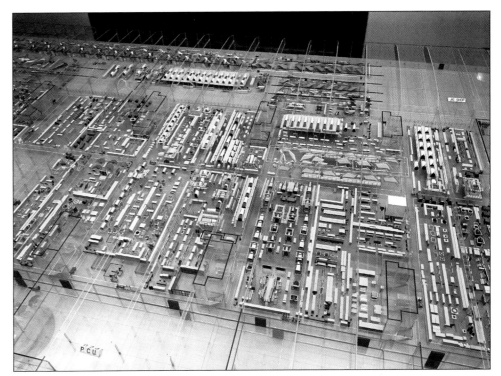

A 1/96-scale model of production facilities was built to model the flow of the F8U through the factory to completed aircraft. Here, some of the shops that build the small parts are modeled.

At the same time the F8U entered production the Regulus I and Regulus II were planned to be in production. This view shows how they would share space in the factory.

Rocket Pack

The testing of the F8U-1's other armament system, the rocket pack, would not go as smoothly. The 2-inch Gimlet rocket, two tandem tubes, firing pins, and detents were tested at NOTS Inyokern to verify the firing pin design. In addition to the two tandem tubes, a production 32-rocket pack (1/2 of the envisioned load of 64 rockets) was to be ground tested at Inyokern.

By November 1954, CVA learned that production of the 2-inch rocket had been stopped. The reason for the production halt was a pending decision to standardize the Navy and Air Force on a single rocket type. Changing the required rocket from the Gimlet to another design would have an effect on the rocket-pack design. All testing at NOTS Inyokern, along with design and development work on the rocket pack, was therefore stopped by CVA and design work began in December on a 2.75-inch rocket pack.

In February 1955, the BuAer requested redesign of the rocket installation to utilize reloadable clips holding 2.75-inch rockets, with provisions for 2-inch rockets. The ability to fire full salvos, half salvos, or single rockets of either type was requested for the new design.

On 11 March 1955, CVA informed the BuAer that it was preparing a rocket pack redesign that would provide for eight reloadable tandem clips containing four 2.75-inch rockets each. At CVA there was too much uncertainty concerning the 2-inch Gimlet rocket to proceed with any sort of design work utilizing those rockets. It was felt that if the Gimlet became the rocket of choice, a design would be prepared at that time. ECP-35 (Engineering Change Proposal) was created to meet only the new 2.75-inch rocket requirements.

ECP-35 proposed a new pack structure to accommodate rocket clusters, changes to the structure and operating mechanism for the

Final assembly area for the F8U. The models were said to be so detailed that time clocks were included.

Finally, the roll-out area where the newly completed F8Us would be towed to the engine run facilities and eventually to the airport area for flight and acceptance testing.

Racks of rocket tubes used to support the rocket pack testing program.

rocket pack, and other aircraft changes due to the different pack and rocket characteristics. Vought accomplished an initial 2.75-inch rocket firing from a clip on 28 July 1955. On 2 August 1955, the Navy requirement was amended approving 32 2.75-inch rockets in a retractable rocket pack. The BuAer added the requirement to approve a prototype prior to flight and ground tests.

The rocket-clip design was created to avoid the blast chamber and deflector door problems that had plagued the F7U-3 Cutlass. The design featured a two-tube, four-rocket reloadable launcher with forward venting of three and a half times the rocket nozzle area. The test program for the rocket pack included successful completion of extensive ground firings prior to any flight test program. The ground firing program was heavily concentrated at Naval Ordnance Test Station Inyokern along with a smaller program at the Dallas factory.

The NOTS testing took place from May through August 1956. A total of 522 rockets were fired out of the total of 534 that were loaded, a successful launch percentage of 98. The causes of the unfired rockets were fairly evenly distributed between loading errors, GFE (Government Furnished Equipment), and CFE (Contractor Furnished Equipment). Two tests demonstrated hang fires and the effects of rocket motor burn through the rocket pack and aircraft structure. In both tests the rocket motors did not burn through the top or side skins of the rocket packs. The burn-through damage was to the bottom skins of the rocket pack as designed. With a bottom skin burn-through, the outside airflow helped cool the damaged area.

The following is a description of one of the hang-fire demonstrations, number 30, toward the end of the demonstration period in August 1956.

"Event 30 was a live warhead-hang fire (retained rocket) demonstration where the number 7 tube was loaded with a live warhead 2.75-inch MK 1 Mod 3 rocket complete with live rocket motor and

A view of the rocket pack extended under the fuselage of an F8U-1. Notice the tight clearance between the ends of the tubes and the fuselage.

fuse. The rocket ahead of it in the tube was a live rocket motor with an inert warhead. The forward rocket was fired with the pack in the retracted position to simulate a hang fire. As the rocket burned through the tube the Fireye infrared detection system automatically lowered the rocket pack. The pack lowering is a safety feature to allow wind chill to help cool the launcher tube in the event of a burn-through. The hang fired rocket moved approximately 2 feet forward and jammed as the pack lowered. After about 19 seconds the rocket motor caused the live warhead of the rocket behind it to cook off with the resulting explosion doing considerable damage to the rocket pack."[31]

BuAer representatives were invited to view the clip firings during the week of 3 October 1955 to meet the prototype requirements. The BuAer granted authority to CVA on 11 October 1955 to proceed with the test program. A further request from the BuAer wanted investigation into the safety of the rocket system during handling and flight conditions. The request also specified rocket malfunction tests such as hang fires and misfires.

The redesign of the rocket pack progressed into January 1956. The problems in the new design were concentrated at first on the redesigned forward bulkhead casting. NOTS also submitted plans in February 1956 for accomplishing the rocket clip air-firing test program without waiting for an F8U-1 airplane. Two clip units were to be mounted to the wings of an F9F-5 airplane and be fired simultaneously. By March the casting problems were diminishing, but delays were occurring with the selector valves and actuating mechanisms. In April, as a result of testing by NOTS, a revision was made to the testing schedule. By June the rocket pack redesign was coming together. The BuAer requested that CVA submit a proposal to install a rocket pack into the No. 14 F8U-1 to supplement the originally planned armament demonstrator, the No. 2 F8U-1. The airplane was scheduled to be ready for rocket firing demonstrations by 22 July 1956. Rocket firing and hang fire testing by July resulted in a number of engineering changes to the rocket pack and tubes. The rocket tubes were redesigned with resulting schedule delays affecting the program until October.

After the engineering fixes had been applied, rocket firing resumed. By mid-October, NOTS was notified that an acceptable number of rockets had been fired to evaluate the safety features of the rocket pack. NOTS recommendations were due by mid-November. By the end of October 1956 the ground-firing program of the rocket pack reached completion. The eventual rocket pack configuration carried 32 2.75-inch folding fin aerial rockets, half the original design load.

The rocket pack was not available for use for the first series of Service Acceptance Trials, conducted 8 August to 10 October 1956 using YF8U-1 BuNo 141338 and 141339. A production version of the rocket fire control system was finally available for evaluation during August 1957. During the second set of Service Acceptance Trials, the Navy commented on limitations of the rocket pack: "Difficulty in tracking in the rockets mode of the Aero 10L Armament Control System."[32]

The comments on this item gave insight to the future of the rocket program in the Navy. "The concept of air-to-air lead pursuit rockets has left much to be desired in all Navy aircraft in which it has been tried. The F8U-1 is no exception. The lead required for rocket firing at a maneuvering target are so great that only about 1¾ g can be placed on the aircraft and still retain the pipper on the reflector plate. This is due to the fact that rockets follow a path into the relative wind rather than a gun-type trajectory. Large leads are also necessitated by the comparatively slow speed of rockets. Lags induced into the system are complicated by necessity for yaw and angle of attack inputs to the system to determine relative wind."[33]

The report also noted: "The less maneuvering a target is doing, the greater the value of the air-to-air rocket system becomes. Obviously, on a large bomber-type target, the rocket system provides reasonable tracking and kill capability. The rocket system does add to the kill capability of the F8U-1, particularly against large and less maneuverable targets so it is retained in the aircraft in spite of deficiencies."[34] The comments ended with, "Difficulties with air-to-air lead pursuit systems in various Navy aircraft have proven so numerous, however, that expenditure of sufficient funds to correct problem areas does not appear to be warranted."[35]

Eventually an Air Frame Change was released deactivating the rocket packs in the F8U-1/1E and F8U-2 aircraft. After all the development work, research, and testing that was performed to get the rocket system to operate properly and reduce hazard to the firing aircraft, the system quietly disappeared.

Fabrication of the First XF8U-1 Begins

The first work orders were released to the shop on 19 February 1954. This was ahead of the scheduled 30 April 1954 date. In general, the detail parts fabrication program remained ahead of schedule throughout the first aircraft fabrication. Shortages of some key details slowed the fabrication of certain subassemblies. As a result of shortages, a number of subassemblies were passed on via so-called "traveler" instructions to their next fabrication point, even though they were incomplete. This was not unusual in the fabrication of the first few examples of a new aircraft. In fact, parts shortages had an effect on the manufacturing of aircraft throughout the production run. Some of the shortages were caused by relatively new materials being pushed into new applications with fabrication techniques still in development. One of the new materials being pushed forward was titanium.

Titanium

In January 1954, management decided to use titanium hardware in the fabrication of the XF8U-1 to save weight. Chance Vought Air-

Engineers Gilmore and Smith review an assembly model of the F8U-1 as part of the factory modeling built to take the F8U into production as soon as possible after first flight. (CVPR-974)

craft was pushing the state of the art in materials with this move; other than for experimental applications, few other manufacturers had used titanium hardware. Because of the high rejection rate on hardware received from vendors, however, only a small portion of the envisioned usage of titanium hardware was actually used in the XF8U-1.

The role of titanium in the XF8U-1 was affected by several other considerations as well. The BuAerrequested that the amount of titanium used in the XF8U-1 be "comparable" to that used in other aircraft production to address concerns about material shortages. A more serious problem developed when the titanium was spot-welded; for example, cracking on the bulkhead for station 595, where the aft section mated to the center section. Evaluation of 34 test specimens led to the determination that cracking problems were confined to thick-gauge material. On thick-gauge material, a good parts fit was required for a successful spot weld. Tack riveting the parts together, followed by spot welding, was not a satisfactory manufacturing method.

Titanium parts also suffered from a delayed cracking problem. High hydrogen content was the primary cause of delayed cracking problems as evidenced by hydrogen embrittlement on the XF8U-1 aft sections. Special processes were established for high-hydrogen titanium stock and titanium producers worked to reduce the hydrogen content of the raw material supplied to Chance Vought Aircraft. Eventually these measures overcame the fabrication problems experienced with titanium parts on the XF8U-1 aircraft.

Another material used in the fabrication of the XF8U-1 aircraft was Metalite.

Metalite

A Metalite trailing-edge-assembly shortage slowed fabrication of the rudder assembly for the No. 1 XF8U-1. Metalite panels were made of a low-density balsa wood core, bonded on both sides to aluminum skin. The skins are formed in molds and then cured in a large autoclave. Once finished, Metalite panels are riveted to fuselage bulkheads or wing ribs depending on the application. Metalite panels reduced the number of ribs, or stiffeners, required for a strong, low-weight structure by providing inherent stiffness in the design. Metalite, which had been used on the CVA XF5U-1, XF6U-1, and XF7U-1 airplanes and evaluated on F4U horizontal tails, now had application in the XF8U-1.

The wing center section fixture was loaded right after tool completion and the first completed center section was unloaded in early October.

The mid-fuselage section fixture loaded in late August, approximately 10 days late. The delay was attributed to a shortage of machined bulkheads and engineering changes to the air inlet duct assembly. Shortages of titanium subassembly parts resulting from detail fabrication problems, and cracking also occurred. The completed mid-fuselage section unloaded from the fixture in mid-October. The mid-section of the fuselage was then loaded into the joining fixture for the addition of the forward section of the fuselage. Work that had not been completed on the fuselage mid-section was continued during joining operations. The joining of the mid and front sections of the fuselage was completed by 30 October 1954.

The aft section, despite continuing difficulties in fabricating parts from titanium, unloaded from the fixture four days ahead of schedule and arrived at the joining rig by the end of October. The nose section was the final fuselage section to arrive for joining operations on 12 November. The nose section had been delayed by the gun blast tube design changes required after test failures.

Negotiations with the BuAer continued over the limited production proposal. The submission was for five aircraft to be delivered at the rate of one a month for the period of August through December 1955. In October, the contract was further amended with the deletion of the third XF8U-1.

Static Testing

Per provisions of the contract, a static test airframe was to be fabricated and tested. The first item delivered to the test lab was the wing in early December 1954. By late December, static testing of the wing center section was in full swing. Testing of the wing center section stopped after 200 cycles of rolling pullout and 600 cycles of the 800-cycle schedule. A crack had formed in the area of rib 21 on the rear beam. The crack originated in an intersection of the wing skin, rear beam, and rib 21, which all shared a common attachment point. The flange holes were opened up and an external doubler added to the wing skin. The wing completed proof load testing of 120-percent

An interesting test rig is a clear plastic model of the fuel system. With this model, all attitudes of the aircraft and their effects on the fuel system could be simulated. The clear plastic allows the engineer to view the fluid flows through the model in the various positions. (CVPR-122)

design limit load by the end of February 1954 and was installed on the static fuselage. Tests were completed also on the aileron control boost, leading edge droop, and the wing incidence actuator.

The static fuselage arrived in the lab in early February and would take several weeks to install into the test fixture. During March the surface controls, speed brake, UHT, canopy, and windscreen all completed static testing.

Maintenance Survey Team

No matter how well an aircraft is designed and constructed, it must be serviced and maintained during its lifetime. Navy requirements emphasized maintainability in the design of the day fighter. The XF8U-1, an aircraft with a variable-incidence wing, featured shorter landing gear and an airframe that sat much closer to the deck than the F7U Cutlass series. Chance Vought Aircraft tried another new idea concerning maintenance on the XF8U-1 design as well.

When the basic design reached 95-percent completion, a Maintenance Survey Team was established. The Maintenance Survey Team included members from the project office, field engineering, field service, and airport operations. The purpose of the Maintenance Survey Team was to study the XF8U-1 aircraft to ensure that proper consideration was given to the maintenance of the finished product. After the first study, the team offered several recommendations for pre-flight, post flight, and maintenance procedures for the XF8U-1 as follows:

- Provide built-in fuselage steps and handholds for easy access to the top of the airplane to reduce the need for portable maintenance stands. Space is severely limited aboard ship and even a simple item such as the large boarding ladder for the F7U becomes a problem to use and store during flight operations. Anything that can be built into the aircraft for access, and in this case dual purpose of allowing the pilot to access the cockpit along with facilitating maintenance, makes good design sense to incorporate into the aircraft.
- Provide access for equipment compartment inspections from the top of the airplane by installing quick-opening access doors in the fuselage spine aft of the cockpit. Ease of access allows an aircraft to be inspected, repaired, and returned to flight status in less time.
- Seal openings around the angle of attack and yaw vane mounting panels to prevent water intrusion. This will help cut down on equipment malfunctions due to corrosion. Sealing openings will also help prevent salt-water contamination of the fuselage that can lead to structural problems caused by corrosion.
- Relocate emergency air system pressure gauge for easy visual check by the pilot prior to flight without having to open an access door.
- Use a standard jack instead of a forward fuselage jack to facilitate nose landing gear tire changes. This change allows one type of jack to be used to change any tire on the aircraft. Fuselage jacks are normally used in combination with wing jacks to allow landing gear retraction tests on the ground rather than for changing wheel assemblies (tire and wheel).

As the design continued to transition from drawings to fabrication, the Maintenance Survey Team continued to meet. The team met twice in June 1954. These meetings concluded with several more recommendations. The highlights of the team's recommendations are listed below:

- Locate utility hydraulic system reservoir sight gauge, emergency air system pressure gauge, and all emergency system fuses for easy inspection through a quick-opening access door.
- Mount air conditioning system air intake screen flush with the engine and duct interior.
- Install a flush-mounted screen at the entrance of the engine oil cooler air intake duct. Several additional recommendations, including stenciling of various markings on the airplane, relocating the engine oil filter, and changing the tolerance of the arresting hook micro switch rigging were made.

Finally, the team identified the need to establish a procedure for ground checking the engine oil cooler door circuit during pre-flight inspection and to incorporate "push-to-test" or similar switches for this check.

Until this point all recommendations were made using mock-ups and drawings. Actual flight-worthy parts of the aircraft would not be assembled in major manufacturing fixtures for another two months.

Final Maintenance Survey Team Meetings

The Maintenance Survey Team continued to function until November 1954. In their summary report, 72 recommendations were made to the F8U project office. The final highlights are listed below:

- Complete a study of the procedure for removing the rocket pack for the purpose of simplifying the installation.
- Redesign the door installation on the lower trailing edge of the wing center section to simplify access to the aileron power control package, which required removal of 277 bolts and screws.
- Produce a written procedure for special tool fabrication and installation to ensure that special tools were available in the field for Chance Vought Aircraft manufacturing to flow from tooling to engineering.
- Improve access to various components in the main fuel cell, which was considered poor because the rocket pack, speed brake, and rocket pack–cavity fire shield had to be removed before the fuel cell access plates could be reached.
- Convene a Maintenance Survey Team for all future aircraft models. These teams should include the project office, field engineering, field service, and airport operations personnel with spares section and quality control participation as required.

Fuselage Coking

While working at NACA, aerospace engineer Richard Whitcomb discovered the principle of "area rule" in 1952 and won the 1954 Collier Trophy. Air will bunch up around the fuselage, increasing transonic drag, in the speed range of Mach .7 to 1.2. Area rule or "coking" (shape of a coke bottle) was important in reducing transonic drag by pinching or changing the shape of the fuselage to allow the airflow over the wings to remain even.

During the challenges of dealing with unexpected high drag during high-speed wind tunnel testing, fuselage coking had been considered a possible fix to reduce drag. Because of the complexity of redesign work, CVA was resistant to incorporate this change, but in February 1954 CVA agreed to explore the possibilities of applying coking build-ups to the fuselage instead of indentations. Indentations had been previously tested with no drag reduction in the transonic range and a slight drag increase in the supersonic range.

On 25 October 1954, the BuAer advised that early and extensive wind tunnel and rocket model testing had provided information that had made it possible to improve the maximum Mach number .07 to .08 without major redesign or weight increase. However, the airplane still did not meet the specification guarantee. The BuAer also noted that additional tests at NACA Langley on a .042-scale

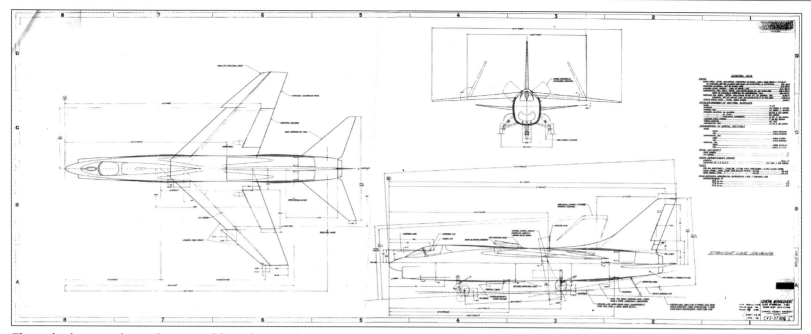

The only drawing the author was able to locate showing an example of coking on the F8U-1 is CVS-37306 with the coking shown in red ahead of and behind the wing. The changes would have aided performance at a considerable design and manufacturing cost. In addition, it would have delayed fleet deliveries of the F8U.

model had been accomplished up to Mach 1.43, in a "sleeved" 8-foot wind tunnel. These results indicated that the desired performance would be obtained by the addition of coking (or area rule) to the fuselage, both forward and aft of the wing. The BuAer desired the incorporation of the fuselage build-up in the production F8U-1 airplane, and requested the following at an early date:

- ECP for production incorporation of the fuselage coking in the F8U-1 model.
- ECP for modification of No. 2 XF8U-1 airplane to incorporate the fuselage change.
- A revised schedule for the XF8U-1 Flight Test & Demonstration Program.

CVA studied the effect of coking introduction on delivery schedules, and prepared schedules based on "expedited" (14th airplane), "intermediate" (20th airplane), and "delayed" coking (incorporation in FY 1957). Based upon the letter of 25 October, CVA developed proposals based on the following conditions:

- Condition I: 18th and subsequent airplanes
- Condition II: 31st and subsequent airplanes
- Condition III: 265th and subsequent airplanes

All departments agreed that the most practical incorporation of coking was at the 265th airplane. That the BuAer would not accept a proposal allowing for several underperforming aircraft (264) to be delivered to the fleet prior to the aircraft that would provide the maximum speed guarantee was a concern. Operating Plans and Control (OP&C) at CVA recommended to management that Condition III be established as the program proposal.

The following arguments were suggested for use with the BuAer:
- It was considered unwise to rush into coking design without more wind tunnel data. The decision should wait until full test data became available, negotiating in the meantime for coking incorporation on a flight-test basis only in one early F8U-1 or XF8U-1 airplane.
- Negotiation for an ECP for production incorporation should await preliminary flight testing since wind tunnel results are not always compatible with actual airplane performance.
- Delay of the production plan until this point would result in its timing tying in closely with the incorporation of other contemplated improvement changes.
- Meanwhile, the Navy would be getting F8U-1 aircraft superior in performance to competitive airplanes, and very close to the guaranteed maximum speed.

Should the BuAer not agree to the proposal and continue to insist on the coking incorporation at the beginning of deliveries, CVA would have to work toward early incorporation as quickly as possible. This would require engineering to start prior to a formal ECP agreement.

CVA wanted the longest uninterrupted run of F8U-1 airplanes

possible before changing to another model, which was the primary driver behind delaying coking incorporation.

On 26 November 1954, CVA replied to the BuAer's 25 October request. CVA's initial estimate of coking cost was $6.8 million for design, tooling, flight, and static testing. This would also cause an increase in average unit cost of $8,700 per airplane through the 250th article.

CVA also stated that three aircraft with glove-fix coking would have to be provided (instead of one) to support flight testing. This would add an additional cost of $300,000. The cost of the first glove-fix airplane, including non-recurring costs but excluding flight test, would be about $600,000. The letter also pointed out the "delays and the jeopardy to F8U-1 fleet deployment which would be caused by the introduction of coking on early production models."

The following recommendations were made:

- Only a program for flight evaluation of the effects of coking be initiated at this time.
- Use an early F8U-1 airplane.
- Action on production coking incorporation be deferred.

Due to the insistence of the BuAer on the high performance to be expected from the "coked" fuselage configuration, engineering work started on 20 December 1954. This work was limited to long lead time items needed for production incorporation of coking. Also included in this work was determination of air loads and preliminary structural analysis of the coked airplane.

On 31 December 1954, in consideration of the facts and specific recommendations presented by CVA, the BuAer advised that it "agreed (reluctantly)" that it would be unwise to incorporate coking any earlier than aircraft 75.

Prior to approving the prototyping area distribution rule on the No. 4 F8U-1, CVA was requested to revise the proposal to incorporate coking on production airplane No. 76 and subsequent airplanes, along with "such other improvements that may be warranted and feasible."

CVA submitted proposal ECP-287 for incorporation of coking not later than the 76th airplane, on 19 January 1955. Along with the ECP, information was provided for incorporation of other performance improvement changes. The coking ECP was limited to engineering design, tooling design, and tool planning only. Firm incorporation would depend upon the results of early flight testing of the XF8U-1. No cutting of metal or manufacturing of fixtures to support coking incorporation would begin until at least midsummer 1955.

XF8U-1 Fabrication Continues

Due to major engineering changes to the trailing edge assembly, the wing outer panel assembly fixture loaded one week late. The first set of outer panels allocated for static testing left the fixture slightly ahead of schedule. The second set of outer panels that would be used on the No. 1 XF8U-1 loaded into the fixture on 6 December 1954 and reached final completion on 14 January 1955. Delivery of the outer panels was delayed five days for incorporation of a late

Work taking place on XF8U-1 No. 1 as the date for shop completion nears. (CVPR-313)

Here, the J57 engine is being prepared for installation in XF8U-1. A significant milestone and a slow process as well. Everything must be checked to avoid damage to the engine or airframe during this delicate mating. (CVPR-310)

A different view of fitting the J57 engine to the XF8U-1 during assembly in the structures test lab at Vought. Everything is accomplished very slowly to prevent damage to the engine or aircraft. The schedule for first flight was tight. (CVPR-311)

After the engine was installed in the forward fuselage the aft section had to be refitted. Here is the careful rejoining of the aft fuselage to the forward, again watching for areas of interference. (CVPR-312)

engineering change that added a structural reinforcement of the wing fold hinge fittings.

The horizontal tail assembly fixture loaded on 29 October and the completed assemblies were removed from the fixture on 9 November, three days ahead of schedule. They were delivered on 19 November, right on schedule.

Finally, the tail cone assembly fixture was loaded on 20 December. Titanium fabrication problems caused delays, but the assembly was completed four days ahead of schedule on 10 January 1955.

By mid-January 1955, the No. 1 XF8U-1 airplane was considered 60 percent complete against a schedule of 69 percent complete. The manufacturing department's ability to regain schedule and meet the 11 February shop completion date was in doubt due to new requirements brought on by mock-up and engineering changes. In addition, three days' delay occurred in aft section installation because of an engineering change requiring beef-up of the titanium bulkhead.

Fabrication Delay Factors

As final assembly started, it became apparent that the 11 February shop completion date would not be met. The Master Schedule

A photo from the hangar rafters showing the massive amount of work being done on the XF8U-1 to complete it on time per the schedule. Ejection seat rails are in work after testing revealed the need for modification. (CVPR-319)

was revised in early February to slip the shop completion date one week to 18 February. No single parts shortage or engineering change can be blamed for the slip in the schedule. The volume of engineering changes during final assembly was sufficient to slow progress. Existing shortages of equipment and parts shortages also contributed to delay shop completion.

Shop Completion, No. 1 XF8U-1

The No. 1 XF8U-1 (138899) was shop completed and delivered to the Structures Test Lab at 7:42 am on 19 February 1955. At this point the aircraft was considered to be 98 percent complete and testing of the installed systems could commence. As the aircraft was 98 percent complete, several major items were still needing completion. These items included cockpit shakedown and stabilization system check-out. The required inspections were completed in conjunction with structures lab operations. Wing fold cylinder rework and replacement of ejection seat tracks were also accomplished in the lab area.

The first operational test of the ejection seat resulted in a broken seat track. A redesign of the track was produced and tested. A second failure also occurred involving rollers; however, the design was beefed up rather than requiring a redesign. The seat track redesign was not released until 18 February, which caused the new tracks to be installed just before the airplane left for Muroc. One last major change was redesigning the air turbine generator to use a Stratos 15 KVA unit because the Eclipse 9 KVA generator had been further delayed by over-speed control problems.

Pre-Flight Operations, Chance Vought Aircraft Dallas

Hydraulic system tests started on the No. 1 XF8U-1 (138899) promptly after arrival in the structures test lab. During hydraulic system tests three major problems arose requiring fixes: (1) freezing of the wing incidence cylinder in the down position, (2) binding between center and outer panel forward skins and droops, and (3) discovery that the wheel brake cylinders were not acceptable for flight. The Weston (brake cylinder manufacturer) representative attempted to repair the brake cylinders prior to shipping the aircraft to Edwards AFB, but was unsuccessful. New brake cylinders were installed on the aircraft prior to the first flight while the aircraft was being prepped at Edwards.

The wing incidence cylinder was also replaced during the reassembly in California. Prior to the first flight, the main landing gear doors needed to be beefed up, along with the outer panel droop support ribs. These changes were completed prior to shipping the XF8U-1 to Edwards.

Delays were experienced during testing, and at one point they were 20 hours behind schedule. However, by working around the clock, tests were completed by 20 February 1955 as scheduled.

Another overhead shot giving an idea of the amount of activity needing to be completed while in testing all around the aircraft prior to delivery of the first article to the flight line. (CVPR-422)

The newly assembled XF8U-1 is now being jacked up off the ground for landing gear and hydraulics testing. (CVPR-314)

Repositioning the XF8U-1 after completion of landing gear testing. Notice the stance of the main gear; this is a trait of this particular type landing gear and was a common sight when the Crusader's cousin, the A-7, was lowered off of jacks. (CVPR-316)

Paint touch up prior to shipping to Edwards AFB. The wing has been removed in preparation for loading in a crate for road transportation, and the fuselage is being readied for the C-124 transport. (CVPR-322)

Upon completion of the hydraulic tests, a series of vibration tests started 25 February and were completed the next day as scheduled. XF8U-1 No. 1 was weighed and fuel system tests began on 27 February. Significant design changes were required prior to first flight. During this period the fuselage aft section was being reworked and the engine was installed in the fuselage. Information from Pratt & Whitney arrived in late January 1955 indicating the afterburner temperatures were approximately 500 degrees F higher than previously supplied. This drove a requirement to change the material of the forward and aft engine heat shrouds from aluminum to stainless steel. It also prompted the addition of an insulation blanket to protect the aft fuselage structure, along with numerous other changes in the aft fuselage, including new forward support fittings, rework of the fire detection system, insulation and reflectors around the fin main beam, and horizontal tail horn assembly housing.

The outer wing panels and rudder of the No. 1 XF8U-1 (138899) were retained by the test lab following power control and vibration tests for use as static test articles. The outer panels and rudder for the No. 2 XF8U-1 aircraft (138900) were installed on the No. 1 XF8U-1 aircraft after the center section and aft fuselage returned from the test lab. Manufacturing made the decision in January 1955 to use the No. 2 XF8U-1 aft section on the No. 1 XF8U-1 airplane because of two important factors: ability to complete No. 2 fin and aft section joining ahead of schedule, and late return of No. 1 aft section from the Engineering Structures Test Lab. Also, No. 2 showed a better titanium cracking history on the aft section.

After completion of the hydraulic tests and vibration tests, the weighing of the XF8U-1 took place. Weight and balance calculations had to be completed prior to the first flight to determine the center of gravity of the completed aircraft. The empty weight of the aircraft was 17, 200 pounds against a design weight of 16,500 pounds. The takeoff gross weight with full internal fuel of the No. 1 XF8U-1 was 25,000 pounds with no armament compared to a 25,160-pound design gross weight including four guns, cannon, and rocket armament.

The XF8U-1 wing center section was crated and loaded onto a truck for shipment to California. (CVA-27937)

Fuel tests involving pumps, indication, switches, and tank leak checks were completed on 1 March 1955. After completion of the fuel tests the wing was removed from the fuselage and prepared for shipment to Muroc. Wing removal was facilitated by removing electrical and hydraulic connections, the incidence actuator attachment, and two pivot pins at the rear of the wing where structurally the wing and fuselage joined. The wing center section then had the outer wing panels, leading edge droops, and flaps removed prior to wrapping and loading onto the truck for shipment to California. Cold war security played a part in keeping "prying eyes" from seeing details of the new design by having the wing and fuselage wrapped before going out in public.

The truck carrying the wing assembly of the XF8U-1 departed the Chance Vought factory on 2 March 1955 at 6:30 am headed for California. An hour and a half later, a Douglas C-124C Globemaster II aircraft arrived at Hensley Field to transport the rest of the XF8U-1 to Muroc for flight testing. Not long after the C-124C parked on the Chance Vought ramp, loading of the fuselage and crated components of the XF8U-1 began. By 11:30 pm that night, the C-124C was loaded and ready for the trip to Muroc.

Here is a final view of the truck carrying the wing center section with escorts preparing to hit the road to California. (CVA-27938)

The wing and aft section removed, XF8U-1 is in final preparation for loading in the C-124. (CVPR-321)

The fuselage of XF8U-1 is rolled up next to the C-124C 52-0982 52nd TCS/63rd TCG. This aircraft crashed on 24 April 1954, a little over a year after this flight.

Mostly covered in a tarp the XF8U-1 is rolled out past new-production F7U-3 Cutlass aircraft. (CVPR-323)

The fuselage is aligned with the ramp leading to the cargo bay of the C-124.

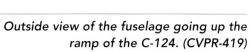

Outside view of the fuselage going up the ramp of the C-124. (CVPR-419)

A view down the ramp of the XF8U-1 entering the C-124.

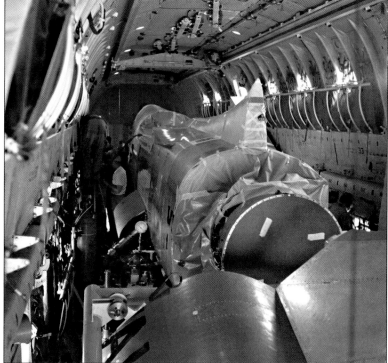

The XF8U-1 fuselage and a multitude of other parts all strapped down and ready for the flight to California. (CVPR-420)

The rumble of four Pratt & Whitney R-4360 radial engines disturbed the late-morning quiet at Hensley Field, Texas. It was 11:25 am on 3 March 1955 and the first XF8U-1 was airborne at last. For the 1950s, it was yet another flight for a workhorse of the Cold War, the Douglas C-124C Globemaster II. However, to the employees of Chance Vought Corporation this flight was very different. The future of the company was contained within the cargo hold of that Douglas Globemaster II aircraft.

The fuselage was transported to Muroc in the cargo hold of C-124C 52-0982 Globemaster II transport assigned to 52d Troop Carrier Squadron, Heavy, stationed at Donaldson AFB, South Carolina. The C-124C arrived safely at Edwards Air Force Base 6 hours and 15 minutes later.

Flight Test Philosophy

It was decided to divide the flight-testing objectives into four parts. The first flight test objective was to conduct a company preliminary evaluation of flying qualities and performance. This evaluation would also highlight any deficiencies and explore their severity. The second flight test objective was to perform the first part of the Flight test demonstration. After those objectives were met the aircraft would be presented to the Navy to perform their preliminary evaluation. In addition, the XF8U-1s would have to demonstrate initial carrier suitability to complete the first phase of flight testing.

No decals here. Touching up the markings on the XF8U-1 prior to its first flight at Edwards.

Along with the flight test objectives, the company decided to install telemetering capability, which was a first for a CVA-piloted aircraft, and all flight test instrumentation would be installed from the beginning of the program.

First Flight Date

The scheduled first flight date of 31 March 1955 was established in February 1954. This was a delay of one month from the original first flight date and was due to a change in forward fuselage lines to reduce the drag of the nose and inlet. Since the XF8U-1 was a completely new and unproven design, initial flight testing at an off-site base was planned from the start. Edwards Air Force Base was selected as the best facility for this because of the safety margin provided by the Muroc dry lake bed. Another factor influencing this decision was the length of the runway at Hensley Field adjacent to the Chance Vought Aircraft plant in Dallas, Texas. The runway was being lengthened, but it would not be completed for several more months.

Reassembly and Pre-flight Operations

By 3 March 1955, all the components of the No. 1 XF8U-1 had been delivered at Edwards Air Force Base. At this point the project was two days ahead of schedule. Reassembly of the aircraft began and reality would soon set in. Depending upon required rework and parts shortages, the program would be back on schedule or a little behind within a week. A tremendous amount of work was accomplished by the California crew working a two-shift schedule. The XF8U-1 had to be reassembled from the pile of parts that had arrived both by air and ground. The aircraft had to be powered up, leak checked, flight controls rigged, and the engine run and trimmed. All this work was completed and the aircraft ready for taxi tests in only 11 days.

An overhead view of the No. 1 XF8U-1 being towed back to the Chance Vought Aircraft test hangar at Edwards after a series of engine tests prior to the first flight. This view gives a good look at the variable-incidence wing in the "up" position, along with the leading edges of the wing in the drooped position. This is the configuration of the aircraft for takeoff and landing.

One of thousands of duct dives that would be performed over the life of the F8U Crusader aircraft. These dives during pre-flight operations allowed for the inspection of the front face of the engine compressor section and the opportunity to make sure there were no loose rivets or other foreign objects in the inlet duct that could damage or destroy the Pratt & Whitney J57 turbojet engine. (CVPR-395)

Mechanics fitting the ground safety screen to the inlet of the XF8U-1 prior to a series of engine runs on the Pratt & Whitney J57. The screen's purpose is to keep ground personnel and foreign objects from being drawn into the inlet by the airflow though the engine. (CVPR-403)

The first attempt to taxi the airplane under its own power was made on 14 March with John Konrad at the controls. After proceeding downwind to the middle of test area, an attempt was made to turn to the right into the relative wind. All attempts to turn into wind by using the throttle, rudder, and brake power failed, and tests were discontinued because of the high wind and tire wear. The Navy required the tight turning ability provided by a fully swiveling nose landing gear to taxi in the confined area of an aircraft carrier deck. The pilot would apply light pressure to either the left or right brake pedal, depending on the desired direction of the turn. The aircraft would then pivot around the wheel on which the brake was lightly applied. This system was common on tail dragger aircraft but was not as effective on tricycle landing gear aircraft like the XF8U-1.

The next day, a second taxi test was made with ground speeds of up to 90 mph attained. Results of this test indicated that general ground handling characteristics were acceptable for the CVA test program. The taxi problems would continue through the first four test flights and the problem was defined as low speed and unsatisfactory ground handling in high winds. John McGuyrt, chief of flight testing, reported, "The nose wheel steering was mandatory and should be incorporated prior to Navy evaluation."

A third taxi test was made on 24 March, the last in the series to be accomplished prior to flight. Tests were completed satisfactorily, and no difficulties were experienced. The No. 1 XF8U-1 was ready to proceed to the first flight.

With the engine running the Vought crew performs leak checks on the XF8U-1 at Muroc.

Chapter 3

FIRST FLIGHTS

The No. 1 XF8U-1 sits on the Muroc dry lakebed in this low-angle photo. This angle features the thin walls of the intake duct that evolved after wind tunnel testing revealed that the XF8U-1 would not meet performance guarantees. When the inlet duct was redesigned, the nose was thinned down to reduce drag and improve the aircraft's performance. (CVPR-361)

The Crusader's first flight was a culmination of 22 months of hard work from the time the contract had been signed. The No. 1 XF8U-1 (138899) was assembled, tested, and disassembled for transport halfway across the United States to California.

On arrival at Edwards, the XF8U-1 began a 5½-year-long flight test career with Chance Vought Aircraft. This airplane would eventually be retired and delivered to the Smithsonian Institution's Air Museum in Washington, D.C., on 25 October 1960.

First Flight on 25 March 1955

Finally, the first flight day had arrived, Friday morning 25 March 1955, six days ahead of contract schedule and only 22 months from the contract between the U.S. Navy and Chance Vought Aircraft being signed. John W. Konrad, chief test pilot for Chance Vought Aircraft, climbed into XF8U-1 No. 1 for the first flight. Under the watchful eye of Crew Chief Rollie Pruett, the mighty Pratt & Whitney J57 engine was started and system checks were carried out. Konrad taxied the XF8U-1 out on the Rogers dry lakebed to the takeoff point.

Once the XF8U-1's system checks were successfully accomplished, Konrad advanced the throttle on the Pratt & Whitney J57-P-11 engine to afterburner, released the brakes, and the first flight began. The XF8U-1 passed the attentive Chance Vought crew on its takeoff roll. The aircraft was visible to the ground observers several times during the first flight.

Russ Clark, assistant project engineer, stated, "The flight objective was to achieve in the order of 1.1 Mach number, which was easily accomplished; in fact, the acceleration of the aircraft through the transonic was smooth, pleasant, and rapid." Naval aviation now had a 1,000-mph carrier-based day fighter second to none in performance. The only reported problem during the first flight of the No. 1 XF8U-1 concerned the yaw and roll stabilization system that would be addressed after further flight testing determined the extent of the problem.

After landing and taxiing back to the temporary Chance Vought hangar, Konrad was seen grinning in the cockpit and gave a confident wink. The aircraft was swarmed by well-wishers offering congratulations. Konrad replied, "Thanks a lot for a good airplane." He continued, "I'm not the one to be congratulated, I just happened to be in the seat." Commander Joe Rees, the BuAer XF8U-1 project officer, was standing nearby. Konrad said to Rees, "Well, Joe, there's your new airplane." To which Commander Rees replied, "She sure looks good."

Within a few hours after the new Chance Vought day fighter landed, comprehensive data on the performance of the engine, flight controls, and other performance factors for evaluation by the Chance

Chance Vought Aircraft engineers for the XF8U-1 program L. C. Josephs and Russ Clark take a moment to pose by the No. 1 XF8U-1 at Muroc. (CVPR-394)

On 25 March 1955 John Konrad moves the throttle forward on the XF8U-1 as evidenced by the black smoke pouring from the tailpipe of the Pratt & Whitney J57 engine prior to afterburner activation. This moment is the culmination of the past 22 months' work, first flight. (CVPR-417)

Like expectant parents, Chance Vought engineers and a U.S. Navy representative watch the first flight of the XF8U-1 along with film crews. The engineers are (left to right) G. K. Johnson, Russ Clark, Joe Silverman, Paul Thayer, and H. B. Sallada. (CVPR-380)

John Konrad takes the XF8U-1 out for taxi tests at Muroc.

Group photo of the Chance Vought Aircraft flight test team taken at Edwards. These are the men who worked long hours to get the No. 1 XF8U-1 ready for flight after its long journey from Dallas. (CVPR-427)

The Spartan cockpit of the No. 1 XF8U-1. Because the aircraft was not armed it did not have a gun sight or armament controls. Also missing in the picture is the Chance Vought Aircraft ejection seat that was fitted during the initial test program and used for many years.

Test pilot John Konrad in debrief with the Chance Vought Aircraft flight test engineering and maintenance staff after returning from the first test flight of the XF8U-1. (CVPR-391)

Brigadier General Holtoner, USAF, on a cockpit tour of the XF8U-1 given by Vought test pilot John Konrad. (CVPR-430)

Vought engineers were available due to an early decision in the program to employ telemetry from the beginning of the flight test program. The Chance Vought team also brought a trailer that contained the equipment to capture and automatically perform data reduction on the information radioed back from the XF8U-1. Telemetry would help the flight test program accurately capture speeds flown, stresses applied, and other functions of the aircraft during testing that cannot all be monitored by the pilot as he flies the test program.

Early Flight Testing of the No. 1 XF8U-1 Begins

The Chance Vought Aircraft team did not rest with the accomplishment of flight number one. In fact, the aircraft flew three more times before the end of March 1955. The test program called for 48 flights between 25 March and 31 May 1955. The first 36 flights were to be dedicated to flight regime investigation, open up the basic flight envelope for the design, and verify earlier predictions based on engineering data and wind tunnel testing. The remaining flights of the original test program would be dedicated to investigating critical items identified in the first series of flights and to prepare for the Navy evaluation flights.

On 2 April 1955, the No. 1 XF8U-1 was put in "work" status (non-flying with maintenance and modifications being performed) for the accomplishment of 18 items considered necessary for flight safety and to support the flight test program. These items included installing a 9 KVA emergency ram-air turbine electric generator (the original specified size), installing the production fuel pressurization system, reworking the stabilization system, and changing the wheel brake valves. The aft section was inspected and cracks in the titanium repaired along with some fuselage reinforcement work. These inspections were prudent given the

The No. 1 XF8U-1 arrives back at the dry lakebed for landing after the 52-minute, history-making test flight in which the XF8U-1 became the first Navy fighter to exceed 1,000 mph on its first flight. Security considerations dictated that the first flight would not be announced by the Navy until three months later in June 1955. (CVPR-438)

The variable-incidence wing is in the up position with flaps and droops extended as this XF8U-1 works on another test point over Muroc. (CVPR-345)

manufacturing experiences working with titanium parts. The work status was extended an additional six days until 12 April, to accomplish all the needed work.

Coking Finale for the F8U-1

The issue surrounding coking incorporation on the F8U-1 production aircraft had yet to be resolved in March 1955. CVA provided additional information to the BuAer on the application of the area distribution rule in response to an 11 March letter. The fuselage structure would be extensively affected by the coking redesign. Many modifications of bulkheads, doors, and other components were required. Certain tests that had already been performed on the un-coked static test fuselage would need to be repeated. This would require an additional fuselage with the coked configuration with vertical tail to repeat the tests already performed.

The Part II structural demonstrations would require 5½ months following the initial flight of the first coked airplane, causing production delays. Preliminary information from the early test flights of the XF8U-1 had indicated that coking might not be required. CVA had reluctantly moved forward a design program with schedules for engineering drawing releases. Production coking drawings were being completed for the F8U-1, but they were not being released. Drawings required for the F8U-1P were being released that did incorporate coking.

During April, CVA continued to work on coking with an eye to early incorporation on production airplanes if the XF8U-1 failed to attain satisfactory flight test performance. The No. 15 airplane appeared to be the earliest practical airplane for coking incorporation should it be required. OP&C recommended CVA delay a deci-

sion on coking incorporation until mid-May to have more time to evaluate the flight test data from the No. 1 XF8U-1.

OP&C issued Master Schedule for Authorized Action on 26 April 1955 establishing overall time spans for advance action on fuselage coking. It established a schedule for engineering production design, tool planning, and design. Kellering (tracer milling) tools and masters, along with material commitments for long-lead precision castings, were included in the schedule.

The BuAer recommended, on 29 April, that the current contract be extended to 75 F8U-1 basic specification aircraft. The F8U-2 designation would be established, reflecting coking and six changes (including Sidewinder In-Flight Fueling), which could be phased in

A high-overhead shot of XF8U-1 on a test flight over Muroc. (CVPR-39)

concurrently with coking. In the FY 1956 procurement plan, 59 aircraft would be procured as F8U-2s. As late as June 1955, the BuAer was holding to its opinions of coking, and on 7 June it approved the engineering design submitted by CVA on 6 April.

Results of the Navy Phase 1 flight tests of the XF8U-1 in June 1955 became available in early July. As a result, CVA decided to suspend all engineering activity on coking. Tentative plans for incorporating coking on the 75th or later airplane continued.

On 18 July 1955, the BuAer advised that coking modifications to the F8U-1 specification would not be required. Engineering had expended 69,584 man-hours on the coking project. A total of 220 drawing packages were in work at the time of project suspension, 80 percent were design-complete, and 109 blueprint packages had been released.

During the work status period of the No. 1 XF8U-1, flight test engineering released a Category A and B listing of items considered necessary in the XF8U-1 prior to Navy evaluation flights. Category A items were considered changes that were required prior to the Navy Phase 1 test flights; the category B items were desirable for incorporation into the XF8U-1. At the top of the Category A list was the higher-thrust Pratt & Whitney J57-P-12 engine. The aircraft acceleration was considered to be slow during subsequent testing, with the test and chase pilots again calling for the up-rated engine. The Pratt & Whitney J57-P-12 would eventually be installed during a work status period in mid-May.

Category A Changes Required for Phase I Navy Flights

- Upgrade the power plant to a Pratt & Whitney J57-P-12 rated at 10,000 pounds of thrust dry and 16,000 pounds of thrust with afterburning
- Revise cooling ejector required with the Pratt & Whitney J57-P-12 engine
- Satisfactory operation of the flight stabilization system
- Aileron up-float fix
- Install an aileron-rudder interconnect in the flight control system. (This helps to coordinate turns to reduce the tendency for the aircraft to skid through the turn.)
- Coordinate operation of wing and droop to minimize the trim change
- Satisfactory brake control
- Reinforce fuselage in the wheel well area
- Production fix to enable canopy to clear the vertical tail during low-speed jettisoning
- Drag clean-up
- Leading edge droop cylinders qualified for 5.0 g
- F8U-1 ejection cartridge
- Unrestricted operation of the Marquardt ram-air turbine for emergency electrical generator
- Satisfactory emergency wheel brake valve

- All items necessary to raise restriction to 650 knots
- Automatic oil cooler door operation
- 9-degree wing incidence

Category B "Desirable for Incorporation" Items

- Nose gear steering
- Reduce landing gear handle loads (The amount of force required to raise and lower the landing gear handle was considered excessive.)
- Canopy air spring (This is a nitrogen pressurized actuator to assist with opening and closing the canopy.)
- Production longitudinal (roll) feel system (This system gives the pilot feedback in the control stick when the ailerons are moved. With a hydraulically power-assisted flight control system the pilot does not get the feedback that he would when using a flight control system of cables and pulleys. An artificial feel system is built into the flight controls to help the pilot gauge how much stick deflection pressure he is applying.)
- Revised nose gear strut
- Satisfactory emergency trim for roll and yaw
- Boost valves with external valve stops in the wheel brake system

Nose Gear Steering

The desirability of providing power steering for the nose gear had been carefully examined during the basic design of the XF8U-1 landing gear system. Prior to the finalization of the detail specification the problem had been discussed in detail between engineering representatives and the BuAer. The discussions resulted in an agreement that power steering would be omitted initially, but would be incorporated as an improvement change if preliminary aircraft evaluations established its desirability. Consequently, a paragraph was included in the detail specification stating specifically that "the nose wheel assembly shall be non-steerable," a standard requirement at the time.

As a side note, CVA's F7U-3 was one of the first carrier-based jets to be configured with nose wheel steering. The necessity for power steering for the nose gear was well-established during the taxi tests and flights conducted during the last week in March 1955.

Flight Test Deficiency Report "Unsatisfactory Ground Handling Characteristics" on 6 April 1955 reported that nose gear steering was imperative, and requested that it be incorporated in all production F8U-1s and that a trial installation be made available for evaluation in No. 1 XF8U-1 prior to the Phase I Navy evaluation scheduled for 31 May 1955.

As a result of the unsatisfactory characteristics established in the flight test, the BuAer informally requested CVA to submit an Engineering Change Proposal (ECP) to incorporate nose gear steering in all XF8U-1 and F8U-1 airplanes. In view of the BuAer request and the flight test report, engineering requested on 2 May 1955 that sales prepare a budgetary cost proposal covering the incorporation of nose gear steering (to which the designation ECP-42 was assigned).

As recommended in April, power steering for the nose gear was installed in the experimental and production models, interim fixes being used on the experimental models.

Electro-Hydraulic Yaw and Roll Stabilization, ECP-67

Stabilization difficulties indicated that the XF8U-1 stabilization system was of marginal reliability. Following the fourth flight of the No. 1 XF8U-1, flight test engineering recommended that the system be improved prior to Phase I Navy evaluation.

Design Decision No. 139, 15 June 1955 (Design Decisions were made to fix problems in experimental aircraft and would integrate into production unless otherwise specified), called for replacement of the electro-mechanical system with electro-hydraulic yaw and roll systems. The No. 16 F8U-1 was selected to prototype the system. If successful the production change would start with the No. 21 F8U-1. ECP-67 was assigned to identify the stabilization system change.

The Management Change Board reviewed the stabilization modification and decided to install an interim yaw electro-hydraulic system as soon as possible in selected aircraft and backfit the remainder. The interim yaw system and reduced throw roll system were considered satisfactory fixes until redesign of both systems could be accomplished. The redesigned systems were to be incorporated by No. 21 F8U-1.

A further Management Change Board in September 1955 met to determine whether to use No. 1 XF8U-1 or a production airplane for the stabilization system modification. The No. 1 XF8U-1 flight schedule was extremely tight and great effort had been made to adjust the schedule to permit it to be returned to Dallas at an early date for the modification. To expedite the prototype installation, the board decided to use the No. 6 F8U-1 production airplane instead of the No. 1 XF8U-1.

On 8 November 1955, CVA submitted its proposal for the dual electra-hydraulic yaw and roll stabilization system after satisfactory simulator and flight testing. The new system offered improved yaw and roll stabilization over the original system.

BuAer's Change Notice Aer-AE-733, 3 April 1956, authorized the proposed system. A flight test was to be successfully accomplished prior to production incorporation. The BuAer did not note that the prototype was now to be the No. 6 F8U-1. CVA requested the BuAer to process a corrected change notice.

On 21 June 1956, the BuAer revised authorization Aer-AE-734 to extend effectivity of the stabilization system change to include all aircraft on Contract N0a(s) 55-170. It also noted the prototype for the system change was the No. 6 production airplane. Immediate production incorporation was also authorized. Flight testing had shown the redesign to be sound with no further redesign anticipated.

Wing Center Section In-Board Flap, ECP-123

A 6 May 1954 Design Decision was published stating that a "plain flap" would be incorporated into the trailing edge of the wing between the inboard end of the aileron and the side of the fuselage. The flap installation was to be designed for the XF8U-1. The incorporation in production and retrofits was to be determined at a later date.

Based on Navy evaluation and CVA flight test results to improve low-speed flying qualities, on 15 August 1955 the decision was made to incorporate the wing center section inboard flap in all XF8U-1 and F8U-1 airplanes. By the end of October 1955 the change was issued for the installation of the inboard flap on the two XF8U-1 airplanes and in No. 21 F8U-1 and subsequent that had not been delivered. Finally, in February 1956, ECP-123 was released to incorporate the inboard flaps into airplanes Nos. 1 to 20, which had already been delivered.

Wing Center Section Spoiler, ECP-178

As a result of Phase I evaluation, with concerns over the roll rate of the XF8U-1, and evaluations of several stiffened wings, a Design Decision was issued 13 November 1955 providing for design and installation of a wing center section spoiler. The spoiler would then be flight tested to measure the level of improvement on the rolling characteristics of the F8U-1 airplane.

The XF8U-1 banks away from the chase aircraft as this photo is taken. The unpainted finish of the aircraft shows the different metal types used in the construction. This picture was taken later in the test program when the last three digits of the U.S. Navy Bureau of Aeronautics (BuNo), "899," were painted below the stripes on the vertical stabilizer. (CVPR-443)

Design Decision No. 56 was issued on 11 July 1956 to install the spoiler on an F8U-1 airplane for flight testing. For flight testing purposes a switch was incorporated that allowed the pilot to select spoilers only for the August system effectiveness testing.

In August 1956 the change was assigned ECP-178 and a prototype of the production installation was to be installed in F8U-1 No. 23; production and retrofit incorporation were slated for F8U-1 No. 17 through 22, 24, and subsequent, and in F8U-1P No. 1 and subsequent. Anticipated production incorporation points were No. 136 F8U-1 and No. 16 F8U-1P.

Center Section Wing Rework ECP-196

Following investigation of a wing failure during static test, changes were released to provide additional strength. Recommended effectivity included F8U-1 No. 1 and subsequent, along with both XF8U-1s. Reissue on 12 January 1956 revised effectivity to the 21st airplane and subsequent.

PC 55319 was issued 15 February 1956 to provide an increase in the static strength of the center section wing. It also authorized the transfer of the F8U-1 No. 15 center section wing to static testing after modification. This PC was reissued four times, the last being on 24 August 1956 when all the releases transferred to and were accomplished under ECP-196.

Reinforcement, Wing Center and Fuselage Mid-Sections, ECP-180

Because of weight increases following the incorporation of numerous changes in the airplane, the chief project engineer issued an engineering memorandum in July 1956 stating that to accommodate these and additional possible changes the BuAer might require, the wing center section needed to be strengthened. The modifications were necessary to meet the detail specification requirements of 6.4 g and 24,000 pounds.

ECP-180 was assigned to the change. Expeditious preparation of the cost quotation and early submittal of the ECP-180 was the change number assigned to the work; the goal was incorporation in the No. 66 F8U-1 and subsequent. The 30 July engineering memo was revised and reissued on 5 September. It now included the reinforcement of the fuselage as well as the wing center section. The fuselage changes included redesign of left and right longerons to increase strength.

The wing center section reinforcement changes involved an increase in skin thickness of the upper panel from .312 to .35 inch and redesign of ribs and stiffeners to accommodate the thicker upper panel.

CVA submitted proposal SS-3P-357 on 16 October 1956 to cover the reinforcement changes to make the wing center and fuselage mid-sections adequate for a 24,000-pound gross weight and main-tain the detail specification 6.4 g requirement. In addition, the proposal provided for potential future tactical improvement changes and incorporation starting with the No. 66 F8U-1 and subsequent, and in No. 5 F8U-1P and subsequent.

Speed Brake Redesign, ECP-11

During flight test the No. 1 XF8U-1 revealed that with the speed brake deployed at supersonic speeds airplane stability was reduced. The F8U-1 project section requested an engineering redesign of the speed brake in October 1955 to improve the stability of the airplane. The experimental shop reworked a speed brake assembly removed from the No. 5 F8U-1 airplane. The redesign added a "V"-shaped notch in the speed brake 25 inches deep and 18 inches wide at the trailing edge. The change was to be incorporated in the No. 1 XF8U-1 airplane for flight testing.

Successful flight testing of the reworked speed brake with the "V" notch indicated it was an improvement over the original configuration. In January 1956 it was decided to incorporate the "V" notch design with the fuselage improvements into the production configuration of the F8U-1.

The following May, CVA requested approval of ECP-110, proposing incorporation of the speed brake redesign in No. 41 F8U-1 and subsequent production airplanes, along with the first F8U-1P and all subsequent airplanes. In addition, the modification would be incorporated in all previously delivered airplanes. The BuAer approved the change proposal in June.

Flight Testing Aircraft Allocations to Support Flight Testing and Development

CVA's testing philosophy for the F8U-1 production airplanes was based on the Proposed Flight Test and Demonstration Program dated 24 March 1954 (and subsequently amended). It designated the first five production airplanes for the following test purposes:

- No. 1 Carrier Suitability Demonstrator
- No. 2 BIS and CVA Armament Tests
- No. 3 CVA Structural Demonstrator
- No. 4 Part II Power Plant Performance and Equipment Demonstrator
- No. 5 BIS and CVA Electrical and Electronic Tests

In keeping with the initial tooling and production plans, the five production airplanes were to be identical to the experimental airplanes. They would include wing fuel dumping installation and any fixes found necessary for the experimental airplanes. Armament for the five production airplanes was modified as follows:

Airplanes No. 2 and No. 5 were built with the gun installation only, airplanes No. 1, No. 3, and No. 4 had all rocket and gun installations omitted. Rocket pack–cavity fairings were fabricated and installed on planes No. 1 through No. 5 for use during flight testing. Upon completion of flight tests the plan was to bring these five airplanes up to production standards with full armament capability.

On 19 April 1955, the BuAer specified certain requirements that had to be accomplished prior to the delivery of F8U-1 aircraft for test and fleet operations. The following F8U-1 aircraft were specified by the BuAer for performance of specification SR-38 Demonstration of Piloted Aircraft:

- No. 1 (BuNo 140444) F8U-1 for structural demonstration and development
- No. 2 (BuNo 140445) F8U-1 for armament development and demonstration
- No. 3 (BuNo 140446) F8U-1 for carrier suitability demonstrations and to be assigned to the BIS Carrier Suitability after Chance Vought Aircraft's demonstrations ended
- No. 4 (BuNo 140447) F8U-1 for power plant demonstration and development flying
- No. 5 (BuNo 140448) F8U-1 for electrical-electronic and fire control system tests and demonstration
- No. 6 (BuNo 141336) F8U-1 to prototype improvement changes

These six F8U-1 aircraft had to perform certain minimum requirements before the next 13 aircraft could be delivered for use by the Board of Inspection Survey (BIS) and the Naval Air Test Center (NATC). The minimum requirements that had to be met before acceptance of the next 13 F8U-1 aircraft could commence included part one of the SR-38 Demonstration of Piloted Aircraft that included aerodynamic and structural tests along with the spin demonstration build-up flights.

Board of Inspection and Survey

The U.S. Navy's Board of Inspection and Survey (BIS) was established by Congress in August 1882 to ensure that the ships of the U.S. Navy were properly equipped for reliable sustained mission readiness. The board also conducts acceptance trials and inspections of new weapon systems for the U.S. Navy. The purpose is to ensure that the contract and authorized changes have been satisfactorily fulfilled. In the case of the F8U-1, further aircraft assignments were identified to support the Board of Inspection and Survey (BIS) trials and inspections as follows:

- No. 7 (BuNo 141337) F8U-1 was assigned BIS Stability and Control testing and would be specially instrumented with strain gauges, stress sensors, and a "photo observer" for recording flight test information. It was scheduled for delivery in March 1956. The photo observer was a panel of duplicate flight instruments that a motion picture camera filmed during flight test.

- No. 8 through No. 11 (BuNos 141338–141341) F8U-1s were assigned for BIS trials scheduled for delivery in March through May 1956.
- No. 12 (BuNo 141342) F8U-1 was assigned to BIS Airframe and Engine Performance testing and would be specially instrumented with strain gauges, stress sensors, and a photo observer for recording flight test information. The 12th aircraft was scheduled for delivery in August 1956.
- No. 13 and No. 14 (BuNos 141343 and 141344) F8U-1s were assigned to Naval Air Test Center (NATC) for Research and Development projects.
- No. 15 through No. 20 (BuNos 141345 through 141350) F8U-1s were assigned to the Fleet Introduction Program (FIP).

In addition to the aircraft assigned to the Fleet Introduction Program, six additional aircraft were earmarked for assignment to the Operational Development Force to help develop combat tactics and operational doctrine for the F8U-1 aircraft.

According to the BuAer, prior to the FIP aircraft deliveries and the Operational Development Force (OpDevFor) deliveries, the spin, armament, and carrier suitability demonstration flights needed to be successfully completed. In addition to those requirements, the F8U-1 had to demonstrate further preliminary flights in the SR-38 testing program to at least an 80-percent load factor and 80 percent of the speed limits specified in the second part of the structural demonstration program.

Difficult Days in Testing

During any aircraft testing program difficulties arise and problems are uncovered. The XF8U-1 testing program was no different. Two flight incidents in May 1955 nearly resulted in the loss of the No. 1 XF8U-1.

On 9 May 1955, during flight number 26, an unexpected event occurred. During high-speed descent testing of the yaw stabilization system, the XF8U-1 became unstable and the aircraft suffered several violent lateral (yaw) oscillations. The test pilot was able to regain control and land the aircraft safely back at Edwards. An investigation of the incident revealed that a setting for the yaw stabilization system was left in the wrong position, leading to the violent oscillations.

The second event in May was just as serious and highlighted a shortcoming in the electrical installation and checkout instructions for the XF8U-1. On 11 May 1955, the day of the 33nd flight, the test pilot attempted to raise the wing at 180 knots of airspeed, which resulted in the pilot nearly losing control. The test pilot decided to land the aircraft in the wing down configuration to avoid re-creating the same set of control problems that would prevent a safe landing of the XF8U-1. The XF8U-1 landed safely on the lakebed at Edwards. The left tire and wheel assembly exploded approximately 15

1X on the ground in Grand Prairie with the latter markings of the last three of the BuNo on the tail and a different arrow on the fuselage. (CVPR-708)

minutes after the aircraft had parked. The left main landing gear was changed after this event.

The control problems resulted from an unusual chain of events caused by the Marquardt emergency generator. It was discovered that two phases of the alternating current (AC) electrical generator wiring were reversed. As a result, the roll gyros in the aircraft flight control stabilization system were rotating backward from their normal rotation direction. The backward rotation of the gyros caused the roll stabilization system to operate in a direction reverse of that needed to keep the aircraft in stable flight. Discussions between Chance Vought Aircraft and Marquardt revealed that neither party had performed phase checks on the alternating current (AC) generator because these were not a part of the checkout specifications for the XF8U-1.

As a result of landing gear damage and the requirement to install the Pratt & Whitney J57-P-12 turbojet engine, the aircraft was put into work status. The new engine would raise the available thrust

from 9,700 pounds dry (no afterburning) to 10,000 pounds and from 14,700 pounds wet (afterburner) to 16,000 pounds of thrust. The No. 1 XF8U-1 had accumulated 35.7 hours of flight time prior to the start of this work status period.

Flight Status Once Again

The Pratt & Whitney J57-P-12 engine was installed and ground checked during the 12-day work status period. The No. 1 XF8U-1 aircraft resumed test flying again on 23 May 1955. During speed brake testing the brake was opened at 35,000 feet at Mach 1.37. An AC (alternating current) power problem occurred and the aircraft entered a series of violent gyrations. The aircraft was put into work status to change the generator and it was decided to leave the Marquardt (RAT) generator switch in the off position during normal flight conditions. The switch would not be energized in emergency operation until the Marquardt had come up to operating speed. The Marquardt generator was producing frequency and current transients while the unit reached operating speed and these electrical transients were affecting the flight stabilization system.

During the first week of June 1955, another braking event occurred that further accented the need for "satisfactory brake control." This item was previously identified in early April 1955. After a landing run of 5,800 feet at a weight of 20,200 pounds with moderate braking, the left brake was observed to be burning and the tires were also sprayed with water to cool them off. The main landing gear wheel temperatures were recorded in the 300- to 400-degrees F range and both of the main wheel and tire assemblies were changed as a result. These events did not further delay the testing program and No. 1 XF8U-1 was back in the air the next day.

1X taxiing out for a flight. Note the slight change to the markings, with "Crusader" now written in cursive on the arrowhead. (CVPR-772)

A nice, static shot of 138899 adorned with "1X" on the vertical tail. It had been referred to as 1X for a while and now was adorned as such. Also of interest, the jet was not officially named Crusader until August 1955, five months after the first flight. (CVPR-980)

1X over Jefferson Blvd. near touchdown at NAS Dallas. (CVPR-1024)

Flight Test Event in June

The 44th flight on 7 June was eventful for both the test pilot and the No. 1 XF8U-1 aircraft. During the flight, a left turn was made pulling 4.6 g at Mach 1.05. The aircraft suddenly rolled to the right about 160 degrees, ending up in a 90-degree right bank. In addition to the sudden direction change, electrical power was lost, along with utility hydraulic pressure. The pilot regained control of the aircraft, switched to emergency power, and returned to Edwards for a safe landing. However, the adventurous day did not end there; on landing rollout the canopy was opened after the airspeed had dropped to 40 knots and it promptly departed the XF8U-1. The left upper landing gear door and left hand aileron were damaged along with a nick to the left-hand unit horizontal tail (UHT).

Understandably, the No. 1 XF8U-1 entered work status again on 8 June. Twenty-four changes were scheduled, with the following highlights: replacement of the canopy, jettison strut, upper left gear door, left aileron, and utility hydraulic pump due to the previous day's event. Another significant change during this work period was the change out of the original 8-degrees system variable-wing-incidence actuator and associated linkages to a 7-degree system. The Marquardt emergency ram-air turbine was changed out and a new 12-bladed unit was installed. Finally, there was a visual and operational check of the flight stabilization system because flight testing was still revealing problems.

Flight Testing Continues

During the period of 14–18 June 1955, the No. 1 XF8U-1 returned to flight status and flew 11 more times to finish the Chance Vought Aircraft evaluation tests prior to turning the aircraft over to the Navy for the Phase I Navy Preliminary Evaluation Flights. During these flights, speed brake characteristics were tested along with level flight speed, military thrust takeoff, combat thrust, and climb to combat ceiling.

Upon completion of those flights, the aircraft entered a final work status period prior to being handed over to the Navy. A Pratt &

138899 arrives back at Grand Prairie after yet another test flight. Of interest, the rear fuselage is painted in the standard Navy Gull Grey over White, and the vertical is painted red.

1X departs for another test flight. (CVPR-1935)

Whitney J57-P-12 engine was installed during the work status, along with replacing the 15 KVA generator with a 9 KVA generator as specified in the contract. And finally, new, higher-flow hydraulic pumps were installed.

On 23 June 1955, the No. 1 XF8U-1 performed an acceptance check flight with no discrepancies and was immediately handed over to the Navy for the start of their evaluation flights. Chance Vought Aircraft had flown 56 flights with the No. 1 XF8U-1 from 25 March 1955 until 23 June 1955. These numbers represented 8 more flights and 23 more days than the original schedule envisioned. However, the XF8U-1 was now ready for the first series of Navy Phase I evaluations. The Navy evaluation flights and the flight testing story of the XF8U-1 continues in Chapter 4. Meanwhile, back in Dallas, progress had been made on the No. 2 XF8U-1.

No. 2 XF8U-1 First Flight

The No. 2 XF8U-1 airplane (138900) was shop completed 22 May 1955, 16 days behind the current schedule. As with the No. 1 XF8U-1, a few open items

No. 2 XF8U-1 inside Convair's Fort Worth hangar with pre-flight testing taking place. (PR-6366)

needed to be addressed during the Engineering Lab checkout period.

The decision was made by Chance Vought management, as No. 2 XF8U-1 aircraft moved to the Engineering Lab, to ferry this and subsequent production F8U-1 airplanes to Edwards. Two factors heavily influenced this decision: the Hensley Field runway extension was not due for completion for another month, and the difficulties and delays anticipated in getting a C-124 cargo aircraft from the USAF. Chance Vought Aircraft made arrangements to fly the No. 2 XF8U-1 airplane from Carswell Air Force Base. Its initial flight was targeted for 9 June 1955 with a ferry flight to Edwards Air Force Base two days later.

In contrast to the way the No. 1 aircraft was handled, the fully assembled and ready-for-flight No. 2 XF8U-1 was loaded on a company lowboy semi-trailer and hauled from Grand Prairie on 7 June 1955 to Carswell Air Force Base on the west side of Fort Worth, Texas. This was the first of several XF/F8U-1 aircraft to make the journey to Fort Worth for their initial flights. At one point in the early years of the Crusader program, Chance Vought Aircraft attempted to establish a flight test facility at Carswell AFB rather than continuing to use the facilities at Edwards and MCAAS Muroc, but was unsuccessful because of the manufacturing activity already at the Convair plant.

While at Carswell in pre-flight testing, the No. 2 XF8U-1 shared a Convair hangar with the mock-up of the GRB-36 and

The No. 2 XF8U-1 during test flight preparations in Conair's hangar on Carswell AFB, Fort Worth, Texas. In the background a mock-up of the GRB-36 and RF-84K combination can be seen. (PR-6366B Collection)

After engine run and hydraulic testing XF8U-1 No. 2 is returning to the Convair hangar.

The No. 2 XF8U-1 being towed with the variable-incidence wing in the down position and the flaps and leading edge droops retracted. This view shows the completely different markings applied to the tail of the No. 2 XF8U-1 aircraft. (PR-6366A Collection)

RF-84K combination. A brown paper wall was constructed around the No. 2 XF8U-1's work area as it sat in the Convair hangar. As a side note, the RF-84K entered service with the 91st Strategic Reconnaissance Squadron (SRS) during 1955.

No. 2 XF8U-1 performed many pre-flight tests while at Carswell. Several items were addressed prior to the first flight including replacement of the right-hand wheel and tire due to a cut tread, bleeding of both brakes, and replacement of a slow-range airspeed indicator.

The first flight of the No. 2 XF8U-1 was completed on 11 June 1955 from Carswell six days ahead of schedule. For the first flight, the aircraft was lightweight, with only the fuselage tanks carrying fuel. The test flight was successful with all objectives met and no problems noted. The second flight was conducted from Carswell on 12 June with full internal fuel, and it was successful as well. With these two test flights completed, the aircraft was ready to join the No. 1 XF8U-1 at Edwards. Preparations began to ferry the aircraft to

Edwards as soon as possible.

The No. 2 XF8U-1 was ferried to Edwards Air Force Base on 15 June 1955. The aircraft was flown to Edwards in two segments; a refueling stop was made at Kirtland AFB, Albuquerque, New Mexico. Both portions of the flight were generally without incident with the exception of wheel and tire overheating that occurred at Albuquerque after two miles of taxiing to the parking area.

And the Name Is

On 20 June 1955 the Navy finally released limited information about the XF8U-1 program. The aircraft did not have a name and not a lot of detail was released initially. Then, in August 1955, the F8U was named Crusader; F. O. Detweiler, president of CVA, made the announcement. The name was selected from a list of 200 suggestions. It was reported that C. J. McCarthy, chairman of the board, made the final decision. The Navy approved the name as well.

Getting close to the first flight of the No. 2 XF8U-1, Chance Vought Aircraft mechanics are seen working on the aircraft while a Strategic Air Command B-36 Peacemaker thunders through the air behind them. (PR-6366C Collection)

Chapter 4

F8U-1: THE CRUSADE BEGINS

Factory Fresh Vought F8U-1 Crusader (142773) landing on a test flight.

Flight testing any new advanced military aircraft is a rigorous program. Successful operation of every onboard system must be achieved and verified, and overall aircraft performance is evaluated in painstaking detail. Any potential problem, no matter how small, must be identified and solved before the airplane enters service with the fleet, and the XF8U-1's flight test program was no exception.

Navy Phase I Evaluation Flights

CVA flew 56 evaluation flights with the No. 1 XF8U-1 (1X) prior to turning the airplane over to the Navy for Phase I of their evaluation. 1X would fly 8 flights between 23 and 27 June 1955 before the Navy returned it to CVA. Phase I of the Navy evaluation created the following summary of unsatisfactory items that were required to be corrected for final acceptance of the airplane: location of fuel transfer switch, aft field of view from cockpit, directional trimming required while accelerating to the climb speed and throughout climb, longitudinal control effectiveness for nose wheel lift-off, trim changes, and airplane buffet associated with speed brake extension. This was found to be acceptable due to the excellent speed brake effectiveness, at 40,000 feet the maneuvering roll control forces exceeded the limits specified by SR-119B and Mil-F-8785.

Here is the summary of unacceptable items that were required to be corrected prior to Phase II Preliminary Evaluation: large longitudinal stick deflection with light forces required for a small amount of control at low subsonic speeds, with cruise droop extended excessive transonic trim changes, sensitive longitudinal trimming between 200 and 400 knots IAS, violent roll produced by simulated stabilization system failure at high gain settings, inadequate roll damping at low speeds, low-speed flying qualities of airplane in 9 degrees wing incidence configuration, ejection seat design requires pad protection under thighs, directional control difficult with only brakes, and wheel overheating due to excessive brake use.

CVA Deficiency List

During evaluation flights by CVA pilots a list of deficiencies was gathered. The deficiencies fell into the following categories: engine, flight controls, and airframe.

The engine deficiencies included afterburner blowout at 55,000, warpage and creep in the afterburner nozzle, low reliability of the afterburner light off at high altitudes, and engine stalls at low altitudes and on the ground.

A summary of flight control deficiencies included poor crosswind-takeoff landing characteristics because of ineffective aileron control at certain speeds, residual yaw oscillations after dynamic stability tests, and inadequate reliability of stabilization systems.

The airframe deficiencies included a canopy snubber that did not prevent shearing of attachment bolts upon opening on the ground in moderate winds, marginal hydraulic power from Marquardt for dead stick landings, lateral sway at high Mach numbers, and low fuel levels due to a lack of fuel cell baffles.

Phase II Navy Evaluation

In October 1955, the Navy completed the Phase II evaluation flights. The evaluation took 17 flights, with 6 using the No. 1 F8U-1 airplane and 11 using the No. 2 F8U-1

140446 was the jet assigned to the initial carrier suitability demonstrations. Here is a good illustration of the wing up and folded configuration during a flight at Grand Prairie. (CVPR-329)

Nose details of 140446 with the cannon ports plugged and the spoked nose wheel. (CVPR-327)

A unique tail view of an early F8U-1, 140446, before the days of ventrals, ECM antennas, and paint. The shiny natural metal finish is in evidence. (CVPR-328)

airplane. Prior to completion of the evaluation, pilot concerns about the rate of roll and afterburner light off reliability were known.

Summary of Phase II unacceptable items: manual yaw gain changer, afterburner light off, wheel overheating, and rate of roll. Reported as the most serious deficiency of the airplane, rate of roll is considered unacceptable above a .9 Mach number below 30,000 feet, and satisfactory below a .9 Mach number at all altitudes.

Summary of Phase II unsatisfactory items: manual operation of the oil cooler door, nose gear steering, speed brake buffet, aft field of view from cockpit, leg clearance, moving stick to right, landing condition, 50,000 feet altimeter, cockpit air ram scoop.

A few of the pilots' comments on items considered "satisfactory": elevator control force gradient and control harmony; wheel brake effectiveness (good); transonic trim change (cruise droop extended and retracted); longitudinal trimming; simulated failure, yaw stabilization system with electro-hydraulic stabilization; roll damping at low speeds; emergency lateral and directional trim rates; power plant starting; compressor stalls (none in flight or during FCLP operations); cockpit entry with T-1 pressure suit worn; location and configuration of new three-position fuel transfer switch (accuracy of fuel quantity gage and totalizer considered "very good"); based on evaluated flight regime (600 knots), pitch damper not required. XF8U-1 airplane "availability" was considered excellent since only three pilot crabs were reported during the 17 evaluation flights.

Here are a few pilot comments that were considered qualified satisfactory, or recommended for improvement: landing gear handle (actuating forces should be reduced); ejection seat (sled tests recommended to ensure clearance above vertical tail after ejection); tail

bump after touchdown expected with aft stick movement (tests to be conducted at Mojave to determine if tail skid required); directional trim change satisfactory except when opening speed brake with Marquardt extended (recommended that CVA investigate this condition); difference in speed brake buffet between 55 degrees and 60 degrees, deflections not discernable but effectiveness of 55 degrees brake not satisfactory.

Buffet considered objectionable, but effectiveness should not be sacrificed to alleviate the buffet; lateral sway at fuel levels below 1,600 and 1,800 pounds becoming worse with speed brake open (correction considered an improvement item); fuel dumping dangerous because of fire hazard presented by overheating of wheels and brakes (recommended action, moving vent aft); afterburner ignition problem solution imperative since ignition on first attempt is necessary for tactical operations; nose gear steering satisfactory in taxiing with cross-winds of moderate velocities (improvement required for spotting on carrier decks).

Other Test Pilots' Views

The Chance Vought team invited a Convair engineering test pilot (C. E. Myers Jr.) to make a couple of evaluation flights in the F8U-1 and report his results,[36] as follows:

"Although not incorporated on the airplane I flew (BuNo 145359), all Crusaders are being equipped with the Specialties Inc. Angle of Attack System. The angle of attack is being detected by a vane such as the RWT on the F-102/106."[37]

II. Test Procedure

A. The evaluation was performed during two flights from NAS Hensley Field, Dallas, Texas. The flight plan included the following:

1. Cockpit and ground handling evaluation.
2. Timed climb from 15,000 feet to 50,000 feet.
3. Level flight acceleration at 38.000 feet and maximum power from Mach .9 to maximum speed.
4. Wind-up turn deceleration at 38,000 feet and 3-1/2 g from maximum speed to Mach .9 Mach.
5. Buffet boundary investigation at 35,000 feet with leading edge extended and retracted.
6. Speed brake effectiveness.

III. Results/Observations/Conclusions

A. Cockpit

1. The general arrangement of the controls and gages is acceptable. The warning lights are barely bright enough to be visible in very bright sunlight. I felt the need for a light to indicate operation in "emergency fuel control."
2. The seat and relation of the pilot to the controls and consoles is excellent. This is the most comfortable fighter I have ever had strapped to my back.

No doubt the most colorful F8U-1, 140444 was the first production Crusader.

The first F8U-1, 140444, during a publicity photo shoot over northern Texas shows off its hot rod red color scheme.

F8U-1 140444 would be involved in the first accident and first fatal accident for the F8U series about five months after its first flight in September 1955.

Little known or covered, 140444 conducted 14 flights paving the way for Project Beta, the Thompson Trophy run. During that time most of the beautiful red paint scheme was removed by hand.

The interesting result of the Project Beta test flights is illustrated in this photo. Eventually all the original red paint scheme was removed and the opposite scheme was applied to the tail. The success of these proving flights would pave the way for the 1956 Thompson Trophy win.

Although 140444 made its first flight at Carswell along with a number of early Crusaders by summer 1955, it was able to receive updates at Vought's Grand Prairie plant. Here, 140444 taxis out for a test flight. (CVPR-689)

    3. Visibility is exceptionally good in all directions except forward where vision is obstructed by the gun sight and occasionally obscured by reflections in the wind screen.

B. Ground Handling

    1. The nose wheel steering and brake are both pleasant to operate and very effective. Nose wheel steering was used on take-off up to 80 knots where upon the rudder was employed for directional control.

IV. Recommendations

A. Investigate the longitudinal pitch problem with an eye toward incorporating a device to decrease elevator deflection when approaching the critical area.

B. Increase drag in the PA configuration to bring the power required during an approach to about 85- to 87-percent RPM (possibly approaching with IR Probe and rocket pack extended would serve as an interim solution).

C. Decrease stick deflection per aileron deflection in the PA configuration.

D. Correct the rudder trim drift.

E. Increase the trim rates of the aileron and elevator systems.

F. Provide "all points ignition"; that is, the capability of obtaining ignition regardless of the throttle position. The F-106 incorporates this feature.

G. Provide a battery for air start ignition.

An early demonstration of the classic Crusader catapult stance, 140446 poised to launch.

H. Add an emergency fuel control light.

I. Glare shield to shade the warning lights.[38]

USAF Evaluation Flights

The USAF performed five test flights using the No. 2 F8U-1 airplane in October 1955. Maj Gen. J. Stanley Holtoner made the first flight on 11 October for 1.08 hours flight time. On the same day, Maj. Childs flew the 1X for .96 hours. During these two flights the airplane experienced a hydraulic fuse problem.

Col. Horace Hanes made the first flight on 12 October and obtained Mach 1.52 at 42,000 feet in a flight that lasted only .68 hours. Col. "Pete" Everest made the second flight of the day for a time of 1.06 hours duration. The final USAF flight of this evaluation was flown by Brig Gen. Al Boyd on 14 October. The general's flight lasted .84 hours and suffered a number of discrepancies. The yaw damper and normal trim went out on takeoff and remained inoperative for the entire flight. When the wing was raised for landing, the wing-out-of-positon light illuminated. Finally, after landing, the inside of the nose gear door was damaged but the reason not known.

The causes for the discrepancies were as follows:

- Nose gear steering drift caused the nose gear door damage; a steering valve was changed.
- The wing incidence light was caused by the wing actuator failing after only 1 degree of movement. The variable wing actuator was replaced.
- The yaw damper difficulty was due to a shorted condenser in the yaw channel and was repaired.
- The 2X airplane was repaired and returned to flight test duties after the USAF evaluation flights.

First Accident, First Fatality

F8U-1 BuNo 140444 was the first production model F8U and was instrumented as a demonstrator aircraft. On 1 February 1956 flight number 50 took off from MCAAS Mojave, California, at 14:53. Weather and visibility were clear and unlimited. The takeoff gross weight was 25,586 pounds, and the wing positioned up. The pilot was Harry T. Brackett, staff experimental test pilot for CVA. The climb to test altitude was routine. Brackett then performed a series of speed brake evaluation runs at Mach 1.20 to 1.45. A scheduled 30-degree dive at normal rated power, speed brake open, was deleted from the flight plan by the pilot. An analysis of directional stability characteristics during a level flight run with the speed brake extended needed to be performed prior to attempting the dive test.

Brackett then proceeded with a planned evaluation of airplane roll characteristics using various combinations of aileron and spoiler at relatively high airspeeds. The experimental spoilers had been installed prior to flight 46. A descent in afterburner was made to attain 650 knots indicated air speed (IAS) at 8,000 feet for the next test. The first test point was to be an ailerons-only roll from 60 degrees to 60 degrees bank in each direction using full stick throw. Telemeter records showed that the roll to the left was accomplished without incident.

When the right roll was started, telemeter signal was lost and attempted radio contact with Brackett was unsuccessful. All communications up to this point had been normal. Edwards started getting reports of an aircraft accident about 30 minutes after contact with the aircraft was lost. Intense sonic booms in the vicinity of the North Base at Edwards captured witnesses' attention. Several aircraft gyrations were noted moments before major structural failure was observed. Witnesses said the fuselage was seen to descend in a slow flat spin with other components floating down for approximately 2 minutes.

At the crash location, the pilot was found fatally injured in the cockpit. He was taken to the Edwards hospital by helicopter prior to the arrival of CVA personnel to the crash scene.

History of 140444

The first flight of BuNo 140444 was made on 30 September 1955. The aircraft had completed 49 flights prior to the accident. Of the 49, 10 were required for shakedown and ferry, and telemetering tests; 19 flights were made to investigate rate-of-roll characteristics of the ailerons and spoilers; 14 flights were made checking high-speed level flight performance; and 6 were made to obtain cruise data. Total aircraft time since new, including the final flight, was 43.34 hours. The J57 engine had logged 109.92 hours. The airplane was assigned to be the structural demonstrator and was completely instrumented for that tasking. The installed instrumentation included a photo observer, oscillography, and telemetering. A perforated speed brake, two-position spoilers set to open 45 degrees on the upper surface of each wing, and readjustment of aileron stops were configuration changes made prior to testing.

H. T. Brackett was employed by CVA since 26 June 1951. He had accumulated 120 hours in the F8U aircraft. He held a master of science degree in aeronautical engineering and was considered by all members of his profession to be superior in his chosen field, both from a personal and professional standpoint.

The accident investigation results determined one probable sequence of events:

Left-Hand Aileron Hinge Fails. Telemeter records show the aileron position of 9-degrees-down rising to an abnormally high position. Structural analysis of the failed hinge revealed it to have failed from repeated loading. Laboratory tests of reverse limit loading on these hinges produced similar failures in a very low number or cycles. Dye check inspection of No. 1 and No. 2 XF8U-1 revealed cracks in the inboard hinges.[39]

Aircraft Vibrates and Starts Oscillating. Telemeter records show rapid end erratic changes in control surfaces and rates and directions of aircraft movement. Dynamic analysis of an aileron with broken hinges, which remained attached to the wing only by the "dumbell" linkage, revealed that a severe vibration of the airframe would be produced by the flapping motion of the aileron. This could produce up to 40 percent limit stress in the wing center section skin.[40]

Electrical Power Lost. Telemeter records stop .43 seconds after failure of the aileron hinges. No radio transmissions were received after loss of telemetering. There are no indications that electrical power was disrupted to any one system prior to the others.[41]

Aircraft out of control in a right roll. The last portion of the telemeter record shows an increase in rate of roll to the right and the longitudinal deceleration is known to possibly produce involuntary pilot-induced oscillations. Yaw stabilization being inoperative due to electrical power being lost also contributes to the gyrations of the aircraft as it decelerates. The one witness who definitely saw the aircraft prior to breakup stated that it was out of control in a rapid right roll.[42]

Variable-Incidence Wing Strut Starts Extending. The strut, as recovered, was extended 11.5 inches of its 16.5 stroke. It is believed that the severe vibration of the airframe caused the internal locks to "walk" and allowed the strut to extend. At the point where the strut had extended 11.5 inches the wing hinges failed. As the wing left the aircraft, it "snatched' the strut from the fuselage at the attachment fitting. Laboratory tests of the VIW strut revealed that a sudden load sufficient to fail the strut fuselage attachment fitting would not cause extension of the strut.[43]

Engine Flame-Out. The engine was flamed out and turning only at 10 to 20 percent on impact. Tests on the J57 engine revealed that on flame-out, a large white puff of incompletely burned fuel will emit from the tailpipe. Many witnesses observed such a "puff" at or slightly before breakup. It has also been determined that application of steady negative g with electrical power off will cause flame-out within .6 to 2 seconds, Oscillatory g forces in all planes could cause flame-out anywhere from .6 to 64 seconds. Tests have shown that this engine will decelerate to 10–20 percent in 25 to 50 seconds with no ram. The trajectory analysis of parts of the aircraft reveal that the time for the fuselage to contact the ground was 25 to 40 seconds after the wing separated.[44]

Wing Fails. The wing hinges failed in tension and bending inward, the wing showing positive g failing loads. Under the flight conditions at the time of telemeter loss, a tension load is present on these hinges and a compression load is present on the VIW actuator. The effect of raising the wing would not be sufficient to fail the wing or its attachments. However, when combined with the forces imposed by the other failures and maneuvers, a sufficient load to cause wing destruction would be imposed. The inward bending of the hinges is the result of the mode of failure of the wing center section as evidenced by the compression failure of the upper skin. As the wing left the aircraft, the VIW actuator fuselage attachment failed in tension. The VIW actuator then struck the vertical tail and failed in bending at the rod end.[45]

Fuselage and Tail Components Fail. Analysis of the forces following wing failure reveal that dynamic response of the fuselage, plus air loads, would be sufficient to fail components such as the left unit horizontal tail, landing gear doors, rudder, equipment compartment door, nose boom, and nose cone. Examination of the left unit horizontal tail actuating rod revealed that a crack existed prior to final failure. However, there is no positive evidence to determine whether the final failure occurred prior to or upon impact. A wreckage trajectory analysis shows that no parts left the aircraft prior to wing failure. It is doubted that any of the escape systems as they are known today would have saved the pilot in this accident.[46]

Post-Accident Return to Flight

Since the cause for the accident involving 140444 was not immediately determined, all remaining XF8U-1 and F8U-1 aircraft were grounded. By the end of February 1956, the No. 3 F8U-1 resumed flying at Patuxent River for Navy familiarization flights and free flight arrestments with a 210-knot speed restriction.

The two XF8U-1 airplanes resumed flying under the 210-knot restriction at Mojave on 28 March. The flights accomplished shakedown after modifications related to the crash, pilot familiarization, and testing of incorporation of the spin recovery parachute for the upcoming spin demonstrations by the No. 2 XF8U-1.

As March progressed, speeds gradually increased, with limited roll tests at 350 knots eventually increasing to Mach .9 to 1.2 at 40,000 feet. Afterburner ignition tests resumed at Mach .77 to .95 at altitudes of 15,000 to 50,000 feet. Finally, at Patuxent River, Phase II carrier suitability demonstrations were successfully completed using the No. 3 airplane aboard the USS *Forrestal* (CV-59) during the weeks of 3–6 April and 16–20 April without a single major complaint.

In April 1956 the long-anticipated improvements to Hensley Field (NAS Dallas) were completed. Test flying of the F8U could now take place from the Grand Prairie plant, and first flights could now take place at the plant instead of having to be trucked to Carswell in Fort Worth, Texas.

The fixes due to the loss of 140444 caused a major shift in the whole program schedule by April 1956. The airplanes for BIS use were delayed four weeks, the FIP airplanes two and a half weeks, the VX-3 airplanes two weeks, and first fleet deliveries were delayed three weeks to 14 December 1956.

Late in April the No. 2 F8U-1 left Grand Prairie for Mojave for gun firing trials, and the stiffened wing showed some improvement in roll rate (spoiler incorporation yet to come).

Navy evaluation to further investigate F8U maximum speed, maximum rate of roll, afterburner relight, afterburner blowout, and specific range had just begun when the loss of the No. 7 airplane occurred on 4 May 1956. The evaluation was terminated after nine flights because of the crash. The cause of the crash was not associated with engine difficulties. The Navy made preliminary checks

A series of four deck handling photos taken during carrier suitability demonstrations aboard USS Forrestal *in April 1956 using F8U-1 140446.*

on specific range and indications were that the airplane would be somewhat short of specification requirements. Engine instrumentation was not available to evaluate engine performance. From the few afterburner relights attempted at high altitude the Navy's general comment was that no improvement had been made to this problem since the previous evaluation in January.

Loss of F8U-1 141337

"The pilot, Major J. A. Feliton, USMC, was engaged in the Navy preliminary evaluation of the rate of roll characteristics of the F8U-1 aircraft. At 14,500 feet, 480 knots EAS (Mach .995), a full-deflection aileron roll from 60-degrees right bank to 60-degrees left bank was completed and a similar maneuver to the right was initiated. After approximately 90 degrees of roll to the right (30 degrees past hor-

izontal), a rapid negative pitch transient occurred. The pilot's normal corrective reaction resulted in a severe pitching oscillation. After two cycles the pilot released the stick, and a steady negative pitch resulted. The wing failed and the structural damage then caused failure of the fuselage. Fuel cells, ruptured as the fuselage failed, then exploded. The pilot successfully ejected at the time of, or slightly after, structural failure."[47]

Once again all XF8U-1 and F8U-1 flying was grounded pending results of the investigation. This accident suspended the Navy evaluation flights that had started at NAS Dallas using 1X and the No. 7 F8U-1.

The aircraft 141337 was the seventh production F8U-1. The first flight for 141337 was 4 April 1956 and it accumulated 16 flights prior to the accident for shakedown, pilot checkout, yaw stabilization evaluation, and instrument records. Total time on the airframe

F8U-1 140446 showing the tight fit on the deck edge elevator of USS Forrestal. (CVPR-764)

"After you," F8U-1 140446 waits its turn to launch after a North American FJ-4 Fury.

Crusader 140446 sharing the deck with Piasecki HUP-2 Retriever, BuNo. 128519 of HU-2.

According to the notes on the back of this photo this is 141337 (No. 7) taking off on its last flight from NAS Dallas. It would be lost less than an hour later on 4 May 1956. (CVPR-683)

up to the time of the accident was 20.01 hours. The accident flight took off from NAS Dallas at 18:05 on 4 May 1956; ceiling and visibility were unlimited. The accident site was approximately 4 miles north of Greenville, Texas.

Some of the findings give insight into the chain of events occurring in the accident sequence. "The first abnormality in the flight was a sudden negative pitch transient. A relatively short period of time (on the order of 5 seconds) elapsed from the initiation of the negative pitch transient until the wing failed." The wing failed due to excessive negative g loading. "The oscillation encountered leading to failure of the wing and then the fuselage were a function of a pitch transient from an unknown cause plus pilot reaction."[48]

"The cause of the accident was a severe and unexpected negative pitch transient of undetermined origin which resulted in inadvertent over controlling due to deficient control force characteristics under the maneuver and flight conditions at the time."[49]

Final Navy evaluation was completed at 27 June and 2 July 1956. A total of 25 flights were flown by four Navy pilots, and the following power plant discrepancies were noted by the Navy:

- Afterburner light off above 40,000 feet was unacceptable.
- Time to accelerate from idle to military power was unsatisfactory. Above 40,000 feet the Navy obtained 30 to 37 seconds for acceleration and 16 to 17 seconds per snap accelerations on the deck.
- Bleed valve operation was inconsistent and erratic and the

Navy definitely preferred the slow bleed settings schedule as flown in the No. 1 X airplane.

Flight testing was resumed and the Pratt & Whitney engine performance program on the No. 4 airplane was delayed by a flashback fire, which occurs with afterburner light off on the ground. A flashback occurs when fuel vapors are apparently drawn into the aft fuselage sections by the reverse cooling system and are ignited by afterburner light off. Airplane No. 1 X was used during the following few weeks to further investigate afterburner relights in conjunction with pilot-induced oscillation problems

During the latter part of the Navy evaluation, on 2 July 1956, high-altitude climbs were made and the maximum corrected pressure altitude of 63,140 feet was obtained on a zoom maneuver. During the highest climb the afterburner blew out at this altitude, but the indicated airspeed was down 165 knots.

Loss of F8U-1 141344

The third F8U accident involving 141344 (No. 14) occurred on 14 August 1956 on the third flight of the aircraft. The first flight of 141344 was 30 July 1956; it had accumulated 2.43 hours of flight time when the accident occurred.

The pilot, John W. Konrad, chief test pilot at Chance Vought Aircraft, was engaged in an evaluation of engine compartment and aft fuselage pressures and temperatures during combat-rated thrust operation from takeoff to absolute ceiling or where afterburner operation could no longer be maintained. At 40,000 feet the TOT rose rapidly from 615 to 660 degrees C. Throttle was immediately retarded, which decreased RPM but did not affect TOT. Throttle was then retarded almost to idle. At 78-percent RPM, the TOT rose rapidly to approximately 800 degrees C, accompanied by violent compressor stalls and followed by flameout. Six relights were made. Each time the TOT rose rapidly; and after the first relight, a maximum of only 40-percent RPM could be attained. At 10,000 feet, the pilot realized he could not reach the field and successfully ejected at 8,000 feet and 215 knots. The aircraft disintegrated upon impact."[50]

The cause of the accident was failure of the first-stage turbine due to an unknown object passing into it from the combustion section of the engine. There was nothing that Konrad could have done to prevent the loss of the aircraft.

F8U-1 Tactical Improvements

The following tactical improvements were identified and incorporated in the F8U-1 design and testing: external sidewinder (ECP-39), in-flight refueling (ECP-65), and limited search radar (ECP-86). Prototype external sidewinder authorization was received 25 August 1955. Authorization for both prototype and production in-flight refueling (IFR) was received 3 January 1956. The proposal for a limited search radar prototype was not submitted to the BuAer until 16 April 1956.

Production incorporation of in-flight refueling and sidewinder occurred with the No. 66 airplane. A flying prototype of the limited search radar was scheduled for 29 March 1957. Production scheduling for the limited search radar was dependent upon GFE radar availability, not expected until the second quarter of 1958. The radar was finally incorporated in the F8U-1E (145416) after 318 F8U-1 aircraft had rolled off the production line.

External Sidewinder ECP-39

Early in the V-380/383/384 the incorporation of the Sparrow guided missile had been a design consideration. Wind tunnel testing was performed with the Sparrow II missiles located in various fuselage and wing positions. It was determined the best wing position with the lowest drag, though impractical, was the wing tip. The lowest drag encountered in the testing was with the Sparrows mounted to the fuselage sides. Aircraft balance and the practicality of launching a missile of the Sparrow size from the fuselage were questions left unanswered by the study.[51]

With the emphasis on the day fighter capabilities of the designs, the Sparrow requirement was removed. This left the F8U to be equipped with cannon and unguided rockets as armament. With the successful flight tests of the Sidewinder 1 missile in 1952–1953 and a contract for production in 1955, the future of aerial weaponry was at hand. The Sidewinder was an obvious choice for incorporation into the new day fighter. It provided a more accurate and longer-range weapon than what currently equipped the F8U.

Demonstration of the tactical improvement of the incorporation of the Sidewinder missile fell to F8U-1 141343. Here, it is taking off on one of the first captive carry demonstration flights of the fuselage-mounted Sidewinder missile. (CVPR-1062)

In-flight refueling testing was assigned to 141346 and added to the requirements of the F8U-1 after the program had started. This resulted in CVA having to design a probe that would fit in the airplane.

An addendum (No. F8U-1) was added to the SR-38E-2, "Specification for the demonstration of Piloted Airplanes," dated 17 November 1954, for testing of an F8U-1 Sidewinder. CVA requested the use of a F8U-1 airplane for flight tests of the Sidewinder missile installation in January 1956.

In-flight Refueling Probe ECP-65

In September 1955, the Navy decided that all its carrier aircraft needed to be equipped for aerial refueling. Space in the F8U-1 was already tight with the incorporation of all the necessary equipment into the smallest airframe possible for the day fighter competition. CVA engineering came up with a retractable probe installation mounted on the left-side fuselage behind the cockpit, which had a bulged fairing to cover it. To refuel, a door would open and a hydraulic cylinder would telescope the probe out away from the fuselage and into the pilot's line of sight. Once extended the probe was flown into the basket at the end of the hose extended by the tanker aircraft to connect and receive fuel. The No. 16 F8U-1 was modified and took place in a testing program from December 1956 to the end of March 1957. The system was also tested by VX-3 and NATC and approved for incorporation in the F8U-1. IFR capability was incorporated with airplane No. 66.

According to Report Project TED No. PTR-PP-3684 Model F8U-1 Aircraft, Determination of the In-Flight Refueling Envelope, Report #1, Final Report, dated 26 February 1959, the in-flight refueling probe on the F8U-1 suffered several discrepancies. Three F8U-1 aircraft (143732, 143740, 143820) participated in the testing, and the discrepancies were noted as follows:

"Failure of the probe to remain locked out when the probe switch is in the OFF position." With the IFR probe in the fully open position, a mechanical lock should hold the probe in the extended position when the hydraulic power is removed and the switch is moved to the off position. This discrepancy resulted from a mis-rigging of the mechanical lock, allowing the lock pit to over-travel the locking slot.[52]

"The interaction between the steel inner tube collar and the probe fitting, which causes the probe to seize in the extended position." A condition can exist where tolerance buildup can cause interference between the inner tube and the collar. The solution is to enlarge the diameter of the collar to prevent interference.[53]

"The critical nature of the proper probe linkage adjustment and the critical probe lubricating procedures." It was found that the detailed instructions for probe rigging had not been incorporated into the Handbook of Maintenance Instructions, and the entire IFR qualification program was completed with no lubrication at all. The presence or absence of grease was not considered a critical item.[54]

The second shows the door open with the probe retracted.

A sequence of four images taken during a ground test of the in-flight refueling probe on 141346. The first shows the probe retracted and door closed.

The final image shows the refueling probe fully extended. An interesting fact about the Crusader series: It was always known for having long legs. It is reported that in some ACM engagements the Crusader could fight two sessions while its contemporaries had to go find a tanker and return.

The third image shows the probe extending.

Limited Search Radar APS-67 ECP-86

Proposal for APS-67, limited search radar prototype, was submitted to the BuAer 16 April 1956. The APS-67 would be incorporated into the deliveries of the F8U-1E, replacing the original AN/APG-30 gun ranging radar and giving it a limited all-weather interception capability. The radome changed to an all-plastic with a gun camera window on the bottom. The F8U-1 radome was identified by its combination of plastic tip with metal body.

F8U-1 Boundary Layer Control (BLC)

Following an informal request by the BuAer in March 1954 to look into the possible application of boundary layer control to the F8U-1 airplane, a series of tests were begun by CVA's Development Section at the David Taylor Model Basin at Washington, D.C.

By January 1955 sufficient data was available to indicate that BLC was workable and should be tested in a prototype F8U-1 airplane. BLC was expected to decrease approach speeds and improve

Tests of the in-flight refueling system were conducted using the Naval Air Test Center's North American A2J Savage tanker. (CVPR-1084)

A closer view of F8U-1 141346 taking fuel from the A2J. The refueling tests were successful and the probe was introduced into production with F8U-1 No. 66. (CVPR-1093)

Right side view of F8U-1 141336 with Boundary Layer Control (BLC) wing surfaces extended. (CVA-43314)

lateral control effectiveness at high angles of attack. Air nozzles on the ailerons and flap route engine compressor bleed air onto those surfaces. At slow airspeeds the air blowing over the surfaces creates greater lift than the forward speed of the aircraft alone. The additional lift allows the airplane to fly at slower speeds for approach. The engine compressor bleed air can be as hot as 700 degrees F, making insulated ducts a necessity for the system.

By February 1955 preliminary results from the BLC studies had shown promise. The point had come for flight testing with a modified aircraft. Since the first proposal, the aerodynamic model of the F8U had progressed from the bulbous, rounded leading edges on the wing, nose, and inlet. The F8U now featured sharper, contoured leading edges and other improvements to reduce drag and increase speed. Because of those changes, the droop-nose blowing-BLC

F8U-1 141336 (No. 6) with BLC wing front view showing the double-droop leading edges and full extension of the flaps and ailerons on 21 June 1957. (CVA-43316)

concept was not nearly as effective as a double-droop leading edge non-blown with blown trailing edge flap and ailerons.

About three weeks before the first flight of the XF8U-1, CVA proposed ECP-38 for a boundary layer control system. The proposal flight tests of BLC could begin in January 1956 if approval was given by the BuAer in March 1955. One modification necessary for the BLC test airplane would be the incorporation of the inboard flap due to the changes in landing characteristics it provides. Testing continued throughout 1955 in CVA's low-speed wind tunnel (LSWT) and the BuAer had yet to approve the proposal.

XF8U-1 flight testing revealed that at slow speeds approaching stall the stability and control of the aircraft deteriorates. Large amounts of aileron control are required at slow speeds to keep the aircraft on course. CVA wanted full-scale flight tests to verify the improvements of a BLC and double-droop modification. The testing would evaluate the changes BLC would bring to low-speed handling. LSWT tests indicated a reduction of 6 knots in the stall speed and 6 to 20 knots in the approach speed at landing weight. Thought was given to the potential for the test aircraft also to serve V-401 (F8U-3) high-lift system development. A year after the initial proposal, the BuAer informally suggested bringing the BLC proposal up-to-date to include data from recent wind tunnel tests, and resubmitting it.

In April 1956, a revised proposal for design, fabrication, installation, and flight testing was submitted to the BuAer. The proposal included modification of the inboard flap and aileron, installation of a blowing-type boundary layer control, installation of an engine-air-bleed manifold and fuselage ducting from the bleed manifold to the flap with an on-off valve operable from cockpit, and a double-hinged nose droop for the center section and outer panel.

The Bureau of Aeronautics Representative Dallas (BAR) commented that "the advantages of BLC with double nose droop appeared particularly attractive in regard to reduction in speed for minimum thrust, and that possible reduction approach speeds of the order of 13 knots appeared highly desirable." The BAR recommended that a decision be withheld until the results of the F8U-1 carrier suitability trials underway at that time had been reviewed.

A proposal request was made to CVA by the BuAer in July 1956 for a wing with ailerons, flaps, and droops, for high-lift research in the NACA Ames Laboratories' low-speed wing tunnel. The delivery date for the wing would be 1 September 1956. The wing would not include most of its control actuators and mechanisms because these were not needed for the wind tunnel tests. Ames was going to be testing several boundary layer control configurations, including CVA's proposal. Ames would be responsible for installing the BLC provisions to be tested. In September 1956, the proposal for the wing was submitted; however, nothing came of this proposal.

On 16 October 1956, CVA proposed to have the BLC installation completed and available for the start of the flight test program in June 1957. For this to happen, a bailed F8U-1 airplane instrumented similarly to No. 6 had to be available for use by 15 February 1957.

Landing Configurations		
	BLC Configuration	F8U-1 Configuration
Flap and aileron deflection	40 degrees	20 degrees
Type of leading-edge droop	Double	Single
Wing incidence	4 degrees	7 degrees

Eventually the BuAer approved a test plan for incorporating BLC into an F8U-1 for testing purposes. By June 1957, the No. 6 F8U-1 (141336) had been modified with a BLC-equipped wing for testing. The improvements were later incorporated in the French Navy F-8E(FN) aircraft to help with approach speeds on their smaller carriers and into the modernization of the F-8E fleet into the F-8J.

Integrated Flight Capsule

The BuAer recognized the need to improve the pilot's environment in the cockpit of increasingly higher performance aircraft. Pressure suits weighing 95 pounds or more were necessary for high-altitude flight. The suits had the negative effect of making it difficult to reach and activate cockpit controls. CVA had been involved in pilot escape systems since 1948, when the first ejection seat design was created for the F6U Pirate aircraft. In September 1958 CVA proposed an integrated flight capsule in response to a

Vought artist's concept of the integrated flight capsule (IFC) ejection sequence. Among the numerous details are the rocket motor location, the deployment of stabilizing fins, and speed brakes. (CVPR-2075)

BuAer request. The BuAer contracted CVA to design, construct, and test an integrated flight capsule. "Such a capsule will provide and internal environment which will permit unburdening of the pilot of cumbersome personal equipment and will also provide escape capabilities from 0 to 120,000 feet at speeds up to Mach 4. It will be integrated into a current airplane of high performance for operational qualification."[55]

The objectives for the integrated flight capsule program were as follows:

- Provide an improved cockpit environment to increase the operational effectiveness of the manned-weapon system by unburdening the pilot of omni-environmental protective garments.
- Design an escape device capable of protecting a pilot and recovering him from any conditions of emergency which may occur within the complete flight profiles of the expected high-speed high-altitude aircraft of the next 10 years.
- Verify this design by installation in operational F8U aircraft and by testing to the degree that engenders acceptance of the capsule as a flight environment and as a reliable means of escape in the event of need.
  - The design criteria developed and qualified by testing will be fundamental and applicable to any present or future fighter-interceptor-type airplane including the F8U-3.[56]

The requirements for the integrated flight capsule were the following:

- The system must have potential to match that of future fighter-interceptor performance.
- The capsule must deliver the pilot to the surface in good condition and with sufficient means to take evasive action and survive until rescued.
- Must be able to provide for ground level escape between 100 and 800 knots
- Must be able to escape from 25 feet of water
- Must be anti-immersion or floatation provisions to raise the main hatch above the waterline
- Anti-g suit to prevent high transverse g forces on the pilot
- Pilot restraint harness and head restraints
- There shall be no collision between the IFC and the abandoned airplane.
- A semi-automatic escape system will be provided in the event of pilot incapacitation (a dead-man switch).
- Air temperatures in contact with the pilot should not exceed 160 degrees F.
- Environmental protection shall be provided for ground temperatures of 80 to –20 degrees F.
- Means provided for sending radio distress signals
- The weight effect on the aircraft due to the capsule shall be minimal.
- The IFC must be subjected to sufficient tests to warrant its acceptance by the Navy and its contractors as a proven concept.
- The capsule must retain its basic intent as a control center yet allow for efficient operation of the airplane.

The flight capsule descending under the triple parachute canopy in this artist's concept. The clean break at the bulkhead is shown. (CVPR-2520)

A scale model of the integrated flight capsule during tests of the floatation system. The canopy has been modified with a hatch for pilot entry/exit instead of an aft hinged section. The framing would have reduced visibility for the aircrafts' primary purpose of performing day fighter duties. (CVPR-2522)

- The cabin interior will be a vessel for maintaining the atmosphere required for the pilot so that the pressure suit and oxygen mask can be deleted.

The capsule for the F8U-1 will include the engine air duct and extend from the nose to station 312.8 inches. The engine air duct with the lower fins will serve to absorb the crash energy of landing. By cutting at the fuselage station, 312.8 inches of space is provided for stabilizing fins, air brakes, recovery system, and boost rockets with the removal of all gun provisions. The shaped charge located along the station line will sever lines, wires, nose landing gear, and the fuselage. Two boost rockets will ensure the capsule clears the airplane. Four fins have separate thrusters to help them deploy to stabilize the capsule. Speed brakes are provided on the capsule side to slow the speed to 425 knots so the first-stage brake parachute can be deployed. At 425 knots the control unit will deploy the first-stage brake parachute, an 8-foot-diameter ribbon-type chute. The brake parachute is ejected by a fired projectile, which will ensure proper opening of the chute. Once the capsule is below 14,000 feet or commanded by other conditions the main chutes will deploy. The main recovery parachutes are a cluster of three 33-foot-diameter parachutes.

Mock-up of the IFC with the fins deployed and still having the single glass cockpit section but set up more like a hatch than rear hinged canopy. (CVPR-2566)

Another view of the IFC mock-up showing the changed shape of the intake and the single-piece windshield. (CVPR-2567)

In Summary Report AER-EOR-12822, written about the IFC, the following recommendation was made: "It is recommended that the integrated flight capsule program be extended to the detail design, fabrication, and test phases to conclusively prove the concept and its application to Navy weapon systems and that this follow-on work be programmed so that the proven concept will be available for operational application by 1963. It is further recommended that if the flight capsule concept is to be incorporated in a production aircraft, this incorporation should be made by writing the requirements in the basic design specification." The last line in the recommendation

A wind tunnel test of the integrated flight capsule leaving the fuselage. (CVPR-2711)

F8U-1 141346 was the donor of an aft section for thrust augmentation modifications. The fairing was built to enclose the rocket engine to boost climb rate and altitude. The design never reached the test phase for either the F8U-1 or F8U-3.

gives a couple of clues as to why the concept ended there. "Design of the capsule systems can be simplified and the installations accomplished much more economically and at a considerable increase in operational reliability."[57]

V-410 Thrust Augmentation Aircraft

During the mid-1950s there was a very real concern that the Soviets would soon have bombers capable of cruising at altitudes above 60,000 feet. Under the category of tactical improvements, CVA sought means by which jet fighters could reach these altitudes and deal with the threats. Zoom climbs and rocket-assisted climbs were a couple of techniques studied.

The idea of thrust augmentation in two F8U-1s was proposed (V-410) to the BuAer on 14 February 1956. CVA submitted a formal proposal to the BuAer in March 1956 to install an 8,000-pound thrust rocket motor in the aft fuselage of an F8U-1 for thrust augmentation. The Navy showed considerable interest for this capability. Under the category of tactical improvements, thrust augmentation received ECP-68 on 28 May 1956. The configuration under consideration would be similar to a future proposal for the F8U-3 where the rocket motor was to be installed at the base of the vertical stabilizer. CVA anticipated that the BuAer would give a go-ahead for this rocket installation. According to the proposal receipt a first rocket engine was scheduled for 15 August 1957. The first flight of the prototype was scheduled for November 30 with the second prototype flying on 31 December 1957.

By early 1957, the plan was to install a rocket engine on the tail assembly of two F8U-1s, Nos. 16 and 23. One airplane would be retained by CVA for flight tests and the other delivered to the Navy. After CVA completed testing the first airplane would be delivered to the Navy. The Reaction Motors XLF-40 rocket motor, which provided 8,000 pounds of thrust fueled by a mixture of hydrogen peroxide and jet fuel, was chosen. In a ground test the XLF-40 exploded, killing two mechanics.

Due to the fatal accident, Reaction Motors pulled out of the project. CVA continued the project with a Rocketdyne XLF-54 engine providing 6,000 pounds of thrust. By February 1959 CVA was expecting a contract for the V-410 (F8U-1F). The maximum performance expected was Mach 1.93 at 55,000 feet and Mach 1.4 at 79,000 feet. Afterburner blowout at these altitudes was not expected to hurt flying characteristics; however, it was important for the engine to stay lit and compressor stall free during the entire flight envelope. By February 1959, the BuAer decided not to go ahead with the V-410. The project never flew and only went as far as installing a dummy engine in a modified F8U-1 tail cone.

Deadstick Landing Tests

The dead stick landing program was conducted at the CVA plant in Grand Prairie, Texas, and at Edwards Air Force Base, California, to investigate characteristics of the airplane wing up and wing down. "The Deadstick Landing Program was conducted to determine the capability of the F8U-1 airplane to be successfully landed with a dead engine, and to establish the most satisfactory glide and approach pattern and the best pilot techniques in landing the F8U-1 airplane with a dead engine."[58]

The aircraft used in the demonstration was F8U-1P 144607 with F8U-1 140455 used as a chase airplane. The Navy flew deadstick test flights using both aircraft. Test pilot LCDR T. Wagner performed the tests for the Navy.

A total of 16 flights were flown, with 4 being from the CVA plant in Grand Prairie for equipment functional checks and 12 for the build-up to and including the two actual deadstick landings. The test flights took place 8–22 August 1958. The flights investigated Marquardt unit performance, dead engine glides, wing down simulated deadstick landings, wing up simulated deadstick landings, wing down actual deadstick landings, and wing up actual deadstick landings.

The actual deadstick landings were performed with the emergency hydraulic pump in the Marquardt unit as the sole hydraulic pressure source for flight controls. The Marquardt is a wind-driven power package that turns a hydraulic pump to supply system pressure. To prevent interference with the test by a windmilling engine continuing to turn the engine-driven pump, a shutoff system was installed.

The following description of the wing down actual deadstick landing is from report E8R-11613: "High key point was established 5,000 feet short of intended touchdown point and was approached at an altitude of 7,790 feet above the terrain at an airspeed of 215 knots EAS in a wing down, landing droop, gear down configuration with the emergency generator switch in the 'LAND' position. Low key point was obtained at 3,970 feet terrain clearance and 204 knots EAS. The 90-degree position was reached at 2,020 feet altitude and 207 knots EAS. Touchdown was made at 179 knots EAS and resulted in a measured rollout distance of 13,500 feet on the dry lakebed. From test results the rollout distance on a dry hard surface runway was calculated to be 15,700 feet. Minimum regulated hydraulic pressure recorded was 1,590 psi which was obtained during rollout."[59]

The following description of the actual wing up deadstick landing is also from report E8R-11613: "High key point was established

directly over intended touchdown point and was approached at an altitude of 7,700 feet above the terrain at an airspeed of 179 knots EAS in a wing up, landing droop, gear down configuration with the emergency generator switch in the 'OFF' position. Low key point was obtained at 3,720 feet terrain clearance and 176 knots EAS. The 90-degree positon was reached at 1,880 feet and 179 knots EAS. Touchdown was made at 138 knots and resulted in a measured rollout distance of 7,900 feet on the dry lakebed. From the test results the rollout distance on a dry hard surface runway was calculated to be 9,100 feet. Minimum regulated hydraulic pressure recorded was 1,180 psi obtained during the pattern and 390 psi obtained during the rollout."[60]

The results of the flight tests concluded: "The emergency power package will supply sufficient hydraulic and electrical power, with proper positioning of the emergency generator switch, to successfully complete a deadstick landing even under the most pessimistic conditions of a frozen engine.

"A deadstick landing can be accomplished in either the wing up or wing down configuration, providing favorable conditions exist.

"The wing up configuration is more desirable than the wing down configuration for a deadstick landing.

"The use of landing droop is more desirable than the use of cruise droop for a wing down deadstick landing."[61]

F8U-1P

The F8U-1P (V-392) is a single place, carrier- or land-based photographic airplane based upon the F8U-1 day fighter aircraft. It retains the two-position wing of the F8U-1 design. The F8U-1P has a modified fuselage to incorporate a flat bottom and lower sides to accommodate windows for the photographic mission. An interesting subtle change is the addition of area rule to the upper fuselage to help with transonic drag. After all the foot dragging and excuse making to prevent area rule (coking) to the F8U-1 it was quietly added to the F8U-1P.

On 9 and 10 September 1954, L. C. Josephs, B. C. Scott, and W. E. Holleyhead Jr visited the BuAer to discuss and negotiate the detail specification for the F8U-1P. In attendance were BuAer personnel: LCDR J Rees, VF Design; Lt. E. Leavitt, Photographic Reconnaissance; LCDR. J. Jones, Airborne Equipment; Lt. L. Polansky and Lt. Renaker, Electronics; M. Redfield, Ships Installation, D. Armstrong Airborne Equipment F. Copeland Design Evaluation, and W. Nurmi, Technical Data. The specification under review by the BuAer was expected to be signed by 27 September.

The first day was spent largely discussing the photographic requirements of the airplane with LCDR Rees and LT Leavitt. CVA's proposal to delete the requirements for the K-47 12-inch cameras, CAS-2a 12-inch cameras, and window washing system was not accepted. LT Leavitt pointed out that the K-47 camera was the only successful night camera the Navy has had. He also stated that the

A new, production F8U-1P executing a missed/low approach. (CVPR-1371)

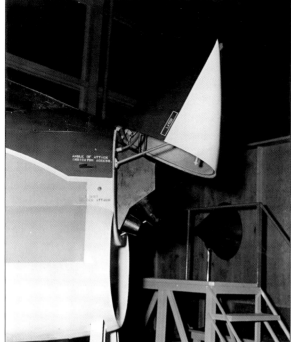

Side view of the F8U-1P mock-up showing how the nose cone opens for access to the photographic viewfinder.

airplane must have a window washing system to ensure clean camera windows. The use of curved glass windows for the forward firing camera and viewfinder was accepted by the BuAer subject to satisfactory operation in service.

Leavitt would not accept the CVA proposal to provide split vertical camera adjustment on the ground for the CAX-12 12-inch and CAX-12 6-inch cameras. He stated that those cameras must be controllable in flight so that the pilot would be able to use any camera position at his discretion. He further stated that the mounts for the K-47 cameras must be adjustable on the ground.

A requirement for CVA to investigate the feasibility of a K-47 split vertical camera installation was written into the specification. Leavitt agreed to eliminate shock mounts from the camera mounts, but CVA would have to demonstrate that the cameras would not be damaged during catapulting, arresting, and flight conditions, and that high- and low-frequency vibrations would result in a circle of confusion of more than 1/100.

Provisions would have to be incorporated in the viewfinder for supplying the velocity/height factor to the camera control system.

In the case of the F8U-1P only a mock-up of the forward fuselage was necessary for the company and Navy mock-up review. Here is the F8U-1P mock-up with the camera windows and a larger radome than was adopted in production.

A radar was not installed in the photo reconnaissance version of the Crusader, which provided room for the photographic viewfinder. This mock-up photo shows the viewfinder installation.

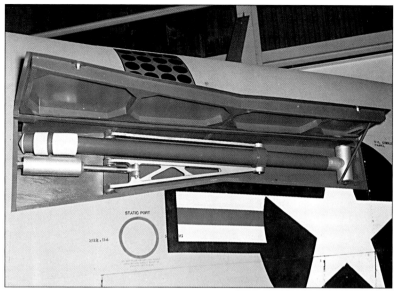

The F8U-1P refueling probe installation varied from the F8U-1 by being fully enclosed in the lines of the fuselage without requiring an aerodynamic faring. This photo shows the door open with the probe retracted.

Leavitt stated that this information would be needed by the pilot when the cameras were operated manually. It was also necessary to provide edge lighting for the flare release controls so the pilot could determine how many flares remained. Space provisions would be required for TV installation. Leavitt stated that "a TV installation is being developed and that probably all but one camera would be removed when the TV system is used."[62]

Schedule

The schedule for the F8U-1P called for a completed mock-up by 22 April 1955, Navy mock-up review board 2 May 1955, and engineering 95-percent point on 25 November 1955. Aircraft fabrication would begin 20 January 1956, with the first airplane shop complete by 2 November 1956 and the first flight by 28 December 1956.

This shot shows the F8U-1P refueling probe in the fully extended position.

Mock-Up Review

The F8U-1P underwent mock-up review in May 1955. The mock-up highlighted the changes from the F8U-1 to the F8U-1P. Included in the mock-up was the aerial refueling probe that had been required for all fleet aircraft just the previous fall. Unlike the F8U-1, the F8U-1P refueling probe did not cause a fuselage bulge; it was completely contained within the line of the fuselage that also featured subtle coking.

Ground testing the Emergency Power Pack (EPP) on a new F8U-1P required air from two jet starters to turn the turbine fast enough to power up the package. (CVPR-P1-598)

The F8U-1P was shop complete in November 1956. After testing the aircraft was ready for first flight. The first flight of the F8U-1P occurred on 17 December 1956 when 141363 took to the air at Grand Prairie.

F8U-1P Aerodynamic Demonstration

The F8U-1P completed Part II Aerodynamic (Performance) Demonstration on nine flights utilizing 141363 (flights 130–138 for 141363) during 5 March to 3 April 1958. One of the demonstration points was maximum speed at combat thrust at 35,000 feet. 141363 attained a Mach number of 1.426 (821 knots) on flight number 130, which exceeded the guarantee maximum combat speed at 35,000 feet by 16 knots. Military-rated thrust maximum speed at 35,000 feet was demonstrated at 566 knots (Mach .983), also on flight 130, exceeding the guarantee by 15 knots.

Combat ceilings at both combat power and military power were established to be 53,000 feet and 44,900 feet, exceeding guarantees by 2,600 and 1,700 feet, respectively. The landing configuration stalling speed with idle thrust was performed at 106 knots. The test was witnessed by a pacing Navy pilot flying AD-5W 139560. The stall speed was 5 knots slower than the guaranteed speed.

The sharply painted F8U-1P aerodynamic demonstrator 141363. It was eventually delivered to the fleet and was lost in 1977 aboard USS America.

Aerodynamic demonstrator F8U-1P was modified from F8U-1 141363 using the forward fuselage shaped like the F8U-1P. Here it is preparing for its first flight.

Lacking camera windows, 141363 launches for a test flight prior to its full conversion and delivery to the fleet as an F8U-1P.

141363 in the red, white, and blue–striped scheme prepares for a flight from Naval Air Station Dallas.

F8U-1P 144610 was also bailed to Vought for testing and demonstration purposes.

F8U-1P Carrier Suitability

The BuAer and CVA agreed that the F8U-1P only need to demonstrate the areas where there were basic differences between it and the F8U-1. The F8U-1 had already successfully demonstrated carrier suitability. The major area of difference between the two airplanes that needed testing was the structural integrity of the camera equipment installation in the F8U-1P. For the demonstrations the aircraft was required to carry a suite of operational cameras. For the catapult launch demonstrations the camera configuration was the following:

- Station I   KB-10A camera
- Station II LH   2 CAX-12 trimetrogon (topographic mapping) cameras with 1.5-inch lens cones
- Station II RH   1 CAX-12 trimetrogon (topographic mapping) camera with a 1.5-inch lens cone
- Station III   1 CAX-12 trimetrogon (topographic mapping) camera with a 12-inch lens cone
- Station IV   1 K-17C camera

For the arrested landing demonstrations the camera configuration was:

- Station I   KB-10A camera
- Station II LH   2 CAX-12 trimetrogon (topographic mapping) cameras with 1.5-inch lens cones
- Station II RH   1 CAX-12 trimetrogon (topographic mapping) camera with a 1.5-inch lens cone
- Station III   1 K-47 camera
- Station IV   1 CAX-12 trimetrogon (topographic mapping) camera with a 12-inch lens cone

Catapult launches utilized the TC-7 steam catapult, a relatively new addition to the Navy testing facility at Patuxent River having been completed in 1954. The land-based Mk-7 Mod 1 gear was used for the arrested landings. During the catapult launching demonstration it was noted that the airplane attitude was practically consistent throughout the power stroke and the transition to flight was smooth with no tendency to pitch up or down. One comment noted the camera system viewfinder limited forward visibility during deck operations but the catapult director did not have any problem directing the pilot to the proper launch position.

F8U-1P BuNo 144608 along with CVA Test Pilot Robert E. Rostine was tasked with the carrier suitability demonstration at Patuxent

A rear landing view of 144610 showing the raised wing, lowered flap (small inboard panel), and aileron (large outboard white panel) in the landing configuration.

Showing the red test markings and nose instrumentation boom, 144610 taxis at NAS Dallas.

A nice action shot of F8U-1P 145645 landing after an acceptance flight.

Crusader 144624 on its Navy acceptance flight prior to "payday" at Vought.

6 inches to the right of centerline with the right main gear positioned 7 inches to the right. A catapult pressure of 450 psi resulted in a shuttle end speed of 152.8 knots and a peak acceleration of 5.4 g. "After holdback release the aircraft moved toward the centerline of the catapult and a small-amplitude oscillation resulted which appeared to dampen before the end of the power stroke. Satisfactory control of the airplane was easily maintained during the launch and transition to flight."[63]

A look at the arrested landing demonstration found the following comments: "The pilot readily maintained control of the airplane on approach and was able to see the mirror landing aid and the LSO at all times up to normal cut position."[64] The aircraft rolled back after arrestment enough to allow the hook to clear the arresting cable. This allowed the tailhook to be retracted. The nose gear swiveled 180 degrees during the roll-back, causing the pilot to use light braking until the nose gear swiveled around and nose gear steering could be used again.

During the carrier suitability demonstration, a two-point high-sink-rate landing was performed on landing number 18. The sink speed was 17.5 fps with an engagement speed of 120 knots, and the longitudinal acceleration was -5.0 g. "After engagement both main landing gears lifted momentarily off the runway while the nose gear remained almost fully compressed; no significant yawing or rolling occurred."[65]

The full or nearly full compression of the nose gear shock strut was a common event during aircraft carrier operations with the Crusader during its service life, along with the main gear shock struts extending or momentarily lifting off.

At the conclusion of the demonstration it was reported that "during carrier-type operations the handling characteristics of the photographic airplane were identical to those of the basic Model F8U-1." The report went on to state, "The pilot was able to see and answer the Landing Signal Officer at all times up to wire pick-up."

River in 1957. This demonstration utilized field catapult and arresting gear instead of an aircraft carrier deck. Two different visits to Patuxent River supported the demonstration. The first, 19–20 June, consisted of six flights and seven catapult launches. The second was during the period of 13 September to 2 October 1957 with a total of 27 arrestment attempts. Between June and September 1957, 144608 was used for BIS photographic, electronic, and electrical trials and to establish a cross-country speed record (Project Bullet).

An example of the catapult launching tests was launch number five, which was to demonstrate a maximum gross weight launch and extreme off-center positioning. With full internal fuel and cameras the weight was 26,720 pounds, and the nose gear was positioned

F8U-1P 144608 posing for a picture with the wing up, droops, ailerons, and flaps down, with unit horizontal tail leading edge down.

An excellent example of an F8U-1P, 144608, all buttoned up sitting on the Vought plant ramp.

Chapter 5

FLEET INTRODUCTION AND RECORD FLIGHTS

View of Crusader 141346 on display at Oklahoma City during one of the first public showings for Vought's new supersonic F8U-1. Note the bevy of fire extinguishers standing at the ready. (CVPR-891)

Like any complex new aircraft, the F8U-1 suffered teething problems during its early flight test program. Despite the loss of three test aircraft and numerous problems identified throughout the program, the Crusader emerged as a successful new entrant into the Navy's jet-powered carrier-based fleet, winning the coveted Collier Trophy for its designers in the process. Now a holder of numerous world records, the F8U-1 began its legendary career.

Several major items failed to meet expectations during 1956, which led to the BuAer's abrupt action in rescheduling the F8U-1 FIP to start on 4 January 1957. The extended time allowed CVA to make progress toward solutions to the J57 engine problems, and investigate forged wasp alloy turbine blades as the solution for hot section distress. Afterburner reliability needed improvement as well, and completely satisfactory F8U-1 weapons system demonstrations had not yet been achieved. OpDevFor and FIP were instructed to conduct their armament tests with restrictions. The in-flight loss of the right trailing edge from the No. 10 F8U-1 Armament Test Airplane, along with delays in the Pre-BIS Armament Test contributed to the delay in the Fleet Configuration Conference and the start of FIP.

Fleet Introduction Program F8U-1 awaiting its next flight. The rocket packs were not part of the Fleet Introduction Program (FIP), only the gun. Staining from gunfire is visible on the forward fuselage of every FIP airplane.

A couple of FIP Crusaders share the Patuxent River flight line with a variety of other 1950s designs.

Fleet Introduction Program

The Fleet Introduction Program started in 1954, and by the time the Crusader entered the program it was the ninth aircraft to participate in the program. Some of the other aircraft that preceded the Crusader through FIP were the S2F Tracker, F7U-3 Cutlass, A3D Sky-warrior, and the FJ-2 and FJ-3 Furies. The F8U FIP was held at NATC Patuxent River and involved the pilots from VF-32 and VF(AW)-3. The FIP had a couple of objectives. The first was an eight-week test of the aircraft in an operational-type environment. Fleet aircraft mechanics and pilots operate the aircraft as they would in an operational squadron. After the men return to their assigned bases they serve as

Alan Sheppard piloting F8U-1 141345 looking a little worse for the wear years after a Project Beta speed run.

After completing the initial carrier suitability trials 140446 stayed aboard Patuxent River and continued to serve in carrier suitability testing. Naval Air Test Center has applied their lettering to her tail. (CVPR-1043)

In addition to NATC tail markings 140446 was adorned with "446," the last three digits of its BuNo, on the sides of the inlet duct. (CVPR-1048)

instructors to the other members of their respective squadrons. The Service Test Division of the Naval Air Test Center hosted the F8U FIP. For the FIP, VF-32 provided 11 pilots and 80 enlisted maintenance personnel. VF(AW)-3 provided 40 enlisted men and 6 pilots. Commander Reid Stone, the commanding officer of VF(AW)-3, assumed command of the FIP joint squadron with the VF-32 skipper, CAPT Donald Gay Jr., becoming the operations officer for the FIP.

As the FIP progressed, the fleet squadron personnel took over the duties of flying and maintaining the six assigned F8U Crusaders. The FIP was initially supported by mechanics from Chance Vought Aircraft until the Navy crews learned the tasks. Vought also supported the FIP with a ground school that was held at the CVA factory in Grand Prairie, Texas. Several additional days were spent in the classroom at Patuxent to get briefings on the latest techniques for flying the F8U and spin recovery techniques. The maintenance crews were in the hangars while the pilots were in class performing acceptance checks on the new aircraft. Many of the maintenance personnel had attended a ground school in Texas and practiced on an F8U mobile maintenance trainer at Cecil Field, Florida.

When the FIP ended, several of the F8U aircraft went home with each of the two participating squadrons for use in training members of their respective squadrons who had not participated in the

FIP. VF(AW)-3 was also taking on the responsibility of becoming a transitional training unit to support squadrons transitioning to the Crusader. With the successful completion of the FIP the Crusader had passed from experimental design in testing to operational squadron use. For a complex, cutting-edge aircraft like the Crusader, 21 months from first flight to fleet use was a remarkable feat. The Crusader would now enter operational service as the Navy's first 1,000-mph fighter.

Summary of 1956 Flight Test and Demonstrations

After three airplanes were lost, schedule delays due to crash investigations, and mandatory changes, the major objectives of the demonstration program were successfully realized. Preliminary BIS trials were conducted successfully and FIP was in progress. The first F8U-1P was accepted in November and had its first flight in December. The Crusader participated in four at-sea evaluation cruises with excellent carrier operational characteristics reported. In actually, the aircraft had challenging approach-speed characteristics: it was difficult to get on-speed. It is entirely possible its career would have been as short as the F7U-3's had it not been for the introduction of the angled deck and mirror landing system.

Spin Demonstration

NavAer SR-38E-2, "Specification for the Demonstration of Piloted airplanes," dated 1 December 1952, specified Part I and Part II Spin Demonstrations. In preparation for the spin demonstrations, XF8U-1 No. 2 (138900) received several modifications. The modifications included a battery-powered ignition system for engine relights in case of engine flameout, a spin recovery parachute, and canard surfaces.

The emergency ignition system was used on flight 137 when the engine was inadvertently shut down while in a spin. A successful airstart was made and the aircraft recovered. The airplane was also equipped with a spin recovery parachute assembly attached to a

The landing of another early F8U-1 serving with the armament test branch of NATC.

Another unit involved with Crusader testing was VX-3. Here, one of VX-3s F8U-1s is riding the forward elevator.

XF8U-1 138900 (2X) being readied for the start of spin demonstration flights at Muroc.

special aft section that was placed on the airplane prior to the demonstration. The anti-spin chute was 28 feet in diameter and designed to fully open at 160 knots without exceeding design limit loads. At 200 knots the system had a reefing system that restricted the canopy to 12½ feet until the airspeed decreased to 160 knots, at which point the chute would fully blossom. Originally, the chute was deployed by the armament pickle switch and the trigger switch. After an accidental chute deployment, the pickle switch was deactivated. The trigger switch was also referred to as the "dead man" switch. The chute was jettisoned by "T" handles (primary and backup) on top of the instrument board.

The aircraft also had canards that were developed during spin tunnel testing of model airplanes. The canard surfaces were installed as auxiliary spin recovery devices. One surface was installed on each side of the fuselage in the same location as the electronics access doors and similarly shaped. Each canard had approximately 600 square inches of surface. When actuated they extended to a horizontal position; they were hinged on top. They were hydraulically actuated with an emergency pneumatic retraction system.

Part I demonstrations (two-turn spins) required only 4 flights with 25 flights leading up to the actual demonstration. Of the flights, 16 were anti-spin parachute deployment tests. The demonstration took place at MCAAS Mojave from 22 June to 9 August 1956. The aircraft performed the SR-38 required normal spins from a 1-g stall, aileron controls neutral, at 50-percent normal rated thrust with spins to the right and left. Also performed were normal spins starting from a 2½-g steady turn at normal rated thrust. During the buildup and demonstration flights four engine changes were required because of over temperatures. A tendency to develop compressor stalls was noted along with a tendency to more easily spin to the right than the left. All Part I demonstrations were successfully completed with satisfactory recoveries.[67]

F8U-1P 141363 all painted up with the spin recovery parachute aft section taxis out for a spin demonstration flight.

Time for a spin again, this time with ventral fins; 138900 is outfitted with the special aft section strengthened for the spin recovery parachute system.

A rear quarter view showing the spin recovery parachute system installation.

XF8U-1 138900 performed Part II (five-turn spins) of the spin demonstration at MCAAS Mojave 20–30 November 1956. The XF8U-1 in a spin was described as oscillatory about all three axes, especially the pitch and roll axes. The longer the spin was allowed to continue the less the oscillations became.

The spin recovery chute was deployed twice during the demonstrations. The first parachute deployment was (unintended as already described) deemed unnecessary. The second spin recovery chute deployment occurred during flight 158 with the aircraft in a right spin. Pro spin controls were held for five turns with the exception of an inadvertent input of full left aileron control for 1½ turns followed quickly by full right aileron control. After a spin of 14½ turns, the minimum spin chute deployment altitude was reached. The pilot pressed the dead-man trigger switch but the chute did not deploy. Finally, after a total spin of 16½ turns the spin recovery parachute emergency mechanical release was triggered. The 50-inch-diameter pilot chute blossomed and deployed the 28-foot-diameter recovery chute and the spin stopped one turn later.

Spins were demonstrated starting with a 1-g idle power, stall to the left and right, both with 1/3 aileron and ailerons neutral. The next series had entry with a 2.5-g steady-rate turn at normal rated power, left and right. Inverted spins from an inverted stall position were attempted 12 times but none successfully developed an inverted auto rotation.

The final series demonstrated an Immelmann turn in which the aircraft climbed from 11,170 to 23,830 feet and was rolled from the inverted position to upright flight at 211 knots with no unusual characteristics observed.

A reliable recovery technique to recover from a five-turn spin was developed and demonstrated. The recovery took place in 1 to 2½ turns after being applied. The control inputs for the recovery involved the following: extending the leading edge droops, applying full opposite rudder, applying aileron control with the spin, and holding a full aft control stick. Engine compressor stalls occurred with spins and the engine needed to be throttled back to prevent over temperatures. Three engine changes occurred during the spin demonstration flights. All Part II spin demonstrations were completed successfully.[68]

In testing news the week of 24 August 1956, a simulated F8U-1P wing fairing that incorporated partial "coking" was flown on the No. 5 F8U-1 for the first time. No. 17, the first FIP airplane, also made its first flight. XF8U-1 No. 1 also flew with wing spoilers for the first time to improve the rate of roll at high speed, low altitude. A solution to the slow rate of roll at low altitude was found.

Robert Collier Trophy

In 1911, the Robert Collier Trophy was established for the greatest achievement in aeronautics or astronautics in America. The criteria were improving the performance, efficiency, and safety of air or space vehicles. The value of the improvement had been thoroughly demonstrated by actual use during the preceding year. Leonard Hobbs of United Aircraft was awarded the Collier Trophy in 1952 for his role as chief engineer in the design, development, and production of the J57 engine.

In 1956, Charles J. McCarthy and associates of Chance Vought Aircraft and Vice Admiral James S. Russell and associates of the U.S. Navy BuAer were awarded the Robert Collier Trophy. The trophy was awarded for conception, design, and development of the F8U Crusader, the first operational carrier-based aircraft capable of exceeding 1,000 mph.

Thompson Trophy (Project Beta)

Project Beta was created to establish a world's speed record for a production military aircraft. The course was 9.3 miles on the outbound run and 9.3 miles on the inbound run with a sweeping, 16-mile 180-degree turn between runs. The average speed from

The first F8U-1, 140444, works to support Project Beta efforts by developing methods for setting a closed-course speed record.

One of the techniques used to give the Crusader the range it needed to complete the run with all the afterburner use was to supercool the fuel. A rig not unlike a moonshiner's still was built and filled with dry ice. The higher-density fuel was then pumped into the 141345 (Windsor's jet) and it was launched.

Commander Duke Windsor posing on the Oklahoma City ramp during the 1956 National Air Show.

the two runs would be used to determine the speed for the record attempt. The altitude changes permitted were a loss of no more than 328 feet or a climb higher than 1,640 feet over the selected target altitude during the runs and turn around.

A sign of the times, the project was under orders by the Secretary of Defense to not exceed 1,000 mph. The restriction was placed to hide the real capability of the Crusader from the Russians.

The No. 15 F8U-1, 141345, was assigned to the project. Except for the installation of a photo-observer, a radar marker beacon, and two barographs, there were to be no changes to the production configuration of the aircraft. The photo-observer and barographs for documenting the record attempt were housed in the ammunition compartments behind the cockpit. The rocket pack fairing was used to house the radar marker beacon.

The lower surface of the outer wing panels, the fin, and rudder were all painted florescent orange to aid ground observers. Instead of ammunition, ballast was loaded in the gun link chute areas and

140444 being towed into the hangar at Muroc for an engine change.

J57 being removed for repairs in the Muroc hangar. This shot really illustrates how long the J57 with afterburner assembly is and how much of the interior of the Crusader is devoted to the engine.

The front face of the replacement J57 during the installation process.

The upper panels tell the story of the work to remove all the red paint off the first production Crusader. By the time this photo was taken, all the paint had been removed; only the Crusader name was left.

An early-morning engine start for another proving run for Project Beta.

four operational 20mm cannons were installed for the flights. The aircraft was flown several times in the Dallas area with the No. 4 F8U-1 to check the airspeed system calibration.

On 11 August 1956 CDR R. W. "Duke" Windsor ferried 141345 from NAS Dallas to MCAS Mojave. The nonstop 1,500-mile flight was completed in two and a half hours with the only maintenance discrepancy being that the main electrical generator dropped offline near Mojave and the Marquardt Emergency Generator supplied electrical power for the landing. About 289 gallons of usable fuel remained on the aircraft upon completion of the flight.

The aircraft was placed in work status the same afternoon as a 30-knot crosswind caused cancellation of a practice flight. The aircraft was fueled with JP-5 fuel and the engine was up trimmed. The up trim consisted of changing the thermocouples and calibration of the turbine out temperature (TOT) adjustment of the fuel control surge and acceleration valve to allow for a 10-second acceleration time with a fuel flow of 6,100 pounds from the standard 13-second and 6,000-pound fuel flow. Also included in the up trim was the

Starting the timing gear for a practice run.

Preparing to start the engine for one of the afternoon practice runs.

For the benefit of publicity, one launching session was filmed both on the ground and in the air.

F8U-1 141345 being towed from the hangar on the day the record was set.

Duke Windsor accelerating for takeoff on the record run in 141345.

replacement of the engine afterburner fuel control with one adjusted for a 15-percent increase in fuel flow and a 5-percent increase in thrust. The generator was changed due to frequency and voltage variations that could potentially cause a stabilization system failure at high speed.

On 12 August the engine was trimmed for the record attempts. The TOT was adjusted to 630 degrees C and the maximum limit of TOT approved by Pratt & Whitney was 670 degrees C for no more than 1 hour worth of operation with the engine time limited to 23 total.

The first test run was flown with CDR Windsor at the controls on 13 August with a takeoff time of 07:13 and landing at 07:45. The outbound leg was flown at 1,020 mph (Mach 1.54) the return leg at 845 mph (Mach 1.28) due to the loss of speed in the 270-degree turn. The aircraft was flown at 40,000 feet utilizing 19 minutes of afterburner time during the 32-minute flight with 2,700 pounds of fuel remaining.

A second flight was completed by CDR Windsor in the afternoon from 13:00 to 13:38. The course was flown at 40,000 feet with an outbound speed of 924 mph (Mach 1.40) and the return leg at 924 mph (Mach 1.40) accelerating to 950 mph (Mach 1.44) by the end of the run. During the run the cockpit pressure regulator failed, allowing the cabin pressure to rise to 32,000 feet while the jet was at 37,000 feet. The obtained airspeeds were disappointing and lower than expected. In debriefing CDR Windsor it was discovered he flew the runs at a 620 degrees C TOT rather than the targeted maximum of 660 degrees C.

141345 flew three times on 14 August, including a practice run on the course starting at 06:52, landing back at 07:30 with 333 gallons of fuel remaining. A second flight was made about an hour later starting at 08:25 landing at

Plotting board for Project Beta aircraft location.

NAA officials installing the official timing watch prior to the start of the record run. (CVPR-863)

An NAA official documenting the time on the stop watch after completion of the record run. (CVPR-866)

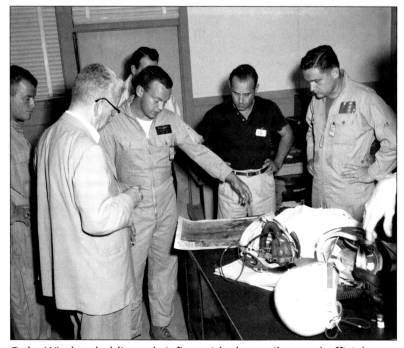

Duke Windsor holding a briefing with chase pilots and officials.

09:00. This time the TOT was 640 degrees C during the run at 41,000 feet. The speed indicated was 1,003 mph (Mach 1.52 to 1.55 with ground speeds of 990 mph outbound and 945 mph on the return leg). No squawks were written against the jet after the flight. The final flight on the 14th was for publicity photos and movie filming of the aircraft. The jet was in the air for an hour and a half and landed with no discrepancies.

Early the morning of 15 August, CDR Windsor took 141345 into the air at 06:47 and landed at 07:19 after 19 minutes of afterburner operation. The reported speeds were 1,023 to 1,056 mph (Mach 1.55 to 1.6) at 40,000 feet on the outbound leg, 1,023 mph (Mach 1.55) during the 270-degree turn and 1,056 mph (Mach 1.60) on the return leg. The radar beacon, which was used by a ground controller to keep the aircraft on course, failed. The cause of the radar beacon failure was damaged wiring.

The flight on 16 August provided some anxious moments when the engine over-temped on takeoff roll about 4,000 feet down the runway. The TOT reached 740 degrees C before Windsor aborted the takeoff by chopping the throttle, dropping the tailhook, and

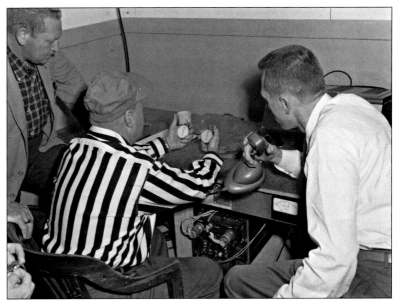

An NAA official checking the time of the Project Beta speed runs.

The Project Beta team posing with 141345 after the record run.

A radar van for tracking Windsor during the record attempt.

Part of the optical tracking systems used during the speed record attempt.

A documentation camera for recording the speed record attempt.

The all-important timing line. The observer lies flat on his back looking up between the two poles at a wire that is the official starting and end point that the flight must cover and with very little altitude variance.

applying heavy braking. The tailhook grabbed the chain gear and brought the jet to a stop. The heaving braking action caused both main tires to blow and reduced the diameter of the wheels by 3 inches. After engine removal, the afterburner nozzle flaps were found to be stuck in the closed position due to damage in the nozzle linkage and actuator system.

The 17th was spent installing a new engine, wheels, tires, and brakes. By midnight the engine had been run and leak checks completed. All that was left was the special setup for the record attempts. After final engine setup on 18 August another practice run was attempted. This run suffered from a UHF transmitter failure, which caused flight termination. After repairs a flight obtained speeds of 924 mph (Mach 1.40) inbound, 910 mph (Mach 1.38) in the turn, and 990 mph (Mach 1.50) on the return leg. As the record attempt neared, two Lockheed TV-2s and one Douglas A3D arrived at Mojave. Each aircraft had two barographs installed as they were to be flown

F8U-1 141346 was on a rotating display at the National Airshow in September 1956 as 141345 flew during the display. (CVPR-889)

at the attempt altitude with NAA officials observing the speed run to verify that altitude limits were not exceeded.

The record was set on 21 August 1956, 1,015.428 mph (Mach 1.54) at 40,000 feet. However, the results were planned to be withheld until announced at the National Air Show in Oklahoma City on 1 September 1956. CDR Windsor Jr. flew 141345 to Grand Prairie to visit the CVA plant on 25 August 1956. The aircraft was flown to Oklahoma City for the National Air Show for aerial display and the award of the Thompson Trophy. It was joined by F8U-1 141347 displayed on a rotating platform.

One interesting side note for the record run: The fuel was pumped through tubing in a 6-foot barrel filled with dry ice to cool the fuel and make it denser for the speed run. The cooling barrel was affectionately known as a "still" because it resembled a moonshiner's still.

Project Bullet

On 16 July 1957, F8U-1P Crusader 144608 piloted by Marine Major John Glenn Jr. broke the transcontinental speed record with a flight crossing from Los Alamitos, California, to Floyd Bennett Field, New York, in 3 hours 23 minutes and 8.4 seconds. The average speed for the flight was 725.55 mph. This also was the first upper atmosphere supersonic flight from the West Coast to the East Coast of the United States. This recon aircraft took photos at regular intervals using six internal cameras, resulting in a coast-to-coast supersonic continuous strip of aerial photographs. This hadn't been done since September 1948 when an experimental prototype Republic XR-12 photo-recon transport flew a speed record flight from Edwards, California, to Mitchel Field, Long Island (located about 15 miles from Floyd Bennett), while photographing its entire route.

Accompanying Glenn on his flight was LCDR Charles Demmler, USN. Unfortunately, during the record run Demmler's F8U-1 143706, suffered damage to the refueling probe and was unable to continue the flight. Glenn was greeted by a Navy band, Navy brass, and his family after landing in New York. Many years later, when 144608

A close-up of the "moonshiner's still" that was built and filled with dry ice to increase the density of the fuel pumped into the 141345 Project Beta jet.

A beautiful in-flight shot of F8U-1P 144608 in Project Bullet markings. The aircraft carries "Major J. H. Glenn USMC Project Bullet" under the left windshield. Another item of note: The aircraft's BuNo is presented twice on the rear fuselage.

A VAH-11 crewmember inspects the drogue from one of the AJ-1 Savage tankers at Naval Air Station Dallas prior to a refueling flight to support Project Bullet.

LCDR Demmler, Major Glenn, and VAH-11 crewmembers review plans for the refueling to support Project Bullet during refueling tests conducted from NAS Dallas prior to the record-breaking flight.

VAH-11 AJ-1 tanker 124160/GN-607 cranking up for a refueling test flight over Dallas with the Project Bullet duo.

LCDR C. Demmler, the USN Project Bullet F8U-1 143706 pilot that was to accompany Glenn on the Project Bullet flight.

Cycling the refueling probe on Glenn's F8U-1P prior to a refueling test flight to support Project Bullet.

A successful number one engine start on AJ-1 122591/ GH-604 prior to a refueling test flight.

Glenn and family on the ramp at Floyd Bennett field after completion of the record-breaking coast-to-coast flight on 16 July 1957. 144608 provides a dramatic backdrop.

A nice in-flight photo of Project Bullet's F8U-1 143706, flown by LCDR Demmler during one of the test flights prior to the record attempt.

Glenn climbing down the ladder having just arrived at the conclusion of the record-breaking flight. Had it not been for refueling probe problems on the F8U-1 there would have been two triumphant Crusaders on deck.

Speaking with the press and military leaders, Major Glenn is visible near the lower rear corner of the fire truck after his record-breaking flight.

Here, Glenn taxies F8U-1P 144608 to a stop at Floyd Bennett Field in Brooklyn, New York, upon the completion of Project Bullet.

Glenn engaged in post-flight shutdown duties in 144608 after landing in New York at the conclusion of Project Bullet. A non-standard camera is installed on the canopy rail as part of 608's test duties.

You cannot have a major public relations event without a band. Navy musicians, including bassoon, celebrate Major Glenn's arrival. The canopy is unlatched as he prepares to open it. It's not clear if the band played the Navy or Marine Corps song.

returned to CVA for refurbishment, the late Senator John Glenn was invited to come see his old ship. His visit was a special occasion and he was presented with the stick grip from 144608 on a plaque.

RF-8G 144608 did not live to see retirement. On 13 December 1972 she was lost at sea following an accident aboard USS *Oriskany*. The aircraft was serving with VFP-63 Detachment 4 at the time of the loss. This is a description of the accident from a CVA field services report:

"Pilot launched on a local photo training flight. Departure was uneventful. Recovery was a moderated pitching deck (3 to 6 feet). Pilot bolstered on first pass. (Arresting hook missed all wires.) LSO comments on this pass were a little low in the middle, pilot was called for attitude and answered, aircraft still a little low in close and pilot over controlled power and attitude, went flat and bolstered.

"On his second pass pilot was advised the wind was 35 knots and to make a manual pass. Pilot started slightly low but was on glide path from the middle to approaching the in-close position. The deck started downward and the pilot was advised and told to put on a little more power. The aircraft impacted the ramp in a nose up attitude with the aircraft main mounts striking just below flight deck level and the aircraft continued up the flight deck and the pilot ejected. The aircraft continued over the angle and impacted the water. The pilot was picked up by the ship's angel and returned aboard the ship."[69]

Sol Love of LTV presenting Senator John Glenn with the stick grip from RF-8G 144608, the aircraft he flew during Project Bullet.

Senator John Glenn viewing 144608 during his 28 September 1970 visit to Vought's Grand Prairie factory.

Chapter 6

F8U-1T: A CRUSADER BUILT FOR TWO

Vought's unique F8U-1T "Two-Sader" takes off for a demonstration flight with heat-seeking AIM-9 Sidewinder air-to-air missiles.

From nearly the very beginning, Chance Vought Aircraft envisioned the Navy purchasing a fleet of two-seat F8U-1T trainer aircraft to support naval aviator's pilot transition to the Crusader. Several attempts were made to sell the fleet on this unique two-man supersonic training aircraft, but to no avail. Two of CVA's proposals are discussed in this chapter.

V-408

In February 1956, CVA developed the V-408 design, a two-place trainer version of the F8U-1. It would have the agile aerodynamic and performance characteristics so that it could be used by fleet squadrons to transition pilots to the F8U-1. The V-408 had the potential to

F8U-1T 143710 awaiting its first flight. In the beginning the aircraft was painted with dayglow conspicuous markings that were later toned down to insignia red.

A close-up view of the F8U-1T cockpit reveals the partial-pressure suits worn by the crew members.

F8U-1T 143710 touching down after its first flight. The aircraft was unique in being the only member of the breed with a braking parachute installation.

serve the fleet as a transition trainer long after the F8U-1was no longer in fleet service. The V-408 trainer airplane would retain as many of the F8U-1 features as possible. A tandem cockpit arrangement was planned with as little rework to the F8U-1 fuselage as possible; this was strongly driven by management.

Presentation of the proposal to the BuAer was scheduled for 16 April 1956. By August 1956 the BuAer plan was to include 30 F8U-1Ts to be built by 1 October 1959.

V-449

In November 1960, the BuAer informally indicated interest in a training version of the F8U. CVA proposed a modified version of the F8U-1 with up to 300 aircraft. It would utilize the F8U-1 configuration aft of fuselage station 357. The forward nose would be modified from the F8U-2N configuration with the additional insertion of a second cockpit seat. The wing center section would be standard F8U-2N. Instead of the bleed air–driven electrical generator, the engine would have a constant speed drive with a 20 KVA generator installed to meet the electrical needs of the aircraft. This change helps with freeing fuselage space for the two-seat modifications.

The forward fuselage would have the most changes because of the addition of the second seat and longer canopy. The lines of the F8U-2N would be retained. The section 180.5 through 357 would be new and include new fuselage lines with bulged nose landing gear doors, and new canopy lines with the canopy fairing into the wing center section. The nose landing gear doors would fair and end at fuselage station 325.

CVA submitted the proposal for the V-449 to the BuAer in March 1961. The proposal utilized a modified F8U-1 and a new F8U-2N; the Navy favored the modified F8U-1 version. The company finally got funding in May and authorization to rebuild the No. 74 F8U-1 airplane, 143710, into an F8U-1T demonstrator. The first flight of the F8U-1T was on 6 February 1962. The aircraft was flown to Andrews AFB and several other bases before being taken to Naval Air Station Patuxent. The tour was well accepted and a BuWeps trainer study was submitted to the CNO recommending the F8U-1T for an advanced trainer buy. The aircraft was extensively tested by the Navy, including carrier trials. F8U-1T carrier trials were successfully completed by the end of October 1962. It was looking like the FY 1963 procurement of 90 F8U-2NEs would be split with 70 fighters and 12 trainers.

A proposal was made to the Royal Navy and the French Navy for two-seat Crusaders. The original French order had 6 two-seaters listed. These were later deleted from the order and only single-seat F-8E(FN)s were purchased. Navy budget priorities caused an initial order for 12 aircraft to be cancelled. By the end of December 1962 there was little hope left for procurement of the F8U-1T. All indications were leading to a subsonic aircraft to fulfill the training requirement. The TA-4J was selected for the training contract.

A cockpit mock-up of the V-408, a two-seat training Crusader based on the F8U-1. (CVPR-3216)

A second view of the V-408 cockpit mock-up with the canopy in the open position. The designers were limited in their options to create a two-seat airplane with a minimum amount of change to the lines of the basic airplane.

F8U-1T 143710 in-flight carrying a single Sidewinder missile on each side of the fuselage.

A left rear view of the F8U-1T showing markings details of the first paint scheme.

Of interest in this tail shot of the F8U-1T are the aft section cooling scoop and the housing for the braking parachute. The housing and mechanism are nearly identical to that used on the TA-7C/A-7K series.

An underside view of the F8U-1T after the test nose cone and boom have been replaced with a regular radome.

A left-side view of the F8U-1T showing markings details of the first paint scheme.

Left front view of the F8U-1T. These images are from a series of walk-around photos that are provided in the Vought engineering reports. For a modeler or historian, they give a great overall look at the aircraft at this particular time.

Low-angle front view of the F8U-1T showing the test boom; 2NE standard nose size and shape.

During NATC operation the F8U-1T is readied for a catapult shot from USS Independence (CV-62).

F8U-1T spotted on the deck of the USS Independence (CV-62) during NATC trials.

In the second paint scheme applied to it, the F8U-1T is landing with a single sidewinder.

The F8U-1T left on 22 March 1963 for a European tour of France, England, Germany, Italy, Greece, Turkey, Sweden, Norway, and Denmark aboard the USS *Saratoga*. The airplane participated in the 1963 Paris Air Show with John Konrad at the controls.

The TF-8A returned to the United States aboard another aircraft carrier and resumed its test work at NAS Patuxent. Eventually, the aircraft was retired from Navy service after many years with the U.S. Navy's Test Pilot School. The NTF-8A was delivered to NASA for use in their programs.

In the late 1970s as the Navy had retired their Crusader fighters, Chance Vought Aircraft picked up a contract with the Philippine Air Force to refurbish two squadrons of F-8H aircraft. CVA would also provide logistics and support for them until 1990. The F-8H aircraft would serve as an interim fighter until a more advanced aircraft could be procured to replace them. To support training of the Philippine pilots, CVA had requested NASA bail TF-8A 143710 back to them. It returned to Grand Prairie for refurbishment and eventually sported an overall white paint scheme with a blue stripe down each side of the fuselage and the Navy BuNo number painted in the stripe on the rear fuselage. The TF-8A was used extensively for training until its loss.

TF-8A 143710 Accident

On 28 July 1978, "TF-8A BuNo 143710 was on a routine training mission with 1st Lt. Ramsey Ramos, Philippine Air Force, in the front cockpit and Vought test pilot Kenneth J. Fox in the rear cockpit.

"The takeoff and flight for the first 45 minutes were normal in all respects. Following a dive to gain speed for overhead maneuvers, the throttle was advanced to 99-percent RPM. The engine experienced extremely heavy compressor stalls at 7,000 feet MSL (mean sea level). The sound (Ka-Boom) was very loud and unlike compressor stalls previously experienced by Fox in other F-8 aircraft. The throttle was immediately retarded to 82 percent, a left turn was made toward home base, a zoom climb to 20,000 feet was initiated, and a report was made to Vought control and Ft. Worth Center of the engine problems.

"Throttle setting at the beginning of the climb was 89 to 90 percent. The engine instruments were normal and the engine was stable. The throttle was advanced to 96 percent to continue the climb to 26,000 feet. Severe compressor stalls were again experienced with an additional loud rumble sound. The throttle was placed at idle and the stalls stopped, but the rumble continued."

"Several attempts to break the stall using normal and manual fuel control resulted in high temperatures, low RPM, but normal fuel flow. Rumble of the engine continued with no response to the throttle. Electrical power and the pilot intercom system were lost. The emergency generator did not restore full electrical power. The only method of communication between the pilots at this point was by yelling. The aircraft was descending during this time, and it became evident that a suitable field could not be reached. Fox informed Lt. Ramos that they would have to abandon the aircraft. At 7,000 feet Fox jettisoned the canopy and pulled the face curtain as he saw Lt. Ramos reach for his face curtain. The ejection for both pilots was normal. The aircraft impacted the ground 5 miles southeast of Tolar, Texas."[70]

The colors have changed from dayglow to red in this in-flight shot of the -1T. Well-illustrated is the height difference between the two seats and the hump that was added to the fuselage to accommodate the rear seat height.

"In the bag" takeoff with rear-seat pilot flying under the hood.

After a promotional tour to East Coast naval air stations, F8U-1T returns with several squadron insignias applied to the side, including VF-174, the East Coast training squadron.

Taxiing out for a flight with an unpainted radome at NAS Dallas is the one and only F8U-1T produced.

A right-side in-flight view with the single Sidewinder missile installed. The only external stores carried by the F8U-1T were single Side-winder missiles.

TF-8A 143710 near the end of its service life in a very sharp white with blue stripe scheme. The aircraft was bailed back to Vought from NASA for the training of Philippine Air Force Crusader pilots.

A nice head-on shot of the F8U-1T illustrating the forward vision available to the two seat locations.

Chapter 7

F8U-2: IMPROVING THE BREED

Prior to the F-8J conversion, the F8U-2NE had single droops and the 7-degree variable incidence setting for the wing. Distinctive markings were unique to the 2NE series.

With the F8U-1 now in service, a natural evolution of the design and expansion of the aircraft's capabilities began in earnest. Advanced radar, in-flight refueling capability, and enhanced armament consisting of up to four heat-seeking AIM-9 Sidewinder air-to-air missiles gave the Crusader an added punch. As with many evolved aircraft programs, Vought's F8U-2N soon became the thoroughbred.

First Attempt

The first mention of the F8U-2 occurred during the discussions between the BuAer and CVA concerning the incorporation of coking on the F8U-1. A BuAer recommendation on 29 April 1954 was that the current contract for 5 basic-configuration F8U-1 airplanes be extended to 75 with an additional 34 being produced out of FY 1956

An NAS Miramar-based VF-124 F-8E getting hooked to the cata-pult for launch. (USN)

The low-speed wind-tunnel model for testing the F-8E with Side-winders and underwing-mounted Bullpup missiles.

F8U-2NE Number 54 and F8U-2N Number 47 ready for delivery. The F8U-2Ns incorporating AN/APQ-94 radar were redesignated F8U-2NE in accordance with BuWeps Notice 13100 dated 5 April 1961. This change caused F8U-2N 149134 and subsequent to be redesignated F8U-2NE airplanes, CV Nos. 1 and subsequent.

Dumping fuel is a little known Crusader ability being demonstrated by 147036 during a test. Prior to its loss on 11 April 1964 F8U-2N 147036 was heavily involved with F8U-2NE/F-8E(FN) testing.

F8U-2 demonstrator 140448 complete with ventral fins taxis out for a test mission. This aircraft was restored by the Vought Aircraft Heritage Foundation and now is on display at McAuliffe-Shepard Discovery Center in Concord, New Hampshire. (CVPR-1628)

with different blocks of F8U-1 airplanes. The radar would eventually be incorporated in the F8U-1E and F8U-2.

Success the Second Time

The reborn F8U-2 program began in the summer of 1957. A list of improvements to the F8U-1 had been developed and needed to be incorporated into the production airplanes. These improvements included in-flight refueling, Sidewinder missile carriage, and the APS-67 radar. CVA wanted to incorporate these into a new model, the F8U-2, but the BuAer wanted incorporation into current F8U-1 production because the performance increases were not sufficient to introduce a new type in the fleet.

The F8U-2 airplane is an improved version of the F8U-1 aircraft. The major modifications incorporated in the F8U-2 include the following:

It appears that this F8U-2 pilot has just elected to execute a missed approach as the afterburner flame is visible but everything else looks like he was shooting an approach. (CVPR-2218)

funds. An F8U-2 designation would then be established that incorporated coking, Sidewinder missile, in-flight refueling, and several other changes; 59 F8U-2s would be built from the remaining FY 1956 funds. The results of flight testing and the determination that coking was not necessary, contributed to the demise of the first F8U-2.

The first iteration of the F8U-2 program was abandoned by the BuAer in October 1955 as the performance and other changes were not sufficient to merit a new model. The incorporation of the Sidewinder missile, in-flight refueling, and APS-67 radar would be done

- The new APS-67 radar and EX-16 fire control system providing improvements in the armament system in addition to improvement of target tracking capabilities
- Two ventral fins that provide additional directional stability for an expanded flight envelope
- A Pratt & Whitney J57-P-16 engine with up-rated thrust
- Along with the engine improvements, two aft fuselage-mounted cooling scoops were added to improve airflow characteristics and for afterburner cooling

Wings folding down while taxiing to the end of the runway, F-8E 150336 provides a different view.

Banking for the camera, plane 145587 is out for a publicity shoot. (CVPR-2292)

Two other less widely known differences between the F8U-1 and F8U-2 involved the unit horizontal tails (UHT). Engineering Change Proposal (ECP) 454 changed the control system for the UHTs to increase the strength of the control system components. It had been discovered that fuselage bending during certain combinations of g and airspeed created unwanted control inputs. The second difference involved the travel of the UHTs, which was reduced by 3 degrees to prevent interference with the new ventral stabilization fins.

The AN/AWG-3 armament control system was incorporated into the F8U-2. The system consists of the EX-16 aircraft fire control system and the AN/APS-67 (XN-3) search and range-tracking radar system.

The EX-16 fire control system was an improvement to the MK-16 fire control assembly installed in the F8U-1 aircraft due to less weight and volume, more accurate lead angle computation, and easier maintenance. The EX-16 system used air data generated by the angle of attack and the angle of side slip transducers mounted on the nose of the aircraft. Additional inputs were airspeed, range to target, range change rate, air pressure, rate of acceleration of the attacker, and the ballistic characteristics of the 20mm projectiles. If the armament selector was in the rockets position, the aircraft angle of attack, sideslip, and angle of rocket firing were all added to the aim point computations. As the computations were made by the fire control system the aim point was presented by a gyro reticle image in the gunsight glass for the pilot to use to accurately aim the guns or rockets.

The radar set AN/APR-67 consisted of 14 electronic assemblies and a scanning-type antenna, all of which were housed in the nose. The radar provided for target detection, tracking, and accurate optical aiming of the 20mm guns and 2.75-inch folding fin aircraft rockets. The AN/APS-67 radar provided continuous scanning of a pie-shaped section ahead of the aircraft up to a range of 16 miles. A cathode ray tube indicator in the cockpit presented detection and range information on targets to the pilot. This information aided the pilot in maneuvering the aircraft to within visual attack range.

145554 heading out for an acceptance flight at Grand Prairie. (CVPR-2149)

Banking away from the camera, plane 145587 is out for a publicity shoot. (CVPR-2277)

F8U-2 145546 during a Sidewinder external carriage test in a late-afternoon mission. (CVPR-2040)

The APS-67 also supplied information to the pilot for the employment of the AAM-N-7 Sidewinder 1/1a missile. (AAM-N-7 is the Navy designation for Air, to Air, Missile, Navy, Seven). The pilot made a cockpit selection of either Sidewinder 1 or Sidewinder 1a, depending on which type was carried. (Few Sidewinder 1 missiles were produced, approximately 240; the normal load of the F8U-2 would have been the AAM-N-7 Sidewinder 1a, which became the AIM-9B when the joint designation system was introduced.) The missile release computer took radar range and static pressure and computed the maximum range for either missile, displaying that information for the pilot. The maximum range for the selected missile was shown in feet from 0 to 30,000, along with the radar range to the target being tracked. This quickly gave the pilot the ability to determine if the target was within range of the Sidewinder missile for proper employment.

Armament Demonstrations

F8U-1 140448 was modified to F8U-2 configuration to help support testing of the new Crusader variant. The modifications included installing an in-flight refueling receptacle fairing; the actual in-flight refueling capability was not added. In addition to the receptacle fairing, 140448 received a F8U-2 radome with AN/APS-67 radar and all associated equipment. Wing tip–mounted documentation cameras were installed to record the firing tests

of the 2.75-inch aerial rockets, 20mm guns, and AAM-N-7 Sidewinder missiles. 140448 completed 49 flights to support the build-up and accomplishment of Part II Armament Reliability tests. 140448 was based at the CVA facility at Edwards, utilizing the ranges at NOTS China Lake and Mojave. The armament demonstration flights were conducted from 19 August 1958 until 14 October 1958.

The Part II Armament demonstration schedule consisted of the following test points: gun firing, rocket firing, and Sidewinder missile firing.

The 20mm gun demonstration required "firing a full load (125 rounds per gun) from each gun with all guns firing while the aircraft

Zuni rocket carriage trials on F8U-2 145546 at Vought's Grand Prairie plant.

Close-up of the two Zuni twin rocket launchers on the fuselage mount of an F8U-2.

A view from the front showing the angles at which the Zuni rocket tubes are mounted to the weapons rails.

flew at an approximate airspeed of 700 knots, and altitude of 15,000 feet while pulling 3.5 to 4.5 positive gs in a turn." The requirement was that there be no evidence of damage to the aircraft structure or equipment due to gun blast or vibration during or after the firing of the guns. Gun firing had been demonstrated during the F8U-1 program after the problems with the gun blast tubes had been solved. The test objectives were satisfactorily demonstrated by 140448 at Mojave. The 20mm Mk 12 installation was identical to the F8U-1's; the testing centered on the expanded flight envelope and vibration level the gun firing caused on the AN/APS-167 radar equipment.

140448 successfully demonstrated gun firing at flight altitudes of 12,000 to 13,000 feet and airspeeds of 700 to 717 knots indicated while pulling 3.9 to 4.3 gs. All electronic and electrical equipment functioned properly and the airframe vibration level was satisfactory.

The second portion of the Part II Armament demonstration required firing a full load of rockets in three separate tests. The first demonstration was firing a full load of rockets with the aircraft flying at 716 knots airspeed and pulling 3 g. The second demonstration required firing a full load of rockets while flying at 36,840 feet at an airspeed of Mach 1.85. In the zoom climb demonstration, a full salvo of rockets was fired at 59,240 feet with an indicated airspeed of 164 knots. The 2.75-inch folding fin retractable rocket pack was satisfactorily demonstrated during the tests.

The demonstrations were not without a little drama. On flight 248 (numbering is the 140448's flight number, not test number), during the post-flight inspection a hole was discovered in the upper surface of the engine air intake. Further inspection revealed damage to the compressor section of the engine. The source of the damage was narrowed down to a fin from one of the rockets fired during

the flight. The concern was a rocket collision after firing. (Collisions and fin losses were a common occurrence during multiple 2.75-inch rocket firings with all aircraft.) The firing sequence was modified to provide more separation between pairs of rockets being fired, and this event did not occur again during the series of demonstration flights.

The third, and final, Part II Armament demonstration objective involved firing AAM-N-7 Sidewinder missiles in varying conditions. During Sidewinder 1A missile firings a maximum altitude, minimum speed demo of 54,960 feet and 168 knots was recorded. Highest airspeed firings were 717 knots indicated airspeed at 14,800 feet and Mach 1.78 at 36,920 feet of altitude. It was discovered that in the 55,000- to 59,000-foot altitude range, firing the Sidewinder 1A at slow indicated airspeeds in the 179- to 180-knot range, missile exhaust could cause an engine flame-out. This problem would be addressed in a later separate test program that included manual derichment by retarding the throttle; eventually an automatic system like that utilized in the F4D was tested.

Four Sidewinder Configuration

A four Sidewinder configuration was being tested on the F8U-2 for application on the F8U-2/-2N aircraft. The missile changes with the semi-active radar homing (SARAH) and infrared active homing (IRAH) Sidewinders required a revision to the Magnavox guidance system but greatly increased the firepower of the F8U. The installation aggravated an already marginal afterburner cooling system due to changes in the airflow along the fuselage blocking the cooling scoops.

147036 provides a view of the differences between the Sidewinder mounting rails between sides. On the left side they are mounted lower to allow the aerial refueling probe to clear the missile.

Zoom Climbs

Testing of the F8U-2N covered afterburner cooling with a revised inlet bleed door schedule and revised missile mounting. The completion of this work allowed the CVA test program to proceed to investigate zoom climb capabilities of the F8U-2N. The zoom flight test program started in early April 1961, and consistent zooms of 70,000 feet were achieved without engine malfunctions. Interestingly, the afterburner still consistently blew out at lower altitudes.

Swiss F8U-2 Proposal

CVA was contacted by a Swiss delegation about a possible purchase of F8U-2 airplanes. CVA advised there would be an 18-month lead time with a go-ahead by January 1958. In October 1957 CVA proposed selling the F8U-2 aircraft to the Swiss government. At the conference Swiss pilots flew an F8U-1 at the Naval Air Test Center, Patuxent River. Deliveries were to start in February 1959, but ultimately the Swiss chose the Mirage III for their requirements.

Japanese F8U-2

A Japanese purchasing commission received an F8U-2 presentation from CVA during a visit in October 1959. No orders were forthcoming from the visit, which eventually led to the purchase of Lockheed F-104 Starfighter aircraft.

British Government Request

In November 1961, the British government inquired about F8U-2s equipped with the Rolls Royce RB-168 afterburning engine. CVA replied that the installation appeared feasible and started a study to look at replacing the Pratt & Whitney J57-P-20 engine with a Rolls Royce AR 168-23 Spey. This would also include minimal changes and certain equipment removed to be replaced with customer-specific equipment.

To optimize the airframe for the installation of an AR 168-23/-23C, several changes were required. The engine air duct would be modified by increasing the inlet area at Sta. 130 and re-fairing the duct with the larger size back to Sta. 180. The guns and in-flight refueling probe would be removed and the structure adjusted with new contour following the installation of fairings.

The engine air duct would be further modified in the Sta. 320 to 335 area to remove a bleed duct opening. The oil cooler installation, ducting, and external exit door would be removed. From Sta. 423.5 to 472 the engine air duct would be replaced with a smaller-diameter duct and extend aft to the front face of the engine at Sta. 493. The engine compartment cooling ducts would be removed and replaced with a distribution collar at Sta. 536. The collar would receive air from the engine low-pressure bleed and distribute it to the present duct system.

The forward engine mounts would be relocated as a new structure to support them would be required between Sta. 515 and 595.

The aft engine mounts would be located at Sta. 611 with suitable structural modifications. A new engine installation track would have to be installed to facilitate engine installation/removal. In the cockpit there would be a few instrument changes, such as the addition of an engine oil temperature gauge and a nozzle position indicator.

The -23 requires an airframe-mounted gearbox to drive engine accessories, which would be mounted in the area of the main gear bulkhead. To properly position the engine in the airframe for center of gravity purposes an extension of 10 inches would be required in the engine A/B area. The aft end of the airplane would be 15 inches shorter to accommodate the larger afterburner nozzle. Specific to the installation of a Rolls Royce AR 168-23C are the engine-mounted accessories that increase the clearance envelope from 42- to 48.75-inch diameter.

To maintain the same thrust line as the J57-P-20, the following modifications would need to be made:

- The four aft fuel cells between Sta. 515 and 595 would be modified with a loss of capacity.
- Access doors would be required at Sta. 590 for engine drains and at Sta. 620 on the lower side for access to A/B hydraulic oil.
- An access door on the bottom of the airplane would have to be provided between Stations 492 and 560 for engine accessories.
- Minimum clearance between the arrestor gear housing and the engine A/B shroud would require shroud modifications.[72]

In January 1962, the British government was furnished data on the Spey-powered F8U-2NE to support its interest in a possible 100-airplane purchase. It was noted that the Spey would be a popular political choice but would add cost to the aircraft for development and flight testing.

Comparative Performance Equipped with Four Sidewinder Missiles		
	J57-P-20	**Spey**
Maximum Mach Number at 35,000 feet	1.62	1.75
Mission Time (hours)	1.87	2.0
Gross Weight (lbs)	29,667	28,880

Mutual Aid Program

For the Mutual Aid Program (MAP), CVA was promoting the F8U-2NE in competition with the N-156F. The quoted price for a mutual aid F8U-2NE was close to $800,000 compared to $890,000 for the N-156F. The program was anticipated to buy up to 400 aircraft with the first 100 to be delivered in FY 1965. Interestingly, there was pressure from the British to use the Spey engine in the MAP F8U-2NE. On 23 April 1962, the N-156F was chosen the winner of the F-X competition, which eventually produced 624 F-5A aircraft. As history would show, CVA would come up short again to Northrop for the follow-on MAP procurement.

The F-8E production line late in the run with around 50 more airplanes to build and deliver.

A nice high-angle view of two Hellrazors Crusaders, 146953 and 145598, lined up to launch with squadron mate F-8D 147059 hitching a tug ride. (USN)

Still carrying the F8U-2N designation under the UHT, 147036 in "clean" configuration. The effects of engine heat are visible on the tail cone.

Delmar Target Towing System

The Delmar Target Towing System could be attached to F8U-1/-1B/-2/-2N/-2E aircraft to support target needs of the fleet. The equipment consisted of a tow reel, fuselage sheave fitting, launcher boom, basket assembly along with a pilot's control box, and target. With the exception of the pilot's control box, all the components were externally mounted. The AERO 43 (DX-4) tow reel assembly was attached to the left-side fuselage using a missile pylon and fuselage support structure. The tow reel was powered by a wind-driven turbine and carried up to 37,500 feet of .040-inch-diameter wire. Several different-diameter wires could be loaded, depending on the target or banner towed. The AERO 38B launcher was attached to the lower left-hand wing near the outer wing panel using two adapters that were bolted through doublers and wing skin into the wing fold rib. The launcher lead the tow wire from the reel to the target and held the target in the proper position clear of the towing airplane when the target was deployed.

The infrared targets utilized in the Delmar system were the AERO-36, AERO-36A, and the AERO-42. The targets were streamlined press-fiber shells with four polystyrene fins. The targets would rotate at three to four revolutions per second when towed at speeds of 270 to 380 knots. For target deployment and recovery the aircraft was limited to 250 knots of airspeed.

F8U-2N 147036 showing off the speed brake and dual Sidewinder installation for the camera plane, prior to modification to F8-U-2NE standard.

F8U-2N

The F8U-2N is a development of the F8U-2 with improved performance and increased ability to detect and destroy targets at night and in foul weather. Among the improvements were the change from the J57-P-16 engine to the J57-P-20 engine with an increase of 1,100 pounds of thrust (18,000 versus 16,900). A three-axis-hold autopilot was incorporated into the airplane along with an

VF-174 F-8C 145598 a second away from an attempted arrested landing during carrier qualifications.

F8U-2NE demonstrator 147036 was the second F8U-2N modified to serve in the F8U-2NE test program.

An F-8E(FN) low-speed wind-tunnel model testing the double droops. The duct for BLC air is visible in the center section.

APQ-83 angle tracking radar. One of the more subtle changes was the replacement of the rocket pack with a 75-gallon fuel cell. The F8U-2 could carry both semi-active and infrared-homing Sidewinder missiles on four fuselage-mounted missile rails. Program tests to further develop the F8U-2N/J57-P-20 resulted in zoom climbs using 147035 of more than 70,000 feet.

At one point an altitude of 75,400 feet was reached even after the engine flamed out at 73,430 feet. It was also discovered that unless manual derichment was used when firing Sidewinder missiles above 60,000 feet, the engine would flame out. Satisfactory engine performance at 70,000 feet could be maintained by deactivation of a converter valve that caused unwanted exhaust nozzle movement above 63,000 feet, a stronger spring in the bleed valve actuator to allow operation above 68,000 feet without compressor stalls, optimizing the fuel control to operation at 45,000 feet instead of the factory setting of 35,000 feet, and tightening production tolerances in the fuel control.

F8U-2NE

The F8U-2NE was an improved version of the F8U-2N with the incorporation of a larger radar dish for the AN/APQ-94 radar housed in an enlarged radome. The larger radome changed the shape of the forward fuselage of the F8U. The F8U-2NE also incorporated an Infrared Search

Confused identity. The tail says "2N" and the nose says "2NE," but the radome and IR scanner say "2NE," which is correct. 147036 after a nose graft.

F8U-2N 147036 without 2NE markings on the nose but with 2NE modifications incorporated. It also carries a pair of Sidewinder missiles. The clearance provided the in-flight refueling probe is visible here.

F-8C 146953 of VF-174 Hellrazors tensioned up on the catapult of USS Forrestal. *(USN)*

Crusader fitted with YAPS boom (yaw, angle of attach, pitch, sideslip), which provides precise air data information during flight test. The wings are folded past the vertical position.

This rear view of F-8E(FN) No. 1 shows clearly the double droop on the leading edges of the wing and the decreased angle of incidence degrees versus the 7 degrees of previous Crusader models. Flaps and ailerons are in the drooped position as well.

Striking the familiar Crusader ground pose, 147036 poses for images used in engineering reports.

149192 ready for delivery. Delivery jets had the Vought production number (black numerals) removed. It carries the F8U-2NE designation dating this picture to after April 1961.

F-8E returning to the ramp after a test hop. Afternoon lighting highlights the folded wings and extended droops. The cone-shaped object over the star is the top of the control tower in the distance.

and Track system (IRST) visible in front of the windshield. This system allowed for passive (non-radar emitting) target tracking and attack with Sidewinder missiles or cannon.

AN/APQ-94 Evaluation

The AN/APQ-94 radar is a range and angle tracking system with a maximum range of 30 miles for detection and 20 miles for lock-on. 147036 was the prototype for the F8U-2NE and was used in the trials of the AN/APQ-94 radar during preliminary evaluation of the airplane. Production F8U-2NE 149135 completed the Navy evaluation of the airplane including the remaining radar test flights. Thirty-one flights were flown to evaluate the system from September to December 1961.

During the tests another F8U was used as a radar target at altitudes of 20,000 to 40,000 feet to evaluate detection and lock-on capabilities. The trials included tail-on, beam, and head-on aspect angles at speeds of Mach .65 to .98. During the tests zoom climbs of 62,000 and 68,000 feet were accomplished with satisfactory radar operation. Finally, additional tests were performed

The pylon leading edge anti-erosion treatment is visible in this close-up of the inert test Sidewinders.

Two views of the larger radome on the F8U-2NE; this aircraft also has the infrared seeker installed.

This F8U-2NE has an aerodynamic cover installed in place of the infrared seeker. It also has a red warning edge painted all the way around the intake.

149137, an F8U-2NE carrying two Sidewinder missiles ready for a test flight. The droop is in the cruise position and the speed brake is hanging slightly open.

With the pendant cable tensioned, 150341 of VF-174 is just seconds from being catapulted off the deck. (USN)

on the home on jam (HOJ) missile release computer and Sidewinder missile integration. Gunfire blast and vibration tests were accomplished by F8U-2NE 149152 at the Navy gunnery range at Corpus Christi, Texas. At Mach 0.85 and 5,000 feet altitude several one-second bursts of approximately 125 rounds per gun were fired with no adverse effects on the system. At the end of the testing the AN/APQ-94 radar operated satisfactorily and was considered compatible with the F8U-2NE.

The F-8E was tested to incorporate the capabilities of the Bullpup missile. Actual results in combat with other single-seat aircraft were less than satisfactory. It was difficult to fly a single-seat aircraft in a high-threat environment, follow the missile flare, and guide it successfully to the target. Quite a number of photographs exist showing test aircraft 147035 and 149192 with AGM-12 Bullpups installed; however, the missile was never used operationally in the fleet.

F-8E(FN)

CVA actively promoted French Navy interest in 40 to 50 F8U-2NE aircraft with J57 engines in January 1962. The French requested that the U.S. Navy demonstrate the F8U aboard the French aircraft carrier *Clemenceau*. By February the formal request was being processed for the F8U demonstration aboard *Clemenceau*, possibly as early as March.

On 16 March 1962 two USS *Saratoga* F8U-2Ns made 10 launches and recoveries aboard the French carrier *Clemenceau* in the Mediterranean. The operations went well and the French were pleased with the operations aboard ship. The order for 40 to 50 F8U-2NE aircraft in 1964 looked very promising.

By April, CVA presented a proposal to the French for 40 F8U-2NE and 6 F8U trainers. Deliveries would start in late 1963, provided a go-ahead was given in September 1962. During May the proposal was accepted by the French Department of Defense and the U.S. Navy. By June, it was up to the French Defense Minister to negotiate funding for the $60 million program. The anticipated start date was 1 September. A French delegation visited CVA and Magnavox to discuss the adaptability of a French missile to the F8U fire control system. The 1962 French legislative elections, with all the turmoil and changes to their process, were finally over and it was felt that a contract agreement would soon be reached.

A Marta R.530 missile mounted on the fuselage for low-speed wind-tunnel testing.

During the testing of the F-8E(FN), mounting the Marta R.530 underwing was tested in the low-speed wind tunnel with plenty of airflow tufts.

YF-8E(FN) 147036 taxiing in after a test flight. The aircraft carries U.S. and French Navy insignia.

F8U-2NE 147036 was used for Marta R.530 carriage testing and was lost in an accident on 11 April 1964. Its place in testing was taken by the first F-8E(FN).

A head-on view of test aircraft with Marta 530s installed.

F-8E(FN) No. 2 and trials companion No. 3 preparing to launch from USS Shangri-La.

A Marta 530 radar-guided version mounted on an F-8E testbed showing the relatively large side of the missile.

A close-up of a Marta 530 infrared version mounted on F-8E(FN) testbed 157036, former YF-8D.

Twice-modified prototype YF-8E(FN) 147036 returning from a test flight carrying Marta 530s.

The French order was expected in February 1963 for a total of 40 F8U-2NEs. The 6 trainer versions were dependent on a U.S. Navy order for the type. The contract was finally signed in February 1963 for 42 F-8E aircraft.

In March 1963, TF-8A 143710 was ferried to Rota, Spain, aboard USS *Saratoga*. It was flown to the French airbase at Istres. CVA test pilot Robert Rostine completed 37 demonstration flights for French Navy officials. Deliveries were scheduled to start in June 1964.

The French Navy incorporated a number of changes into the basic F-8E. These included the double leading-edge droops; boundary layer control, which decreased the variable-incidence wing from 7 to 5 degrees; and a larger UHT. In addition to the normal cannon and Sidewinder armament, the Marta R.530 missiles were carried on the fuselage sides. The R.530 came in an infrared- or radar-guided version and necessitated the change to a Magnavox AN/APQ-104 radar and modifications to the AN/AWG-4 fire control system.

F-8D 147036 was modified to serve as a F-8E(FN) prototype for the aerodynamic improvements. The aircraft was redesignated YF-8E(FN). The first flight of 147036 was 27 February 1964. The

French Navy F-8E(FN) No. 2 (151734) prepares to be catapulted from the USS Shangri-La *(CV-38) during aircraft and weapons testing off Mayport, Florida, in 1964. The aircraft is carrying two inert AIM-9 Sidewinder missiles.*

Still wearing some of its former unit marks, F-8H 148681 (former VMFA-112) arrives via rail from MASDC for use in the Philippine Air Force (PAF) program. It became "F9" PAF 308.

Once flown by the Hook magazine's own "Purely Wholesome," LCDR Jack Woodul's name is still on 147060, which eventually became "F6" PAF 305.

148649 F5 PAF 304, 147070 No. 1 Spare, and 147060 F6 PAF 305 in the hangar at Vought after their trip from Arizona.

F-8H F2 (148661) PAF 301 and F3 (148628) PAF 302 undergoing rework.

The modification line for the Philippine Crusaders; nearest the door is F7, which is the former 148705 PAF 306.

aircraft lasted only 21 flights before being lost in an accident on 11 April 1964. F-8E(FN) was fitted with the instrument test boom and took over the prototype flying program. The Marta firing program took place at China Lake and the carrier suitability trials took place on USS *Shangri-La*. Testing was completed and the aircraft approved for service by late 1964.

During the life of the F-8E(FN), several changes were made, including replacing the Marta R.530 with the smaller and more capable Marta R.550. Because of the time required for the development of the Dassault Rafale, a total of 17 F-8E(FN) were overhauled and modernized to F-8P configuration. The new configuration included new electrical, hydraulic, avionics, and internal navigation systems. The F-8P would serve the French Navy until December 1999.

Philippine F-8H

The government of the Philippines contracted with CVA to remanufacture 25 F-8H aircraft. The Philippine government would purchase 35 F-8H airplanes and spares from the U.S. government. The U.S. government also would loan the NASA-owned TF-8A to the Philippine government for flight training. The 35 F-8H aircraft were in storage at the Military Aircraft Storage and Reclamation Center (MASDC) in Tucson, Arizona, and were shipped to Grand Prairie by rail. Of these, 25 aircraft would be made flyable with the additional 10 used for parts reclamation to support flight operations at Vought and in the Philippines. The TF-8A was to be refurbished to bring it up to current specifications for use in the training program. The first aircraft were inducted into the refurbishment program in late 1977 and all aircraft delivered by the middle of 1979.

F8 148684 PAF 307 and F9 148681 PAF 308 are visible in this overhead shot of the rework line at Vought.

"F1" fresh out of the paint shop at Vought prior to first flight and squadron markings being added.

A Vought test pilot crosses over Jefferson Boulevard piloting PAF 300 at NAS Dallas.

PAF F-8H 300 cleaned up and accelerating after takeoff.

PAF 300 headed for takeoff: wing up, droops down, and canopy open without the strap that keeps it from over-extending.

"F1" on the compass rose at Vought. The aircraft is aligned with known compass headings painted on the ground and the aircraft compass readings are compared. The deviations of the aircraft are noted and are written on a "Compass Card" that is attached to the airplane for the pilot's reference.

F-8H 147806's wing still had the fairing for the Bullpup missile; however, the capability was not included in the F-8H program for the PAF.

PAF 7th Tactical Fighter Squadron insignia on the tail of an F-8H.

An in-flight view of F-8H 148649 on a training flight near Dallas. The "F5" on the rudder is the Vought production sequence number.

PAF 304 testing the landing configuration with wing up and gear down.

PAF 301 on a test flight over north Texas illustrating the location of the Philippine national insignia of the upper wing.

The clean lines of the F-8H show in this image of PAF 301 banking toward the camera.

PAF 301 148661 being towed down a flight line filled with TA-7C and A-7E aircraft.

F8U-1 143793 VX-4 XF-55 PMTC Point Mugu, California, 19 May 1962 with the Delmar target-towing package installed. (Clay Jansson via Jim Sullivan)

F8U-3: A SUPER CRUSADER

A Pratt & Whitney J75 engine on its transportation cradle awaiting installation in the No. 1 F8U-3.

As the Navy entered the age of the fleet defense fighter armed strictly with missiles, Vought engineers faced an uphill battle in a challenging competition with McDonnell for a production contract to build the Navy's new frontline fighter. That St. Louis–based company was building a new Mach-2 aircraft designated the XF4H-1 Phantom II. Would the Phantom's twin engines and two-man crew become the decisive factors in determining the victor? Only an intense head-to-head fly-off competition could provide the answer.

All-Weather Fighter

Just after the first successful flights of the XF8U-1 in April 1955 CVA learned through their Washington contacts that the Navy was interested in an all-weather, missile-only fighter. The fighter would perform the Combat Air Patrol (CAP) mission as part of the envisioned 1959–1963 Task Force Air Defense System.

EM-1617 (10 May 1955) suggested that based on this information, work start immediately on a proposal for a high-performance missile-carrying version of the F8U. In addition to hearing about the new fighter request, CVA learned that the BuAer was strongly interested in utilizing the Pratt & Whitney J75 engine in the new fighter. During the mid-1950s there was strong competition between CVA, Douglas, and Grumman aircraft companies. In CVA there was a real concern that the maximum speed of the Grumman F11F powered by the GE J79 could reach higher speeds than the F8U-1 by 1958.

The Navy had requested allocation of J75 engines for 1957 delivery for three programs, one being the F8U aircraft. The assumption was the Douglas F5D would be another recipient of the engine. This aircraft had been a strong competitor in the day fighter competition that the V-383 had won. Knowing the competition would be fierce, engineering started work on incorporating the J75 engine into the F8U.

Substantial improvements to the F8U-1 would be required to approach the Mach 2.5 maximum speed potential of the J75. Five significant technical problems had to be resolved for the new design to be successful: the directionally unstable configuration of the F8U-1 at speeds approaching Mach 1.9; possible relocation of the duct inlet for satisfactory performance over a wider Mach number range; submerging or semi-submerging missiles to exploit the performance capability of the airplane; larger radar to provide adequate detection range; and significant aerodynamic heating problems for many parts of the airplane.

Solving these technical problems required extensive changes to the F8U-1 configuration. Certain information could be carried over from the F8U program to help the V-401, but the expectation was that the end product was going to be an entirely new aircraft. However, the BuAer had advised that due to the budget environment, appropriation could not be expected for the purchase of a new airplane. The V-401 should be considered a logical development of the F8U aircraft. CVA would use performance, cost, and scheduled availability to sell the V-401 to the Navy.

V-401 Development Program

By June 1955, the development effort was focused on a J75-powered missile-carrying day or all-weather fighter based on the F8U design. The project was given the internal mode number V-401; it would later be known by the BuAer designation F8U-3. From CVA's viewpoint the V-401 program had three goals:

1. To extend CVA's share of the fighter market to include all-weather as well as day fighter aircraft
2. To exploit the basic configuration and experience developed on the F8U-1
3. To extend the life and sales potential of the F8U configuration by expanding performance and mission capabilities to meet future fleet requirements

Timing of the V-401 program and the sales potential of the airplane were prime considerations in reaching the decision to submit a proposal because of the current F8U-1 program that was in its infancy.

The F8U-3 was not considered as a competitor to the F8U-1 and not expected to have a negative effect on F8U-1 sales. By "phasing in" during the expected peak of the F8U-1 production, the F8U-3 would reach production quantities in late 1960 or early 1961 after the F8U-1 had been in service several years.

CVA engineering released an estimated cost figure of $228,049 in July for the preparation of the V-401 proposal, including engineering labor requirements, experimental shop cost for fabrication of proposal models, wind tunnel model, and direct charges, with allowance made for a number of key personnel to be placed on an overtime basis during the final phase of the proposal. Plans were made to present the proposal to the BuAer by about 21 September 1955.

Formal Request for Proposal

On 11 August 1955, CVA received from the BuAer a formal request (BuAer Conf. Letter Aer-AC-2 SerNo. 014439) for the design, construction, and demonstration of an all-weather version of the F8U, armed only with air-to-air guided missiles. It requested that the following requirements be considered:

Performance
Greatest premium of maximum speed over broadest possible altitude band, and on acceleration and maneuver capability at all altitudes, particularly high altitudes.

Minimum Performance Armed
1. Combat ceiling, 55,000 feet
2. Maximum speed of at least Mach 2
3. CAP cycle time of 3 hours (with JP-5 fuel)
4. In-flight refueling provisions
5. Arrested landing requirements armed, 1.3 minimum speed and 15 knots wind over deck

Primary Weapons System
1. APQ-50 radar, modified to provide CW radar illumination
2. Missile auxiliaries permitting the efficient storage, combat operations, and launch of Sparrow III missiles
3. A battery of four Sparrow III missiles submerged, semi-submerged, or externally positioned to reduce drag[73]

The BuAer also requested studies on weight and performance penalties incurred by the provision of a second seat for a radar operator/navigator. This request was more important, as time would tell, in the BuAer thinking than merely the cost-benefit factor to which CVA responded.

Engineering Proposal

The engineering proposal was submitted to the BuAer (CVA Conf. Letter SS-3P-8) on 12 October 1955. It contained description, technical aspects, and performance guarantees for the V-401 as follows:

- Maximum speed: at 35,000 feet, maximum thrust, level flight, combat weight of 28,420 pounds, 1,265 knots (not less than Mach 2.2)
- Combat ceiling: minimum altitude for 2.5 minutes at 1.5 g at combat weight of 28,420 pounds at 58,000 feet
- Stall speed: with power off, in landing configuration and a landing weight of 24,150 pounds at 108 knots; empty aircraft weight of 20,244 pounds

The V-401 Project Plan

In a new direction for CVA, top management decided in early 1956 that prior to the preparation of a proposal for a major project, management would discuss the philosophies under which the project would be undertaken. Following establishment of a philosophy, program objectives would be established and instructions developed for the proposal.

The V-401 proposal (12 October 1955) had not initiated in this manner, but it was decided that prior to submission to the BuAer the project philosophy and objectives would be established.

Program Control issued the V-401 Project Philosophy and Plan on 19 January 1956, which stated the following departmental philosophies:

Design: The V-401 was to exceed the requirements for an all-weather missile-only fighter and provide a significant improvement in performance over the F8U-1, this to be accomplished with a minimum increase in cost and time.

Materials: Procurement policy was to retain the Project Control System and material control (which assigned responsibility of over-all materials coordination to a materials project man) developed during the F8U-1 program.

Objective: To reduce time lost through misinterpretation between vendors and engineering. Other factors in the procurement plan included use of standard "off-the-shelf" items and equipment actually used in the F8U-1 whenever practicable.

Tooling: To be based on an absolute minimum program to support a rate of 2 airplanes per month for the initial 10 aircraft. A production concept was planned to the extent that all tooling would be of a type and quality capable of producing larger quantities commensurate with rates up to 30 per month.

Manufacturing: An accurate direct labor cost control system was to be set up for the V-401 program to alleviate work stoppages and wasted man hours.

Ordering for the initial contract: To be done from one source in change and manufacturing scheduling, designed for a production program, to avoid repetition of the confusion caused on the XF8U-1 by split responsibility.

Detailed fabrication: To be done in the production shop to eliminate fixture down-times and disruptions in the line flow caused by moving fixtures from experimental to production shops.

New aircraft components: To be done in experimental shop to eliminate functional and production problems prior to subcontracting.

Instrumentation: To be done on the production line to allow logical in-station planning and eliminate costly tear-out and reinstallation.[74]

The project philosophy and plan was approved simultaneously with the proposal.

Preliminary Design Decisions

A series of CVA department manager meetings were held during July and August 1955. The purpose was to resolve certain preliminary design problems. The more important decisions are summarized below:

Directional stability: Folding ventral fins would be used to provide positive static directional stability at all points within the design limit V-G diagram.

Two-place versus one-place consideration: The V-401 would be designed as a single-place airplane because size and weight increases caused by a two-man crew were not sufficiently compensated for by increased effectiveness in performing CAP (combat air patrol) missions under CIC (combat information center) control.

Wing configuration: Wing area would not exceed 425 square feet and would provide a carrier approach speed of 130 knots based on 1.2 times the stall speed. Boundary layer control (BLC) would be incorporated and a double leading edge would be provided.

Ejector nozzle configuration: Incorporated to obtain as much thrust for acceleration and maximum-speed performance and to obtain as favorable a relation as possible between the airplane and engine center of gravities.

Additional problems settled by the departmental meetings included: inlet duct configuration, inlet shock system, longitudinal stability and airplane balance, armament control and electronics complement, proposal weight philosophy, and proposal weight freeze.

On 12 September 1955, engineering released weight comparisons between the original V-401, revised V-401, and the XF8U-1. This data was later revised by 26 September to add 104 pounds to the proposal gross weight. This was due to a 4-percent change in the vertical tail, increased fuselage weight, increased size of exhaust ejector, and addition of an anti-icing circuit.

Weight Comparisons

Item	XF8U-1	V-401 Original	V-401 Revised
Total Structure	7,071 lbs	9,526 lbs	9,602 lbs
Surface Controls	900 lbs	1,031 lbs	1,031 lbs
Total Propulsion	5,974 lbs	7,744 lbs	7,769 lbs
Total Equipment	1,506 lbs	1,839 lbs	1,842 lbs
Weight Empty	15,451 lbs	20,140 lbs	20,244 lbs
Useful Load	9,145 lbs	15,656 lbs	15,656 lbs
Gross Weight	24,596 lbs	35,796 lbs	35,900 lbs

V-401 Design Philosophy

"The V-401 was designed to provide a large improvement in performance over the F8U-1. To do this required the use of the larger J75 engine and resulted in an increase in manufactured airframe weight of about 31 percent over the F8U-1. While this large performance increase is essential for competitive reasons, it is also necessary that we accomplish it with minimum increase in cost over the F8U-1. For those reasons the basic policy used in the preparation of this design proposal was to use the F8U-1 configuration, wherever practicable, in order to get maximum carry-over of learning from the F8U-1. By doing this we believe that the V-401 should be considered a somewhat larger and heavier version of the F8U-1, rather than a new experimental airplane.

"In this respect the cost experience with the F7U-3 may well provide a more appropriate basis for estimating than the experience with the XF8U-1. This is because the V-401 in relation to the F8U-1 program should be similar to the relationship between the F7U-3 and F7U-1 experience. The effect of the greater performance improvement accomplished with the V-401 should be largely offset by the increased learning due to greater production of F8U-1 airplanes."[75]

By 7 October 1955, when report 9874 "F8U-(3) (V-401) Design Philosophy" was released, a clearer description of the F8U-3 had emerged. "It was determined that a general arrangement similar to the F8U-1 was most suitable for the V-401. The V-401 is powered with a Pratt & Whitney J75 afterburner engine. The airplane has a two-position incidence, swept wing mounted high on the fuselage.

"The wing planform is the F8U-1 planform moved outboard 17.3 inches from the centerline of the airplane to provide an area of 425 square feet. The horizontal tail planform is the same as the F8U-1. Ventral fins are used to provide good directional stability at high Mach numbers and high angles of attack.

"The airplane has a length of 58.7 feet, a span of 38.7 feet, and weighs 35,900 pounds at takeoff with three Sparrow III missiles. The missiles are carried in a semi-submerged position in an armament bay in the lower fuselage, which can be replaced to provide for alternate incorporation of other missiles, or rockets."[76]

Detail Specification Negotiations

CVA submitted the first draft of a detail specification for the F8U-3 to the BuAer on 12 October 1955. It was contained in engineering report 9879. The draft contained examples from the new design philosophy–guided approach to major projects. The philosophy for the F8U-3 was written in engineering report 9872.

A few specific examples of the application of the design philosophy in the selection of major equipment items follows:

- Two of the same alternators used on the F8U-1P
- Ram air turbines similar to the F8U-1 type but with higher capacity
- Two F8U-1 air conditioning units, requalified to slightly higher bleed and ambient air temperatures
- AN/APG-19 electronics package developed for use in the F4H or specified alternate electronics equipment to provide the same functions if unable to effect a price reduction with Collins
- Same wheels and tires used in the F7U-3M and alighting gear similar (but one-third heavier) to F8U-1 gear
- Same tail warning unit as proposed for F8U-1
- Power control cylinders similar to, but larger than, those used in F8U-1
- In-flight refueling as proposed for F8U-1

Specifically, the V-401 differed from the F8U-1 in the following aspects:

- Installation of J75 engine, instead of the J57
- Increase of internal fuel capacity from 1,261 gallons to 2,000 gallons
- Incorporation of fuselage "coking," and substantially larger air duct through aircraft structure
- Installation of Collins (CFE) electronics package in lieu of Douglas
- (CFE) package and other electronic equipment
- Installation of AN/APQ-50 radar in lieu of APG-30A
- Provisions for carrying three Sparrow III missiles in fuselage pod; no provision for guns; deletion of Mark 16 fire control system
- Incorporation of a new material (Gafite) for canopy
- Increase in unit horizontal tail area from 93.5 to 130 square feet
- Increase in wing area from 375 to 524 square feet
- Incorporation of tail ventrals for additional directional stability
- Incorporation of double leading edge wing droop (F8U-1 provides single droop)
- Utilization of BLC over aileron and inboard flap
- Incorporation of separate cooling units for cockpit and electronics compartment.[77]

On 1 July 1956, the BuAer indicated that a contract would be forthcoming for the F8U-3. CVA management authorized a full-scale go-ahead for the production program.

During the detail specification negotiations, in early August 1956, CVA learned that BuAer technical personnel considered the F8U-3 a new airplane rather than a development of the F8U-1. As a new airplane, the BuAer was attempting to write features into the specification that did not conform to the original design philosophy. CVA therefore felt that negotiations were hampered by indecision on the part of the BuAer's fighter branch as to the philosophy to be followed. This contributed to difficulty in negotiating the detail specification and was also a funding concern because money for a "new program" had not been appropriated.

Several specification items remained unresolved: weights; performance, landing fuel, wind over deck requirements for landing, armament control system, starting system, electronics package, emergency escape system, fuel gauging, cockpit leakage and temperature gradient, and removal and replacement items.

Since the original proposal by CVA for the V-401 the previous August, a number of major changes had occurred that affected proposal weights and performance: The engine had changed to a slightly lower thrust version, from the JT4B-21 engine (25,000 pounds static sea level thrust) to the JT4A-27 engine (24,500 pounds static sea level thrust); flight test results of the F8U-1 showed higher low-speed drag; the weight of the F8U-1 was increasing due to incorporation of spoilers that were applicable to the V-401, and finally, changes resulting from detail specification negotiations.

Fuel-related items that added weight included an increase in landing fuel from 1,850 to 2,500 pounds, a decrease in landing wind from 15 knots to 10 knots, and an increase in combat fuel from 45- to 50-percent takeoff fuel.

Equipment items that added weight included more voltage protection and increased overload capacity to meet specification XEL-907, added GFE dead reckoning navigator and GFE infrared detection, added autopilot and ground-level escape capabilities, and provisions for improved engine accessory access.

Summary of Weight Changes	
Weight Empty Increase	1,137 lbs
Fuel for Three-Hour Cycle Time	476 lbs
Total Take-off Weight Increase	1,613 lbs

The airflow needs of the Pratt & Whitney J75 engine are well-illustrated in this head-on photo of 146340.

Detail Specification Approval

On 3 October 1956, the BuAer signed the Detail Specification NavAer Spec. SD-525-1. The delay in signing (scheduled 9 August) was attributed to the concern of the BuAer's production division over engine and fire control system availability compatible with airplane requirements. On 12 October 1956 a development-only contract was received from the BuAer.

The appearance of the F8U-3 changes dramatically with the aircraft configured for low-speed flight with the surface area of the flaps and ailerons showing.

With the canopy and windshield still covered against scratches during the production process, 146340 is posed outside the hangar in the clean configuration.

The variable-incidence wing is in the landing configuration with the double-droop leading edges and trailing edges extended.

Application of "Area Rule" to the F8U-3

Engineering Memo EM-3768 written by J. D. Louthan gives great insight into the study and research about area rule (coking) and its potential in the F8U-3 aerodynamic design.

"During the F8U-3 proposal work, a basic design objective was to achieve the lowest possible total airplane drag consistent with a sound structural and aerodynamic design in the Mach number range from 1.0 to 2.0."[78]

He went on to write, "The greater the speed potential of the airplane, the less a given change in transonic drag can affect performance, and the greater the chance of adverse effects of 'coking' at speeds near equilibrium."[79] (Equilibrium being the point where thrust and drag equal themselves out and no further acceleration is possible unless something changes.)

For considering "area rule" in the F8U-3 design he wrote of two decisions made: "Make maximum use of the area rule possible with no increase in the drag level at Mach 2.0," and "increase the design Mach number over that considered in F8U-1 work. The result of this work would be to reduce the potential gains available transonically, but also to reduce the chances of compromising the drag level at higher supersonic speeds. The design Mach number selected for distribution consideration on the F8U-3 was approximately 1.4."[80]

The preliminary layout of the F8U-3 fuselage provided only the impression of being "coked" due to the target Mach number of 1.4. Louthan discussed the F8U-3 "coking" philosophy with NACA personnel at Langley and Ames. He discussed the F8U-3 with R. T. Jones and Harvard Lomax of the theoretical aerodynamics section at Ames. These are a summary of the points of general agreement:

146340 displays the amount of aerodynamic change required to get a Mach 2–plus jet fighter slowed down enough to land on an aircraft carrier.

The third Sparrow missile is showing below the fuselage. Notice how the shape of the nose fairs down into the inlet opening.

This rear view in the clean configuration highlights the size of the engine afterburner and just how much the engine dominates the size of the F8U-3.

Like the F8U before it, when the wing is raised on the F8U-3, the UHT adjusts to help control the pitch changes caused by the change in lift. The wing view also shows how the shape changes with droops and trailing edges extended.

A high wing arrangement somewhat limits the reductions in supersonic drag that might be obtained by coking the fuselage. From a drag standpoint, the most important considerations at supersonic speeds are the development of high fineness ratio fuselages with nose and boat-tail slopes as small as possible. A design Mach number of 1.4 was felt to be about right for an airplane in the F8U-3 category.

"Due to the lower thickness ratios of all surfaces, the potential reductions in wave drag due to 'coking' on the F8U-3 are somewhat less than on the F8U-1."[81] On 2 August 1956 the F8U-3 configuration was presented to R. T. Whitcomb at NACA Langley for comments and suggestions. The conclusions reached in this discussion were substantially in agreement with those drawn at Ames. Whitcomb suggested that perhaps some additional reductions in drag in the low supersonic speed range might be obtained by slight additional "filling in" of the area immediately ahead of the wing root. The writer pointed out that this was considered and was not done because of possible risk of compromising the drag level at Mach 2.0. Whitcomb agreed that this was a possibility. The general conclusion reached was that any worthwhile reductions in drag would be uncovered by a "cut and try" testing program on the configuration. Whitcomb was in complete agreement with the design Mach number and the design procedure employed on the F8U-3.[82]

In conclusion Louthan wrote: "It is felt at the present time that no significant reductions in supersonic drag can be made by this method without danger of compromising the drag at Mach 2.0."[83]

Mock-Up

Construction of the airplane mock-up began on 24 August 1956 and was completed 16 November. The cockpit and vision mock-ups construction started 24 August and were completed 16 November and 28 November, respectively. CVA evaluations of all three mock-ups started on 22 November was complete and inspected during the week of 23 November 1956. The official mock-up review with the Navy occurred on 3 December 1956.

The nose section of the F8U-3 mock-up during lighting tests. The formation light can be seen over the aft bar of the national insignia.

The cockpit steps on the F8U-3 mock-up are extended. The Sparrow missile in the photo is extended. The aircraft jack is being used to support the mock-up.

The engine removal and installation frame mock-up used for fit testing.

Design Operation Problems

By early December 1956, problems affecting the F8U-3 that were encountered and successfully resolved in agreement with the BuAer included use of the J75 engine and the fire control system. The definition of an acceptable design configuration, detail specification approval, and mock-up board review were successfully resolved. A rocket thrust augmentation plan was still being negotiated.

Electronic Design Program

Electronics engineering prepared and released initial schedules in July 1956, covering the following major systems: V-401 electrical power system, CNI system, V-401 power control, V-401 stabilization and autopilot system, antennas, airborne missile control system, MA-1 magnetic compass and AN/APN-22 radar altimeter, extension of F8U-1 tail warning system, nose gear steering system, and IR search tracker.

The addition of the autopilot and higher temperature, weight, and vibration requirements prevented the incorporation of the F8U-1 systems as originally planned under the "minimum change" philosophy.

Major items that failed to meet expectations by December 1956:

- Missile fire control system: To be developed late in the program (increasing basic design problems)

The aft section of the mock-up with the bulged fairing for the thrust augmentation rocket motor installed.

Designed for operations on an aircraft carrier, the F8U-3 was equipped with the same wing-folding capability of the F8U. This is one of the few images of the F8U-3 with the wings folded.

A rear quarter view showing the thinness of the wing along with the larger engine-exhaust opening of the F8U-3.

From the rear one can imagine the larger flame the J75 would produce in afterburner pushing a fairly clean aircraft with a thin wing.

Reliability Program

Under the F8U-3 reliability program, qualification tests were conducted on CVA-fabricated electrical and electronic assemblies. Environmental qualification specifications were prepared and several vendor component qualification reports reviewed for compliance. Malfunction analyses were conducted on several systems prior to basic design freeze.

Reliability testing was focused largely on the evaluation of components. From December 1956 to July 1957, 17 F8U-3 components were evaluated in the laboratory. In addition, 36 acceptance test specifications and 11 procurement specifications were written during this period.

Reliability analyses were made to determine the number of failures (statistically) that could be expected in F8U-3 systems prior to design freeze. By 1 April 1957 analyses had been completed on three systems with the following results: Nose gear steering was redesigned; stabilization system was redesigned; and infrared tail warning system was discontinued.

F8U-3 Performance Guarantees

The final draft (30 August 1956) of the detail specification had the following performance guarantees:

- Maximum speed at 35,000 feet, maximum thrust, level flight, combat weight 30,462 pounds, (not less than) 1,151 knots (Mach = 2.0)
- Supersonic combat ceiling, maximum thrust, combat weight 30,46 pounds, (not less than) 52,000 feet
- Combat ceiling, military thrust, combat weight 30,462 pounds, (not less than) 45,500 feet
- Longitudinal acceleration at 35,000 feet, maximum thrust, combat weight 30,462 pounds, elapsed time from M =. 9- to 90-percent maximum speed (not greater than) 2.95 minimum
- Maximum specific range, combat weight 30,462 pounds, (not less than) 0.165 nautical miles per pound of fuel
- Stalling speed with approach power (power is that required for level flight at 1.2 times the power-off stall speed in the landing configuration) landing weight 25,924 pounds landing configuration, BLC operating (not more than) 108 knots

A 22 May 1957 Program Control Revision to the V-401 Project Philosophy and Plan changed the proposed contractual guarantees.

The No. 1 F8U-3 during assembly at the Grand Prairie plant prior to roll out and transportation to Muroc.

- Location of antennas: Delayed six weeks due to redesign of the fuselage resulting from reconfiguration of the inlet duct
- The nose gear steering system was redesigned due to the change in location of the nose gear

In February 1957 the BuAer rejected the proposed autopilot specification submitted in the airplane detail specification. The proposed specification called for a simple cruise relief autopilot with manual engagement and disengagement. The BuAer required a design for a more complex autopilot with control stick override, and an ECP for accomplishing the program was requested.

The flight stabilization system design and performance remained satisfactory, and the nose gear steering design and fabrication of development units had been completed by early July 1957.

All antenna designs were in production drawing status. Studies were initiated for placement of an infrared search-track device on the F8U-3 integrated with the AN/APQ-74 radar.

Contractual Guarantees		
	Original	**As Amended**
Maximum speed at 35,000 feet	1265 kts (Mach 2.2)	1151 kts (Mach 2.0)
Combat ceiling, military thrust	47,000 ft	45,300 ft
Cycle time	3.0 hours	2.9 hours
Weight empty	20,244 lbs	21,668 lbs

In addition, the May revision called for space provision for thrust augmentation; tooling capability to support a production rate of 25 units per month in contrast to 30 stated in the original program plan; and fabrication of additional wind tunnel models.

Wind Tunnel Program

Prior to submission of the V-401 proposal, CVA conducted wind tunnel tests using a company-fabricated .020-scale high-speed model of the XF8U-1 adapted to the proposed V-401 configuration. These tests were conducted at the Naval Supersonic Laboratory at MIT 26–29 September 1955. The initial tests were run primarily to determine directional stability at Mach number ranges of 1.71 to 2.25.

Results are summarized below:

- Directional stability proved approximately as estimated at Mach 1.99 and 2.25.
- Longitudinal stability appeared slightly higher than estimated (both with and without Sparrow missiles) and longitudinal effects of ventral fins were shown to be small.
- Elevator effectiveness indicated as being slightly better than estimated.

A short series of "coking" effects tests were run on the .020 model 7–8 October 1955, with results substanti-

The wind tunnel model for the aft section and controls. Sparrow missiles are fitted to measure the resulting disruption of airflow on the tail surfaces.

ating proposal estimates of longitudinal stability, lateral-directional stability, and drag. However, after the discussions at NACA nothing was changed on the actual design.

Approved Flight Test Plan

According to planning, the scheduled first flights of the first three airplanes were on these dates: F8U-3 No. 1, 14 June 1958; No. 2, 29 August 1958; No. 3, 5 October 1958.

On 22 May 1957, Program Control issued the Program Plan, F8U-3 (Revision No. 1), which contained the Flight Test Plan, developed and approved subsequent to the 2 July 1956 go-ahead, as follows:

The low-speed wind-tunnel model of the F8U-3 in landing configuration during a test run at CVA's wind tunnel.

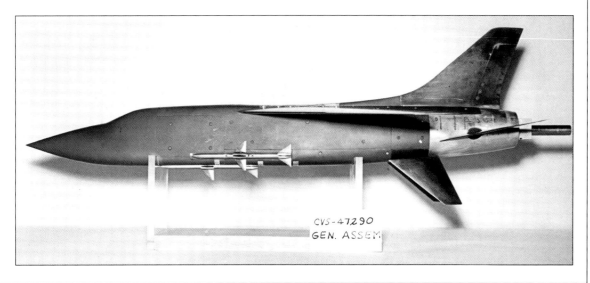

CVS-47290
GEN. ASSEM

Scope: A complete SR-38 specification program. Program increased about 10 percent as compared to the F8U-1 as a result of the BuAer requirement for completion of all major demonstrations prior to BIS and FIP. Approximately 20 months and 1,000 flights required. Spans of various elements of the test program consistent with F8U-1.

Initial Evaluation: Determine flying qualities and nature and extent of any deficiencies. Operate power plant at maximum power and evaluate airplane's handling characteristics over speed range during first month. No interruptions for change incorporations except as dictated by safety of flight consideration. Approximately 30 flights required.

Flight Test of Changes: A two-month period for flight testing corrective changes planned following the initial evaluation, limited to work and flight test necessary prior to Phase I Navy Evaluation. Approximately 30 flights required.

Part I Flight Test Demonstrations: To be performed using two airplanes over an approximate 15-calendar-months span.

Navy Evaluation: Phase I planned at completion of contractor's preliminary flights. Phase II Navy flights approximately three months later. Preliminary Navy evaluation prior to preliminary BIS trials to be performed after completion of Part I demonstrations.

With the aircraft on jacks and hydraulic power applied, the ventral fins are extended. The rudder and UHT have rigging boards mounted to measure the amount of surface deflection for flight control rigging.

Off-Site Operations: Use of Edwards Air Force Base planned for all Part I demonstrations and Part II spin tests. All subsequent flight tests and demonstrations, except those normally conducted at off-site naval facilities, planned at Dallas. Return of aircraft from Edwards subject to review; however, after completion of the Navy Phase II program.[83]

Under the flight test plan the first 33 airplanes were to be allocated for trial and demonstration as follows:

- Airplane Nos. 1 through 9 (BuNos 146340, 146341, 147085–147091) Contractor Tests & Demonstrations
- Airplane No. 10 (BuNo 147092) Rocket Thrust Augmentation Tests
- Airplane No. 11 (BuNo 147093) Raytheon Test
- Airplane No. 12 (BuNo 147094) Pratt & Whitney Test
- Airplane Nos. 13 through 18 (BuNos 147095–147100) BIS Evaluation
- Airplane No. 19 (BuNo not allocated) Point Mugu Test
- Airplane Nos. 20 and 21 (BuNo not allocated) PTR (unassigned)
- Airplane Nos. 22 through 27 (BuNo not allocated) Fleet Introduction Program
- Airplane Nos. 28 through 33 (BuNo not allocated) OPDEVFOR Evaluation
- Airplane No. 34 (BuNo not allocated) was to be first fleet delivery

Test and Demonstrations Revisions were proposed with the J75-P-6 engine as follows:

- Airplane No. 7- Part II Power Plant & Equipment Demonstrator, all demonstrations with J75-P-6 engine (original equipment)
- Airplane Nos. 1, 2, 3, 5, back fit with J75-P-6 engines
- Airplane No. 12, Point Mugu Test
- Airplane Nos. 13 and 14, PTR (unassigned)
- Airplane Nos. 15 through 20, BIS Evaluation
- Airplane No. 21, Pratt & Whitney Test

This assignment would allow initial deliveries with J75-P-6 engines in the fourth, fifth, and sixth BIS, the Pratt & Whitney test, all FIP, and all OPDEVFOR and fleet airplanes. It was anticipated that following the negotiation of the SR-38 Addendum, the flight test plan would be revised as necessary.[84]

V-401 Thrust Augmentation

A comparison was made of the V-401s performance at very high altitudes compared to the F8U-1 with a liquid-fueled rocket boost. A V-401 with 4,000 pounds of thrust rocket boost did not increase performance as much as was calculated on the F8U-1. The V-401 only gained Mach 0.4 with very little altitude advantage, whereas the F8U-1 gained Mach 0.5 and 10,000 feet of altitude over no rocket. A

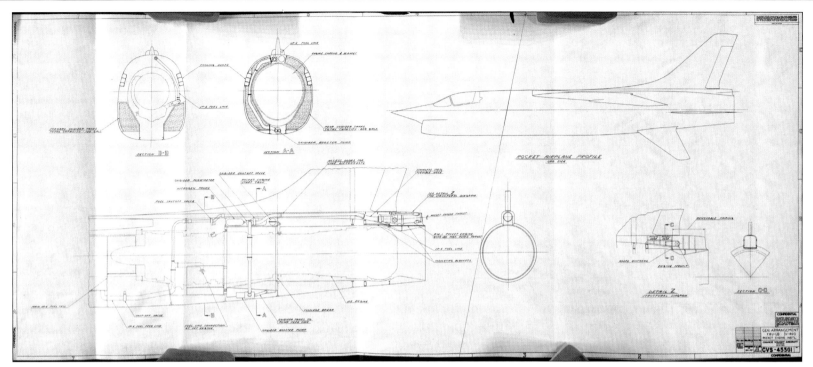

A CVA drawing of the thrust-augmented F8U-3F with a rocket engine mounted above the J57 for additional climbing speed and altitude. The concept never went beyond the drawing stage for the F8U-3.

A front view of F8U-3 146340 on a significant milestone day, shop completion.

With the shop completion sign covered with complete signs, the first F8U-3 is ready to roll out of the hangar.

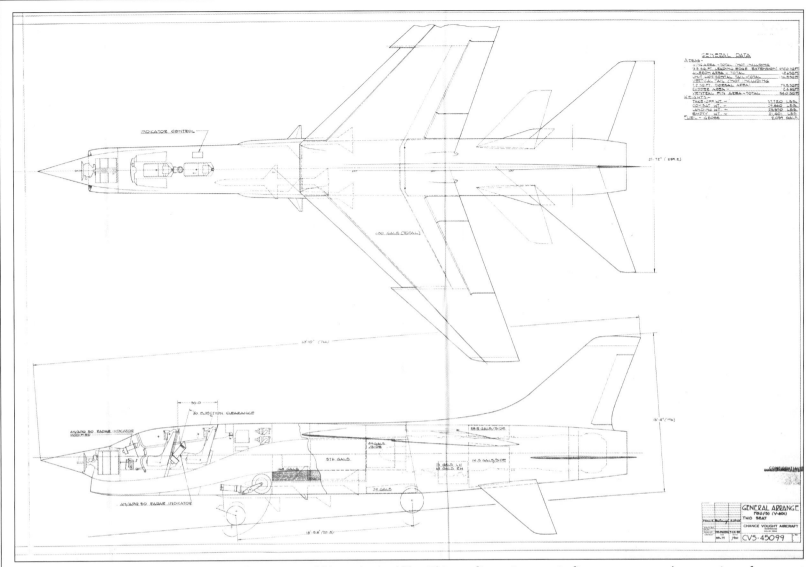

A CVA drawing of what a tandem-seated F8U-3 would have looked like. This configuration was in first response to the question of one seat versus two. Later this configuration was the basis for several strike fighter concepts and an air defense interceptor proposal for Canada.

zoom maneuver was studied on both the V-401 and F8U-1. A zoom maneuver did not benefit the F8U-1 as much as the rocket boost; however, the V-401 saw a greater benefit from the zoom maneuver than the rocket boost.

The zoom maneuver involves pulling gs to obtain a lift coefficient for maximum lift/drag (L/D), which gives the most gs per pound of drag. The load factor varies from 2.5 gs at 50,000 feet at the beginning of the zoom to .7 g at 70,000 feet. It was noted that to zoom at this L/D required a difficult piloting technique. A more practical piloting technique would provide similar results. The maximum altitude was limited by the estimated J75 flame-out altitude of 70,000 feet.

The zoom could provide more than 3 minutes of level supersonic flight at 65,000 feet against a performance guarantee of 2½ minutes at 58,000 feet in supersonic flight.[85]

One or Two Seats

Extensive time, research, and analysis had gone into the design problem of making the F8U-3 a single- or two-seat aircraft. According to an enclosure to Engineering Memo E8M-564 on 11 February 1958 the list of organizations contacted by CVA for information of the subject was quite extensive. The list included the BuAer, the Chief of Naval Operations (CNO), Patuxent River, VX-3, Point Mugu, the Fleet All-Weather Training Unit Pacific (FAWTUPAC), and the Naval Research Lab (NRL). They also contacted the following USAF organizations: Air Research and Development Command (ARDC), Wright Field, Eglin, Edwards, Air Defense Command, and the Air Force Chief Scientist, along with Convair, San Diego. Last on the list of organizations was NACA Ames.

A view of the right-hand nose of the F8U-3 showing the intake design that it shared with the Regulus II missile. Quite a change over the Crusader and Crusader II.

The summary pretty well tells the story of the one- versus two-seat argument: "There is no real quantitative information on this problem. Qualitatively, a case can be made by either side. The people at NRL feel that a maximum gain of the second place is in the order of 5 percent in detection range. But, this is an upper limit and it could be zero. Either system can be made to work, but both systems will require a determination on the part of the prime contractor to ensure that all the problems of logistics supply and training are adequately solved. In the overall sense you have a more efficient weapon system with a single-place than you have with a two-place airplane."[86]

Special Delivery Once Again

Following in the footsteps of the XF8U-1, on 14 May 1958 the first F8U-3 was transported by C-124 to Edwards. This time the trip was a little different, with the wing being bolted to a special fixture installed in the aft elevator bay of the Globemaster II. Once again, models, cradles, and containers were all built to accommodate the transportation of the newest member of the Crusader family out to California for its first flight.

The No. 1 F8U-3 being towed out of the hangar after shop completion for publicity and engineering report photographs.

Taxi tests toward the first flight started on 24 May 1958 with low-speed runs made into the wind, downwind, and at crosswind to check handling.

High-speed taxi runs started on 30 May 1958. First, 360-degree turns were made in the 20-knot wind with gusts to 30 knots.

The high-speed taxi was with boundary layer control (BLC) on, rudder effective at 58 knots, and nose gear lifted at 115 knots. Lift-off occurred at 122 knots and 146340 flew for 100 yards at approximately 5 feet off the ground. On the taxi back the left brake started grabbing. After taxiing back over 1.5 miles the left tire overheated and blew. The blown tire damaged the lower main wheel door and started a small hydraulic fire that was extinguished by the crash crew.

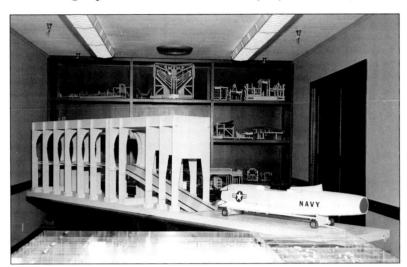

The transportation mock-up for the F8U-3. The box and ramp represent the C-124 and the clearance available for loading the fuselage into the cargo bay.

Towing the F8U-3 out to load on a cradle for C-124 transportation to California. The radome has been removed and other markings and openings covered in preparation for loading and flight.

The F8U-3 wing center section on a flatbed truck for loading onto the C-124. This was a change over the transportation of the XF8U-1 where the wing center section was boxed up and shipped by truck to Muroc.

A crane is preparing to pick up the fuselage of the F8U-3 and place it on a shipping dolly that is parked in front of the C-124. The dolly was necessary to enable the fuselage, less radome, to stay intact for loading and still make it through all the height limitations of the ramp and cargo compartment.

The fuselage is carefully fitted into the transportation dolly right in front of the C-124. It is interesting that this step was accomplished so close to the aircraft and not in a hangar.

The F8U-3 is slowly moved up the loading ramp into the cargo compartment of the C-124. Utmost care needed to be taken because of the potential for damage to both aircraft.

Nearing the top of the hill the whale has almost swallowed the entire F8U-3 fuselage. It would have been interesting to see how close the two came to each other as the loading progressed.

Very close to task completion, only a small section of the F8U-3 can be seen. The crate on the right of the airplane contains the vertical tail assembly that was removed from the aft section for loading.

The tail of the F8U-3 is crated and being readied to move up the ramp into the C-124. It will be placed on the right side of the cargo compartment near the front of the aircraft and is visible in the fuselage loading photos.

Raising the center section of the wing into position below the aft cargo elevator shaft on the C-124 for transportation to California.

The center section of the wing after attachment to the C-124. This solution necessitated only one transport aircraft and eliminated the hazard of moving a wide load on the roads.

An ingenious aerodynamic fairing was built for attachment in the aft cargo elevator opening of the C-124. It smooths out the drag from the center part of the wing that is exposed when the wing is raised for landing on the F8U-3.

Emerging from the flight test hangar at Edwards, the first F8U-3 is fitted with an ingestion screen on the inlet in advance of ground engine testing. The screen helps prevent foreign object damage to the J75 engine.

Towing out to the engine run-up area, the natural metal surfaces of the F8U-3 reflect the California sunshine.

A lot of activity around the jet as the engine is started in preparation for power-on electric and electronic system checks, flight control checks, moving the wing, and engine and hydraulic system leak checks.

The date of the first flight has arrived and 146340 moves from the hangar to the flight line. All systems checks after reassembly are complete. The aircraft is fully reassembled and ready for flight.

Chief Vought test pilot John Konrad smiles from the cockpit of the F8U-3 prior to the first flight.

First Flight F8U-3

The first flight of the F8U-3 146340 took place on 2 June 1958. John Konrad, chief test pilot, lifted off the north lakebed at Edwards for a .80-hour test flight. The length of the flight was limited by a throttle quadrant malfunction. The aircraft did reach a speed of 350 knots at 20,000 feet; not impressive for a machine with such high potential performance. The F8U-3 was escorted by two USAF aircraft and a company TV-2 photo chase aircraft bailed to CVA from the Navy. One of the features of the "sugar scoop" inlet design of the F8U-3 was inlet bypass doors on the top of the inlet just past the end of the inlet scoop. During the first flight the bypass doors were closed, which caused a high-frequency airframe vibration, the doors were opened slightly and the vibration ceased. The chase pilots also reported ventral tail vibrations in the landing configuration at speeds above 160 knots and tail down with the speed brake extended. The flight successfully landed back on the north lakebed

The electrical power cart is hooked up along with the start cart in anticipation of engine start for the first flight. The low sun angle creates an air of anticipation.

146340 taxies to the end of the runway for a flight. At the end of the runway a last check will be made to see if any leaks or other problems have developed that would endanger the flight.

Later in the short life of the F8U-3 program the first aircraft is seen arriving in Grand Prairie. The size of the BuNo on the tail has decreased and a stripe has been added to the fuselage sides.

Chief test pilot Konrad briefs company leaders and engineers right after landing the F8U-3 for the first time. A binding throttle cut the flight short with obvious concerns.

With the natural metal fuselage and dayglow orange visibility markings the F8U-3 makes for a nice color photograph.

This family portrait of the No. 2 XF8U-1, 138900, and the first F8U-3, 146340, shows the advancement in the Crusader series in only three short years. When this picture was taken the F8U-1 had only entered fleet service about two years earlier.

The No. 2 F8U-3, 146341, shares the flight line with newly built F8U airplanes awaiting fleet delivery.

This table was compiled on 20 August 1958.

	F8U-3	F-104A	F-105B	F-106A	F-108A	F-101B	F4H
Engine Designation Sea Level Static Thrust	J75-P-6 26,000	J79-GE-5 15,600	J75-P-3 23,500	J75-P-6 23,500	J93-GE-1 24,800	J57-P-35 16,900	J79-GE-2A 16,900
Gross Weight, Take Off (lbs) Fuel, Internal (gal/lbs)	38,772 2036/13844	18,337 760/5160	35,462 1490/10132	33,500 1323/8996	100,000 7100/47570	43,000 2128/13832	44,260 1972/13410 600/4080
Maximum Speed at 35,000 ft, CRT (Mach) MRT (Mach) Combat Ceiling, CRT (ft) Time to Accelerate at 35,000 ft from Mach 0.9 to 2.0 (min) Radius of action (GP Fighter) (NM) Cycle Time GPF (hours)	2.52 0.96 58,100 3.64 (3.33) 548 2.87	2.26 1.06 60,000 2.0 30 0.7	2.06 1.06 51,000 4.02 235 1.6	2.04 1.01 52,000 4.92 236 1.6	3.0 80,000	1.9 0.98 300 1.9	2.15 1.08 57,500 2.33
Landing Weight (lbs) Stall Speed at Landing Weight (kts)	27,426 113	14,300 132	27,830 133	26,753 123		34,600 146	28,929 102
Armament	3 Sparrow III (also 4 Sidewinders)	T 171 Gatling Gun (also 2 Sidewinders)	T 171 Gatling Gun (internal bomb bay)	4 Falcon + 1 MB-1 Genie	3 GAR-9 (internal)	2 Falcon + 1 MB-1 Genie	4 Sparrow III
First Flight	6-2-58	2-28-54	10-22-55	12-26-56	3-1-61	3-27-57	5-27-58

despite the throttle problems. One of the ventral tail fiberglass tips vibrated loose in flight.

Unlike three years prior with the XF8U-1, Konrad reported the nose wheel steering system and main wheel brakes as excellent. On the second flight, 11 June, Konrad successfully took 146340 through Mach 1, and on 18 August, Mach 2.

The most interesting test flight came during a zoom climb test. John Konrad took the F8U-3 climbing at Mach 2 to 60,000 feet. He then pulled back on the stick for a 30-degree climb. At 71,000 feet the engine compressor stalled and failed. The climb continued reaching 75,960 feet before he flew the aircraft back to Edwards for a deadstick landing.

Internal PR

A September 1958 department correspondence from Russ Clark to Fred Detweiler listed a number of suggested party lines for CVA concerning the F8U-3 when in contact with the "customer's organization" (Navy).

"We can confidently state that: The F8U-3 All Weather Fighter Weapons System compared to the F4H-1 has superior performance and maneuverability at high altitudes for supersonic operations; it is

The relative size difference between the two Crusader models is evident in this high-angle shot of the Vought flight line. It starts to show why some in the Navy considered the F8U-3 to be a new airplane instead of a natural development of the Crusader.

The first F8U-3 taking off under the watchful eye of a flying company helicopter at NAS Dallas.

a simpler, lighter weapons system utilizing 20-percent less carrier deck stowage space and 30-percent less fuel per mission, and is at least 20-percent less expensive to build and to operate in the fleet.[87]

"The F8U-3 has a mission cycle time of three hours on internal fuel. The F4H-1 has only 2.1 hours on internal fuel and requires the undesirable logistics feature of 600 gallons of external fuel to match the F8U-3 endurance.[88]

"The F8U-3 has optimized, reliable automation to simplify the pilot's task such that only one man is needed to accomplish the mission. To successfully combat a Mach 2.2-plus fighter against supersonic invaders, the time of combat engagement is so short that automation is requisite and a second man is redundant. Electronic countermeasure techniques are so advanced that automatic opposition to them is required."[89]

A comparison view of the nose and inlet style differences between the Crusader and Crusader III.

F8U-3 assuming the classic Crusader stance while awaiting engine start for yet another test flight at Edwards.

Ventrals extended and wing retracted, the F8U-3 is ready to accelerate to the speed of heat.

A low-angle view of the Crusader III decorated with dayglow orange test markings against the blue sky at Edwards.

With smoke and heat emitting from the tailpipe, an F8U-3 sits at the end of the runway undergoing "last chance" inspections for leaks or other damage that could have occurred during engine start and taxi operations.

The first F8U-3 passes over Jefferson Boulevard as it arrives at Grand Prairie. For many years, drivers were treated to the sight of Corsairs, Cutlasses, Crusaders, and Corsair IIs approaching or departing NAS Dallas.

Last of the breed to fly, the No. 3 F8U-3, 147085, heads for the runway for one of its few flights prior to program cancellation.

Navy Preliminary Evaluation

LT William Lawrence flew the F8U-3 to Mach 2 on 15 September 1958 to become the first Navy pilot to reach that speed in an aircraft designed for fleet usage. This occurred on an evaluation flight from Edwards. Lawrence was the Navy project officer for the F8U-3 at Edwards.

The results of the Navy Preliminary Evaluation (NPE) dated 9 October 1958 point out some outstanding characteristics of the F8U-3 along with major discrepancies. On the outstanding side of the ledger were control harmony, control response and feel, speed control in the approach configuration, maximum speed, rate of climb, and maneuvering capabilities at high altitudes and Mach number. On the discrepancies side were some familiar problems from F8U/J57

days: engine stall, unreliable afterburner light, and erratic nozzle operation. In the flying qualities area: inadequate stall warning, ineffective speed brakes, poor transonic acceleration, and slow acceleration on a military-rated thrust takeoff. A couple of interesting notes about the cockpit: the stick is too far aft, lateral motion is restricted by pilot's leg, and having to shut off the air-conditioning to be able to close the canopy.

In a departmental correspondence 28 November 1958 R. C. Blaylock compared the performance of the F8U-3 and the F4H. The maximum speed comparison was Mach 2.1 for the F4H and Mach 2.44 for the F8U-3. Rate of climb at Mach 2.0 at 35,000 feet was 15,000 feet per minute for the F4H and 31,500 feet per minute for the F8U-3. He went on to write: "The maximum world's speed record is 1,404 mph held by the F-104. The F8U-3 can attain 1,588 mph. The speed record is relatively straightforward to do on the F8U-3. It probably could be accomplished in 3 to 4 weeks from the initiation of the program. The current world's altitude record held by the F-104 is 91,249 feet. The F8U-3 should be able to achieve an altitude of about 96,000 feet. This latter record, however, is more difficult to do because of engine stall and equipment problems."[90]

Loss of Contract

The competition between the F8U-3 and the McDonnell F4H had been extremely close, with hard-fought arguments by both sides on capabilities, performance, and especially cost. The F8U-3 was an excellently performing program with outstanding performance. In the end, the Department of Defense news release brought the bad news for the F8U-3 program. "McDonnell's F4H-1 wins Competition for Navy All-Weather Fighter." The decision came down to the two engines, a radar operator, and fleet experience with all-weather airplanes having a radar operator given an advantage over a single-pilot airplane.

The F8U-3 program was extinguished with three aircraft built and two partially assembled airframes still on the production line. 146340 had flown 132 flights, 146341 (No. 2) had flown 49 times, and 147085 had flown only 9 times by the time cancellation of the program occurred. The last CVA flights of the F8U-3 delivered the No. 1 and No. 2 aircraft to NASA Langley, the No. 3 aircraft was delivered to NASA Moffett. The unfinished No. 4 also went to Moffett, by rail, for spares support of No. 3, and No. 5 went to Langley by rail for the same purpose.

The second F8U-3 undergoing maintenance between flights at Edwards with the radome and various access panels open.

The first F8U-3 banking away from the camera, headed into history asking, "what if" the F8U-3 had won the competition and entered production with or instead of the F4H?

An overhead photograph of an F8U-3 later in the test program, when the effects of sun exposure and flight testing can be seen on the dayglow surfaces.

Chapter 9

MODERNIZATION

A beautiful in-flight color study of RF-8G 146898. After service this aircraft was displayed at the USS Alabama memorial in Mobile, Alabama, until damaged by Hurricane Katrina. Subsequently it was saved from scrapping by the Fort Worth Air Museum, where the aircraft is proudly displayed today.

As successful as the Crusader was in the late 1950s, the demands of a new war dictated that a series of upgrades and improvements be made to the design as the F8U's missions expanded to include photo reconnaissance and electronic countermeasures (ECM) operations. A more powerful engine generated the need for additional control surface area, and the Crusader now sported rakish ventral fins among other visual changes and enhancements.

Designations Change

BUWEPS INSTRUCTION 13100.7 dated 18 September 1962 changed the aircraft designations to a system shared by all United States Armed Forces to avoid confusion. The BuAer's decade's old system incorporating a unique letter for the manufacturer was now abandoned.

The NATC-assigned F-8E 149218 moves toward a catapult during a test aboard ship with an inert load of Zuni rockets mounted on the fuselage "Y" pylons.

F-8E 149218, nicknamed "The Mad Bomber," is towed on USS Forrestal (CV-59) during carrier testing with a load of 2,000-pound bombs and Zuni rockets.

Crusader Designation Changes

Old Designation	New Designation
F8U-1	F-8A
F8U-1D	DF-8A
F8U-1E	F-8B
F8U-1KD	QF-8A
F8U-1P	RF-8A
F8U-1T	TF-8A
F8U-2	F-8C
F8U-2N	F-8D
F8U-2NE	F-8E

Modification Program

The F8U series was one of the first to undergo major modifications to increase service life. Previously, fighter aircraft had a life span aboard ship of 5 to 7 years with replacements in development on a regular basis. The original 4,000-hour life was surpassed by a large percentage of the fleet. As aircraft became more technologically advanced, expensive, and lacking significant changes in technology, they could be used longer, provided there was sufficient airframe life remaining. The potential for upgrading in the F8U was a tribute to the foresight of the men who designed the aircraft and negotiated with the Navy on the original day fighter proposal back in 1952–1954.

During the mid-1960s, with the increasing involvement in the Vietnam War, the U.S. Navy decided to retain several of its Essex/Ticonderoga–class carriers, notably the USS *Shangri-La*, USS *Intrepid*, USS *Hancock*, USS *Ticonderoga*, and USS *Oriskany*. To equip the Air Wings, which would man these carriers, the service life of many of the Crusader aircraft would have to be extended. CVA was asked to develop a remanufacturing program for various models of the F-8 to replace fatigue-critical structural components, focusing on the wing and nose landing gear, along with any other components that had reached the limits of their service life. In addition, various navigational, fire control, and communications system were upgraded, and electronic countermeasures systems (ECM) were added.

Pendant and hold back cables are tensioned; 149218 is ready for launch from USS Forrestal.

A good view of the pendant and catapult as 149218 taxis into position for hookup.

A nice view of 149218 being readied for launch. Note that the "Y" pylons are not symmetrical due to the in-flight refueling probe on the left side of the aircraft.

The F8U-1P (RF-8A) was the first Crusader model to be introduced into the mod program in early 1965. A group of 53 aircraft were refitted with a new wing, which included the "hard points" for carrying wing stores and external fuel tanks. With the increased thrust came increased speed, and ventral fins were added to provide the required directional stability at the higher speeds. The increase in available electrical power from the larger generator enabled additional camera configurations and electronic countermeasures (ECM) systems. The first of the modified RF-8A J57-P20 engines, with their constant-speed drive and 20-kva generator aircraft, were re-designated RF-8G. The first flight was 31 August 1965. A second group of 20 additional RF-8As were modified during 1968–1970. The RF-8Gs would undergo several modification and service life extension programs. These would include reconnaissance system upgrades, higher-thrust engines, landing gear improvements, and electronic countermeasures upgrades to keep them viable into the 1980s.

The next group of F-8s to enter modification at CVA were the F-8Ds, which began modification in July 1967. Again the modifications featured a new, 4,000-hour wing fitted with weapons carrying hard points. Additional rework for individual aircraft was performed as required to bring modifications and repairs up to date.

The most extensive modifications were made on the F-8E. These aircraft were modified and re-designated as F-8Js. The Navy elected to modify 136 of their -E aircraft to add the BLC system after the success of the French Navy F-8E(FN). This required modification to the wing and the UHT

The moment of truth as 149218 nears the end of the deck during the weapons carriage carrier qualifications. UHTs are set full nose up.

Modified Airplanes		
Model	Quantity Modified	Model Re-Designation
RF-8A	73	RF-8G
F-8A	6	F-8M
F-8B	61	F-8L
F-8C	87	F-8K
F-8D	89	F-8H
F-8E	136	F-8J

ALQ-31 ECM jamming pod while being tested on RF-8G 145622. Not normally a test aircraft, 145622 has the test nose cone and boom installed.

One of the upgrades to the RF-8 series was the addition of a hardened wing with a pylon-carrying capability. In addition, they were wired to carry the ALQ-31 jamming pod. Here is a close-up of an ALQ-31 during carriage testing of RF-8G 145622.

A rarely used wing pylon and the ALQ-31. It is also interesting to note that the jet kept its VFP-62 markings, with the exception of the tail code, during the trials.

VMCJ-2 RF-8A 145632 was one of a small handful of RF-8As to be field modified with ventral strakes.

RF-8G 146889 of VFP-63 arriving at Grand Prairie for a rework visit.

The first F-8J conversion rolling out for its first flight. The light reflects off the different panels, having been exposed during paint stripping as part of the rework process.

149203 looking better in a fresh coat of paint and engaged in weapons testing of the new attack capabilities incorporated in the F-8J.

The double-droop leading edges are on display along with the 2,000-pound bomb on the wing weapons pylon.

The first F-8J, 149203, taking off with 300-gallon drop tanks. This capability was added to the F-8J Crusaders only.

An aerial view of the flight line during F-8J modernization. The line is shared with factory-fresh A-7 aircraft waiting for engines, shades of the F7U-3 days.

RF-8G 144608 awaiting a test hop on the Vought ramp with a slight problem: The BuNo on the right fuselage identifies the aircraft as 146408, which was an F9F-8T. Considering all the Project Bullet attention this aircraft received upon induction into the modernization program, this is interesting.

The aft section of RF-8G 145632 after an overhaul visit to Vought. The AFC 512 ECM antenna is located on the vertical after the removal of the bulky forward-fitted ALQ-51 antennas.

The forward fuselage of RF-8G 145632. In addition to the stencils, the modification to the hot air exhaust for the oil cooler is visible behind the fuselage star. This was an area of constant erosion and heat damage. Many units painted this area black to mask the discoloration caused by the heat.

surfaces. The guidance system for the Bullpup missile was also installed on the upper surface of the wing center section and covered with a low-profile fairing. However, the Bullpup missile was never used by operational F-8 squadrons.

Finally, in December 1968, the program got under way to modify F-8B/C aircraft into F-8L/K models. The modification of these aircraft was less extensive than the F-8E's and included a new, 4,000-hour wing with the ability to carry underwing stores, and revised cockpit lighting to improve the night operation characteristics. The F-8K models were fitted with ventral fins for increased directional stability, but the F-8L were fitted with only the fuselage attach fittings, which would permit the future installation of ventral fins if a more powerful engine were to be installed later.

RF-8K

In 1967, as the RF-8A/G modernization was beginning, a proposal for an RF-8K was submitted to the Navy by Vought. The proposal offered to remanufacture a sufficient number of RF-8As and F-8As into RF-8K configuration. The major differences between the RF-8G and RF-8K were the addition of data annotation on the film, infrared sensor, autopilot, and direct lift control onto the RF-8K.

The front view of an RF-8G showing the clean lines of the design. The viewfinder window can be seen under the nose along with the number one camera station under the air intake.

Conversion from the Two Different Base Aircraft	
RF-8A to RF-8K	**F-8A to RF-8K**
Fuselage Structural Improvements	Fuselage Structural Improvements
Ventral Fins	Ventral Fins
New Wing Center Section	New Wing Center Section
Hard Harness Wiring	Hard Harness Wiring
Permanent Installation APN-153	Permanent Installation APN-153
Extended Service Life	Extended Service Life
IRAN	IRAN
Autopilot	Autopilot
Shoehorn	Shoehorn
Direct Lift Control	Direct Lift Control
Data Annotation	Data Annotation
Infrared Sensor	Infrared Sensor
CSD Electrical System	CSD Electrical System
Camera Station Modernization	Manufacture New Nose and Front Sections (FWD of Station 423.5)
	Rework and Revise Equipment From Removed Sections

The remanufacturer would add 10 years or 3,000 hours of fatigue life to the fuselage, surfaces, and systems. The hard harness wiring would reduce maintenance man hours and increase reliability. The Constant Speed Drive (CSD) electrical generator would be engine-driven rather than the air turbine drive used in the F-8.

CVA was looking for a 60-aircraft contract with an $88,792,700 price tag. If the go ahead was given by 1 October 1967, the first delivery would take place in January 1969.

Final mention was given to a "Super K" proposal that added F-8H/J improvements in a new airframe that would be delivery ready in 24 months. Other improvements included the more powerful J57-P20 engine, Philco DPD-2 side-looking radar, AN/APQ-116 forward-looking radar that was becoming operational in the A-7A, and F-8J nose and main landing gear. Neither proposal was extensively studied by the Navy nor encouraged for further development.

RF-8G 145613 after modernization at Vought. Included in the updates was the AFC 497 Part III Shoehorn "B" antenna fairing on the leading edge of the vertical.

RF-8G 41 landing with the EPP extended during a flight test.

RF-8G "146408" (144608) taxiing during a post-modernization Vought test flight prior to final paint touchup.

145625 landing after a Navy acceptance test flight at NAS Dallas after modernization.

Chapter 10

PAPER AIRPLANES

"If it looks right, it flies right," as the saying goes, and if this mock-up of the V-507 looks strangely similar to Grumman's F-14 Tomcat, that's because it was developed to meet the same fleet requirements. Hence, the V-507 became Vought's entry in the fighter competition that led to the F-14.

Adding advanced features and expanded capabilities are part of any operational military aircraft's career arc, although some of the more radical design studies never leave the company's drawing boards. Among those for the Crusader were an all-weather attack version, a two-place strike variant, and a supersonic interceptor that could carry a large air-to-air missile armed with a nuclear warhead.

V-400

The V-400 was a proposal to incorporate an all-weather capability into the F8U series. The aircraft would be armed with Raytheon Sparrow air-to-air missiles and either the Aero 11B or Aero 19A fire control system. The rocket pack would be removed and the space utilized for Sparrow fire control electronics. The aircraft would have

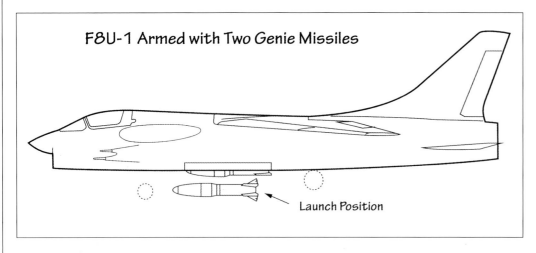

F8U-1 Armed with Two Genie Missiles

Launch Position

Tommy Thomason drawing of the Ding Dong installation proposed on the V-400 (F8U-1).

version commenced. The V-400 was an F8U aircraft with modifications to the fire control and electronic systems to accommodate the Sparrow III missile system and all-weather operation. The changes required by the Sparrow III missile system were compatible with the equipment needs of "Ding Dong." Ding Dong is one of the code names for the Douglas MB-1 Genie nuclear armed air-to-air missile. The MB-1 carried a 1.5kT nuclear warhead and was an unguided missile with a range of about 6 miles. The MB-1 became operational with the United States Air Force in 1957. The MB-1 was part of the standard armament on the F-101 and F-106 interceptors for the USAF.

Vought published their engineering study (Report Number 9784) in April 1955. To enable maximum speed and range the MB-1s were to be installed semi-recessed in the area previously occupied by the under-fuselage rocket pack. Required changes also would be to remove two of the guns and ammunition to help maintain the airplane's center of gravity, the speed brake, and electronics for the Sparrow missile that were to be located in the rocket-pack cavity on the V-400. A four-bar parallel linkage would displace the missile down 27 inches and forward 17 inches in preparation for firing. The linkage had a hydraulic actuator capable of deploying the missile up to, and including, the maximum speed of the aircraft.

been equipped with strengthened attach points on the forward fuse-lage sides for Sparrow carriage.

In response to a request by the Bureau of Aeronautics, a feasibility study of the installation of "Ding Dong" on the F8U all-weather

The takeoff gross weight for the V-400 was to be 25,947 pounds. With the Ding Dong modifications the gross weight grew to 27,616 pounds. The maximum speed at 35,000 feet at combat thrust

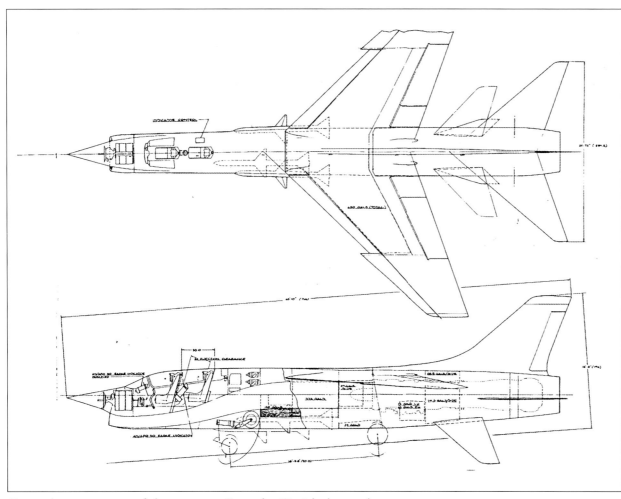

General arrangement of the two-seat Crusader III with the tandem-seat arrangement.

setting was Mach 1.53 for a clean V-400 and Mach 1.44 for an aircraft loaded with Ding Dong missiles. At 50,000-foot combat thrust the maximum speed dropped from Mach 1.25 to .99. The combat ceiling for the V-400/Ding Dong combination was 200 feet less than the projected clean V-400 ceiling of 43,500 feet. At combat thrust the V-400/Ding Dong combination was projected to reach 51,800 feet, about 1,800 feet lower than the clean V-400.

The report concluded that "the installation of Ding Dong rockets on the F8U configuration is feasible with appropriate fire control modifications. Since space provisions were made in the V-400 airplane for either the Aero 11B or Aero 19A fire control systems, the installation of Ding Dong rockets, should they be desired, would be a straightforward addition."

V-401 Two-Place Configuration

In 1955 a study was conducted of weight and performance penalties associated with a two-place configuration versus the single-seat configuration. Two twin-seat configurations were considered in this study, a tandem and a side-by-side arrangement. For the study the wing area was adjusted to maintain a 130-knot approach speed, three-hour combat air patrol cycle, and strength of 6.5 g.

The tandem arrangement had the smallest impact on performance but the largest weight penalty because of the fuselage length increase. The fuselage length increase also drove a need for more fuel, which increased the fuselage area with the fuel tanks and increased cruise drag. The side-by-side arrangement was lighter in weight but had a greater impact on performance. A maximum speed of Mach 1.99 (versus Mach 2.2 for the basic F8U-3) was all that was possible, and the maximum ceiling reduced to 49,600 feet (versus 55,000 feet for the basic F8U-3). The blunt-nose cross section increases fuselage drag, causing the reduction in performance. An additional penalty to the addition of another seat is the need for additional thrust to maintain performance.[91]

V-401 DF Day Fighter

Armament changes to the V-401 DF consisted of removing the Sparrow III missiles, the radar continuous wave injection, range interlock computer, and launch rails. The primary armament for the V-401 DF is the Sidewinder missile. Four fixed-fin Sidewinders were carried in a semi-submerged fuselage weapons bay as an alternate armament. They were mounted on rail launchers that extended and retracted by a parallelogram launching mechanism. The four Sidewinders of the primary armament were folding fin versions that were carried fully in the fuselage in a box container that the front end lowered into the airstream like the original F8U-1 rocket pack.

This same Sidewinder arrangement was offered on the F8U-3 all-weather fighter as well. The avionics for the V-401 DF would essentially be the same as the all-weather variant except for removing the APN-22 radar altimeter and the Black Maria IFF system. The radar system would be the AN/APQ-50, the same radar that equipped the all-weather airplane, except that the CW injection and range interlock computer would not be needed in a Sparrow-less weapons configuration.

Space was also being provided for infrared tracking equipment as it was in the V-401 all-weather airplane. This equipment, under development at the same time as the airplane, would allow for passive search and Sidewinder aiming. It could also be used against a target that dives for low altitude to avoid radar detection.[92]

F8U-3 "V" Versatility

A report was written in March 1958 in an attempt to sell the F8U-3's ability to perform a multitude of roles and not lose its all-weather fighter capabilities. The highlights of the report were multi-mission capability with the ability to perform the missions of several airplane types with one type. It would offer simplified logistics, having fewer types of airplanes to support aboard ship. The baseline fighter capabilities advertised were: three Sparrow III, four Sidewinders, and two MB-1 Genies or special missiles up to 850 pounds. The added capabilities included one 2,000-pound special weapon and two anti-radar Corvus missiles.

Other attack missions could utilize 1,000- and 2,000-pound bombs, Bullpup missiles, Zuni rockets, and gun pods. For special missions, photo and ALQ-55 radar mapping pods, Elint pods, and external fuel tanks could be carried. Even with the attack and reconnaissance loadings the top speed at 35,000 feet remained more than Mach 2.1.[93]

F8U-3F

The external configuration of the F8U-3F was the same as the basic F8U-3. The addition of the Reaction Motors XLR-40-RN-2 rocket engine on top of the fuselage below the rudder required an increase in the width of the dorsal and fin fairings. The internal changes included oxidizer tanks in three locations: forward mid-fuselage, forward rear fuselage, and lower aft mid-fuselage for a total of 385 gallons.[94]

V-413 All-Weather Fighter

CVA was informally requested to provide the F8U-2 with all-weather fighter capability. This was envisioned as an interim design for the period of 1958–1962. By that time a true all-weather fighter like the F8U-3 would be operational with the fleet.

The design philosophy of the Model V-413 was to provide the best all-weather capability possible, using proven existing equipment and with minimum change to the basic F8U-2 configuration. This was accomplished by replacing the APS-67 "limited search"

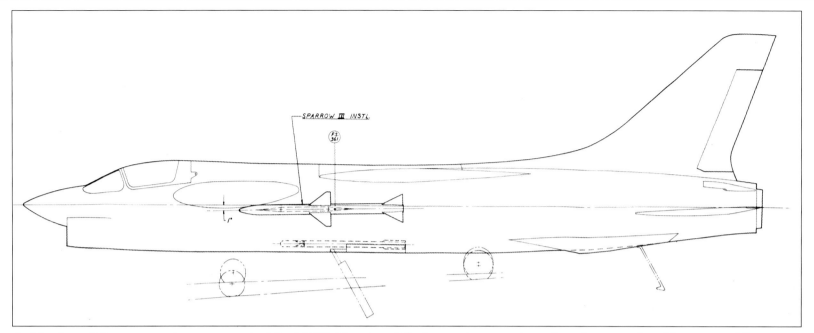

A side view of the armament arrangement of the V-413. The aircraft features a larger radome for a better radar, side-mounted Sparrow III missiles, and folding fin Sidewinder missiles in the former rocket pack location.

radar with the APG-51B all-weather radar and by adding two Sparrow III missiles on fuselage pylons.[95] The 20mm guns and ammunition of the F8U-2 were removed. The V-413 all-weather airplane had an all-missile armament. It was armed with two Sparrow III missiles, mounted externally on fuselage pylons, and two folding fin Sidewinder missiles carried in a missile pack (former rocket pack). In an overload condition the missile pack could carry two additional Sidewinder missiles for a total of four.

To incorporate the Sparrow III missile firing system into the V-413, the Hughes AN/APG-51B Radar, Raytheon AN/APA-127 CW Injection Radar, and AN/ASE-1 Missile Launching Set were squeezed into the F8U-2 airframe. The only changes to the airplane lines were the fuselage forward of the windshield bulkhead. The nose was extended 7 inches and the nose lines were re-faired to provide space for the APG-51B radar. The proven F8U-1 inlet and duct configuration was retained and pilot vision over the nose, though slightly reduced, was entirely adequate.

The Sparrow III system had been in flight test for 9 months and with many successful firings. The changes to the F8U-2 cockpit were minimal. On the main instrument board the APG-51B radar scope replaced the APS-67 scope. Changes were made to the armament control panel for Sparrow missile carriage. The other major changes to the cockpit were the addition of radar controls for the APG-51B radar set to the left-hand console and removal of the APS-67 radar controls.

The AN/APG-51B radar could be used to enhance firing Sidewinder missiles by the scale of the radar presentation. A radar target could be placed within +/– 1 degree of the aircraft armament datum line by use of this presentation. This was well within the field of the

Target Presence Indicator (TPI), a small infrared detector that evaluates the infrared potential of a target. When the TPI indicated proper infrared signal amplitude and alignment, Sidewinders could be fired.[96]

The internal arrangement of the V-413 airplane was identical to the F8U-2 with a couple of exceptions. The APG-51B radar was installed in the nose and gun compartment areas. The APS-67 radar, four guns, and ammunition were removed. This allowed equipment located immediately forward of the main fuel cell to be moved, making space for a 30-gallon fuel cell installation. Some fuselage structural improvements were added to support the external Sparrow III missile pylon installations.

Maintenance access to the APG-51B was accomplished by removing the nose radome and sliding the equipment forward on rails. Radar and missile equipment installed in the former ammunition and gun compartments was accessible through existing access doors. The V-413 added only 600 pounds to the takeoff gross weight over that of the F8U-2 while adding significant capability.

V-1000 International Fighter

The V-1000 was proposed as a candidate for the U.S. Air Force International Fighter Aircraft (IFA) competition. The competition was in response to widespread deliveries of the MiG-21 to client states of the Soviet Union. Countries aligned with the United States needed a high-performance fighter that was easy to fly and maintain.

The V-1000 was designed to exceed all mission requirements. The proven air-to-air combat capabilities of the F-8 Crusader combined with lighter weight by over 3,800 pounds and switching,

A model of the V-1000 in the colors of the South Vietnamese Air Force.

ironically, to the J79 engine. The General Electric J79-GE-17 engine was selected for its worldwide support, a result of its use in the F-4 Phantom.

The J79 engine was smaller than the J57, allowing for a better fit into the airplane. The engine size allowed for ease of access to accessory gearbox-driven pumps and generators. The engine weighed 950 pounds less and had reduced fuel consumption compared to the J57. Wing folding and aerial refueling were omitted due to the aircraft being land-based; most envisioned countries that would benefit from the V-1000 did not have aerial tankers.

Several improvements were made to increase the reliability of the hydraulic system, including steel flex hoses and an improved hydraulic pump. The electronic countermeasures (ECM) system and radar would be removed. In the avionics system, off-the-shelf components would be utilized to further ease logistical support and commonality. Aluminum skin panels would replace those that were currently magnesium to increase maintainability. Only two 20mm guns would be supplied in a weight- and complexity-reducing move.

The change of engine negated the need for the aft fuselage cooling scoops. Internally, a 45-inch extension to the engine air intake would be required because the J79 engine is shorter in length. To increase subsonic maneuverability the leading edge droop setting was -4 degrees, -3 degrees more than the standard F-8. More than 300 hours of testing was performed in the Vought Air Combat Simulator in support of the proposal.

The competition was fierce as the contract potential meant a steady flow of work for many years to come. After a couple months' delay and considerable speculation, Northrup was awarded the IFA contract on their F-5A-21 design. On 20 November 1970, the F-5A-21 was redesignated the F-5E. Newspaper reports at the time stated that the Pentagon had been under heavy pressure from Chairman L. Mendel Rivers of the House Armed Services Committee to undertake the project. It was also reported that General John Ryan, Air Force chief of staff, had wanted a hotter airplane than the F-5A-21. Ryan's recommendation was overruled by Air Force Secretary Robert Seamans Jr. Reports also indicated that the V-1000 had won the Air Force competition three times. David Packard, deputy defense secretary, opted for the less capable but cheaper-to-build F-5A-21, overruling the Air Force recommendation. LTV fought the decision in the court of public opinion but failed to cause any change to the contract award.

Attack Crusaders: V-395 All-Weather VFA Airplane

A description of the fighter/attack aircraft (VFA) concept is presented in the design philosophy report of September 1954: "A new class of military aircraft is the fighter-attack type. Attack airplanes need higher performance and greater radius of action to be fully effective in the delivery of special weapons."[97] The report goes on to describe the need for supersonic speeds to attack heavily defended targets to reduce the time the attacking aircraft is vulnerable to the defenses. In

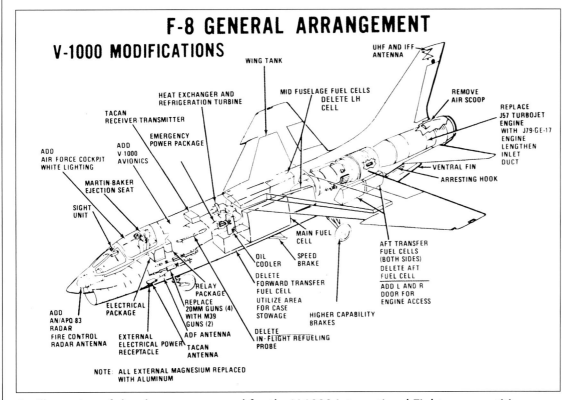

An illustration of the changes proposed for the V-1000 International Fighter competition.

the VFA concept the aircraft could also be used to defend the fleet by having the ability to intercept enemy aircraft by performing combat air patrol at greater distances from the carrier as attacking aircraft speeds increase. Greater endurance was identified as a need in the fighter role.

The design objectives for the V-395 were as follows:

- High supersonic speed while carrying special weapons to decrease the enemy's reaction time and ability to intercept. Estimated maximum speed carrying a special weapon was Mach 1.44.
- Proper equipment for rapid and effective bomb delivery to minimize time for target identification and weapon delivery. A mapping radar, internal navigation, and a dive/toss bombing computer all were planned to support this objective.
- Radius of action while carrying a special weapon of between 700 to 800 nautical miles. As a fighter the radius of action was projected at 640 nm; as a special weapons carrier it was 750 nm.
- Fighter performance should not be compromised significantly as to enable the V-395 to compete effectively with contemporary fighters. The top speed as a fighter was Mach 1.51 and combat ceiling was 52,500 feet.
- The airplane should have the versatility to perform many types of missions by carrying a wide variety of air-to-ground weapons: bombs, rockets, napalm, Bullpup, and special weapons. In the air-to-air role, 20mm cannons, Sidewinders, Sparrows, and unguided rockets would be carried.
- Satisfactory carrier suitability basically mirroring all the OS-130 specifications for C11 catapults, Mk 7 arresting gear, and 130-knot approach speed. Operating from Midway class carriers, the USS *Hancock* and USS *Forrestal*.

- Low cost and rapid development by taking advantage of the basic design from the F8U along with equipment and power plant from that program. The benefit of the wind tunnel testing done to support the F8U-1 coking request will be realized on the V-395.
- Development and growth potential as the V-395, sharing the same basic arrangement as the F8U with the opportunity to install new engines, avionics, and other technological improvements as they are brought to the fleet.

The V-395 design was developed while the first two XF8U-1 aircraft were being assembled and was presented in September 1954 when the first flight of the XF8U-1 was still six months away.

The V-395 configuration was nearly identical to the F8U day fighter, taking advantage of the work done to support that airplane. New features on the V-395 included the semi-submerged stores cavity in the lower fuselage and boundary layer control for the wing and flap leading edges. Interestingly, the same "coking" that was resisted in the XF8U-1 design was now to be utilized by adding fuselage bumps just fore and aft of the wing. It was estimated this would reduce drag by approximately 14 percent in the Mach 1 to 1.2 range.

The V-395 proposal was discussed with the chief of the BuAer. In that September 1954 discussion interest was expressed in a two-seat version of the V-395. CVA submitted Engineering Report 9571 "Study of a Two-Seat Arrangement of the V-395 Airplane" in December 1954; however, the proposal went no further.

V-456 Attack Crusader

In September 1961, CVA considered an attack version of the F8U-2N (V-455) with folding wing tips, double nose wheels, nose

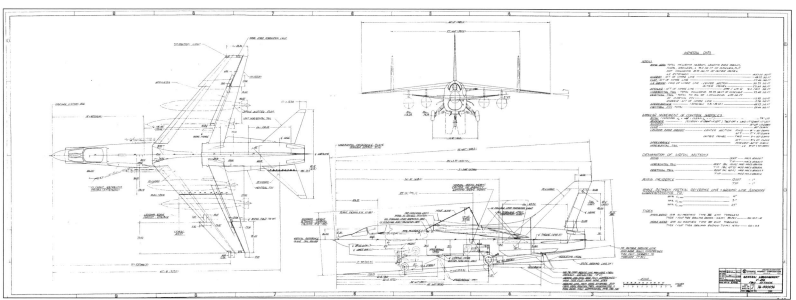

The general arrangement of the V-456 Attack Crusader, Vought's attempt to sell an interim attack aircraft. See end papers for enlarged detail. (76-000056)

tow catapult system, and two seats. However, with a J75-P-20 engine the performance of the aircraft was disappointing and the design went onto the shelf. In 1962 the Navy released a requirement for a carrier-based attack aircraft with all-weather and supersonic performance to replace the Douglas A-4 Skyhawk. CVA had conducted a number of limited war studies with an eye toward future weapon procurement needs during the early 1960s. Using the research information and studying the requirements of the VAX (Heavier than Air, Attack, Experimental) requirements, CVA developed an interim solution to the problem. A VAX winner would require a number of years to develop and improved attack capability was needed at that time.

CVA sensed an opportunity in 1962 and accelerated development of a proposal called the V-456 "Attack Crusader." The V-456 was presented to fill the gap until the winner of the VAX aircraft competition could come on line in the 1968–1969 time frame. The V-456 was based on the F8U-2NE fitted with a larger wing that had two external stores stations under each wing. To enable the design to reach production in a short time and reduce cost, the existing -2NE fuselage and tail assembly were used.

The 25-square-foot-larger wing was required to carry heavier weights and retain the desired approach speeds. The new wing sweep was only 37 degrees versus the 42 degrees of the standard F8U-2NE. The wing was also a little thicker to increase fuel capacity and structural strength. The aircraft was strengthened to 7.33 g and a fatigue life of 3,500 hours. To further enhance the performance of the new wing, full leading edge double-droop flaps and 57-percent span trailing single-slotted flaps were utilized.

The stroke of the main and nose landing gear was increased to compensate for the greater weight of the design. The weapons load was to be a maximum of 6,282 pounds loaded on the four wing and two fuselage external load stations.

The V-456 retained only two of the original four cannon. The two cannons were mounted on the left side of the fuselage; the right side was taken up by an avionics bay. Two versions of the V-456 were proposed: an all-weather attack airplane and a fighter with attack capability. The all-weather attack version of the aircraft was equipped with an AN/APN-149, AN/APQ-94, or AN/APQ-89 radar. The fighter with attack capability was to be equipped with the AN/APQ-94 radar.

The V-456 was scheduled for fleet deliveries 22 months after go-ahead or 6 months after first flight. A couple of features were offered for possible incorporation. The first was nose gear catapulting incorporating twin nose wheels and a tow bar and hold back socket, features to become mainstream in the near future. The second feature offered was a deceleration parachute installation like that used on the TF-8A to reduce landing distances when the airplane was shore-based.

A major accident data comparison of the F8U-2/2N versus projected information for the V-465 showed four accidents per 100,000 hours for the F8U-2/2N and only three accidents per 100,000 hours for the V-465.

Artist's concept of the V-456 Attack Crusader along with a couple of other Vought products, the C-142 and the Gamma Goat Army transport.

A low-speed wind-tunnel model of the V-456 carrying bombs under the fuselage along with four wing-mounted stores locations.

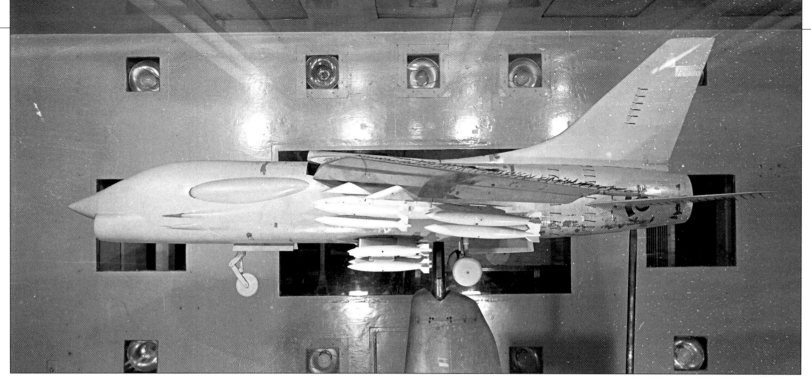

A side view of the low-speed wind-tunnel V-456 model loaded out with bombs.

A side view of a V-463 Attack Crusader model. This version features eight wing-mounted and two fuselage-mounted weapons stations.

VAL (Heavier than Air, Attack, Light) competition that started in 1963.

V-463 Attack Crusader

The V-463 was CVA's answer to the Navy's request for a proposal for a VA(L) light attack airplane. The F-8 design as a basis, hardware and program experience to reduce costs, and the desire for an early delivery to fleet squadrons were drivers of the V-463 design.

To meet the requirements of the VA(L), the V-463 is a single-seat, carrier-based light attack airplane. Compared to 17,580-pounds empty weight for the F-8E, the V-463 weighs 14,296 pounds. A non-afterburning Pratt & Whitney TF-30 was the engine chosen to power the V-463. An innovative change from the airplane's Crusader heritage is the ability to change the engine without jacking or removal of the aft section. The V-463 did not need a variable-incidence wing to meet its performance requirements. The aircraft was shortened approximately 10 feet in length by a shorter intake duct and the removal of the afterburner section.

Utilizing a lower fuel consumption turbofan engine enabled the V-463 to operate long distances with an internal fuel volume of 1,500 gallons. Heavy loads could be carried on two fuselage stations

CVA proposed the V-456 to the BuAer on 29 June 1962 as an interim to the VAX. Interest and discussions with the Navy continued late into 1962 with discussion around the projected long take-off distance of 5,000 feet for the land-based version. CVA requested a higher-thrust engine from Pratt & Whitney (J57-P-20A) for the V-456. With the TFX decision expected soon, a decision on the V-456 was not expected anytime soon.

A study by the Navy about the VAX requirements determined the cost for going supersonic was not going to equate to greater survivability. The VAX competition was canceled and replaced with the

for Sidewinder missiles along with eight under-wing pylons that could carry a variety of weapons loads. In addition to the external loads, two MK 12 20mm guns were carried internally.

The avionics system required to make the V-463 an effective attack aircraft was extensive. It included delivery circular error point (CEP) computation, internal navigation, and terrain-following radar for low-altitude flight. The avionics compartments were waist high mounted on the fuselage sides, accessible through large quick-latch doors. Potential future improvements included a digital central computer, Doppler inertial navigation, and cockpit-mounted heads-up display.

The V-463 also adopted the new nose tow catapulting capability with twin nose wheels and a launch bar and holdback fitting. The basic F8U design was now evolving into a single-place attack

The V-463 and F-8E models, giving a comparison of the size and shape differences between the two aircraft.

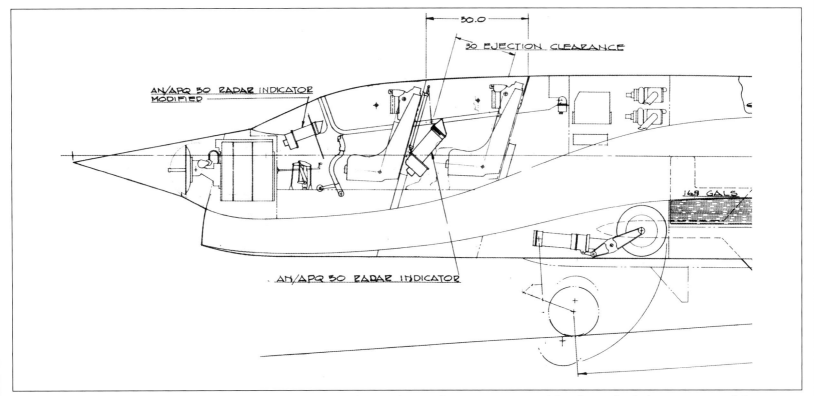

Close-up of the interior arrangement of the two-seat Crusader III. This configuration was used for the strike fighter variants of the F8U-3 as well.

airplane, first for the U.S. Navy and later the USAF and Air National Guard, the A-7 Corsair II.

F8U-3 Advanced II Two-Place Strike Aircraft

The last known proposal utilizing the F8U-3 design was a concept for a two-seat strike fighter aircraft in the 1967–1968 time frame. The

Comparison of F8U-3 and V-507 ADV				
	F8U-3	**F8U-3 ADV I**	**F8U-3 ADV II**	**V-507 ADV**
Engine Scale Factor	J75-P-6 1.0	GE1/10FB2 1.09	P&W STF-304A-21 1.61	GE1/10FB2 1.0
Combat Weight (lbs)	30,578	31,186	29,163	47,268
Loading (SW/ SPARROW/RD)	0/3/0	2/0/600	0/4/0	0/4/0
Mach Sea Level 35,000 Ft	1.05 2.26	1.07 2.21	1.20 2.43	1.20 2.29
Ceiling Combat Cruise	55,800 44,300	51,100 42,700	63,300 44,600	58,800 42,100
Sustained Maneu- vering g Mach 0.9 at 35,000 Ft	2.5	2.32	2.77	2.37

Pratt & Whitney F100 engine replaced the J75 in the F8U-3 ADV II. The retractable ventral fins were replaced by a two-positioned UHT; the same design was used on the V-507 VFAX (competition that led to the Grumman F-14). The aircraft also had both crew members under a single canopy like the one used on the TF-8A.

A 32-inch electronic scan radar with an advanced radar, integrated fighter-oriented avionics, and a central computer accounted for the upgraded avionics suite. Armament included four Sparrow missiles, two Sidewinder missiles, and an M61 20mm cannon. The wings were strengthened for the carriage of external stores.

The winner of the VFAX competition was Grumman's F-14 Tomcat. No production or development contracts were given to the V-507 or the F8U-3 ADV II.

LWST

Large Scale Winged Target (LWST) was an ambitious proposal in July 1988 to recycle the retired F-8 airframes to serve as visual simulators of MiG-23/27 aircraft for the U.S. Army. The remaining F-8 aircraft in storage would be brought to Grand Prairie and a new nose and inlet system installed to replicate the MiG-23/27. The "MiGs" would then be used in air defense exercises for training U.S. Army troops with man-portable missiles. This proposal never gained traction toward a contract.

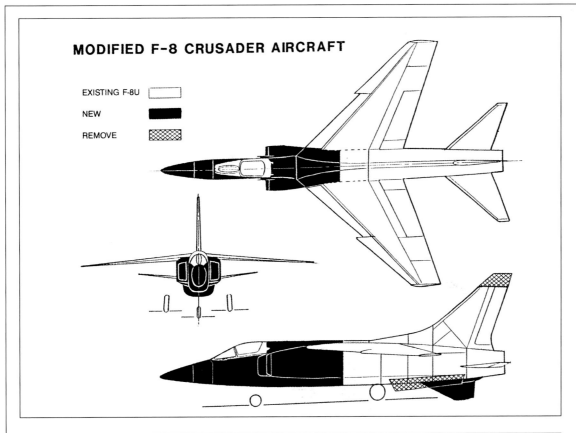

MODIFIED F-8 CRUSADER AIRCRAFT

EXISTING F-8U

NEW

REMOVE

These changes to the basic F-8 create the visual illusion of a MiG-27 in flight for target training U.S. Army air defenders.

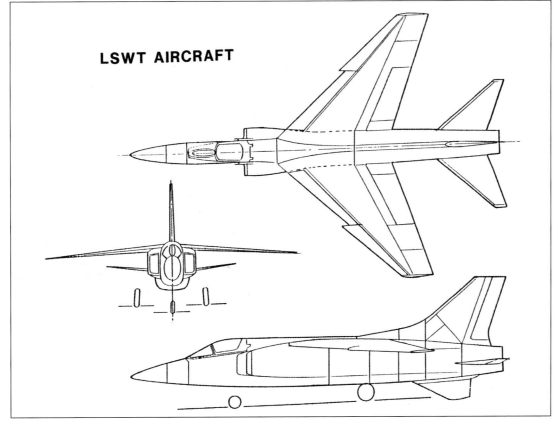

LSWT AIRCRAFT

The general arrangement drawing of the LSWT (Large Scale Winged Target) based on retired Crusader airframes.

Chapter 11

A DATE WITH NASA

A radical-looking underside view of the NASA F-8 Super Critical Wing research demonstrator aircraft showing the drastic change to the wing shape this research program evaluated. (NASA)

M any well-known military aircraft have ended their operational careers in service to the National Aeronautics and Space Administration, or NASA. The Crusader followed that proud tradition by participating in, and dramatically advancing, several new technologies. Almost every new aircraft flying today employs a digital flight control system and supercritical wing airfoil, and both revolutionary features were pioneered by F-8s flying with NASA at the Dryden Flight Research Facility (FRC) located at Edwards, California.

NASA 810 Super Critical Wing demonstrator on the ground at NASA Dryden prior to a test flight. (NASA)

Toward the end of its research career in 1973, NASA 910 picked up a sharp-looking blue and white paint scheme with a broad blue cheat line. (NASA)

The Navy had a policy of turning over an example of an early production fighter aircraft to NACA for flight evaluations and research. NACA took delivery of F8U-1 141354 on 10 December 1956 and flew it until 6 November 1958. During its time with NACA 141354 investigated variable-wing-incidence actuator loads, deflection of the fuselage under g loading, and other stability concerns.

Supercritical Wing

The high wing design of the Crusader has inspired the imagination of NASA engineers for use in aerodynamic studies and programs. One such program was the use of F-8A BuNo 141353 for supercritical wing research. Numbered NASA 810, this F-8A was fitted with a new supercritical wing that had a span of 43 feet. The slender, long-span wings changed the appearance of the aircraft uniquely with curves and a more graceful wing. This type of airfoil reversed the shape of the conventional wing by having a flat top surface and curved bottom surface. Such a wing allows an aircraft to cruise at speeds closer to Mach 1 without buffeting. NASA 810 was retired to display at NASA Dryden Flight Research Center on 23 May 1973.

New Flight Control Technology

Four F-8s went on to serve with NASA and helped bring revolutionary change to aviation. The Crusaders supported the digital fly-by-wire (DFBW) flight control system. The program had the goal of utilizing a digital computer to control an aircraft without the cumbersome control cables, push rods, and mechanisms of traditional aircraft control systems. A successful program would help aviation by providing a control system that saved weight and the

ability to stabilize an aircraft artificially with smaller control surfaces. The DFBW program started in 1969 and was supported in NASA by Neil Armstrong. It is reported he started the requests with the Navy to obtain surplus F-8 aircraft to use in the testing.

Two of the selected airframes were BuNo 145385 and 145546. TF-8A 145385 became NASA 816, which served as stock flying F-8 for practice missions and pilot proficiency. F-8C 145546 transferred

The 802 during the digital fly-by-wire research program. The conventional mechanical control system was replaced by a series of wires and computers. (NASA E73-25554)

NASA 802 and 810 in a rare formation flight over snow-covered California mountains. Both aircraft served to move the science of aviation forward in their respective research programs. (NASA E73-3495)

on 24 May 1971 to become NASA 802, the flying laboratory for the DFBW program.

An unidentified third airframe served as the "iron bird" simulator for the program. The iron bird allowed for testing of the flight hardware and systems along with acting as a flight simulator for the program pilot, Gary Krier. He would "fly" more than 200 hours in the simulator before piloting 802 on the first flight of DFBW. Modifications to the airplane included wire controls to all the flight control surfaces, Apollo flight computer interface, and two computer

systems. The first flight took place on 25 May 1972. Krier flew the Crusader off the dry lakebed and completed the first of many flights without problem.

The flight was as significant to aviation as previous X plane and other test flying but did not generate the same amount of excitement as those flights. Only a small community really understood the importance of the DFBW program. Things learned from the program enabled the control systems in the Space Shuttle, F-117, F-22, B-2, and commercial airliners.

A color image of NASA 802 in the striking white paint scheme with blue lightning bolt. Later, an A-7D was modified for further digital flight control research. (NASA ECN-3276)

The prototype Shuttle Enterprise is released from the shuttle carrier aircraft 747 NASA 905 on its fourth flight on 12 October 1977. The digital fly-by-wire F-8 did the test flying of the software to make these flights as safe as possible. (NASA ECN-8923)

Another notable achievement for NASA 802 was support of the space shuttle approach and landing test (ATL) program. The program was important because the final approach and landing for the shuttle were flown without engines, even in the 747/Enterprise flight tests. The shuttle flew at high speed and steep angles difficult for conventional aircraft to replicate. The shuttle was also designed to be a DFBW aircraft; however, a normal test program would be too dangerous and expensive to perform. NASA 802 was the perfect platform to use to reduce the risk. The software for the space shuttle was loaded into the computers aboard the Crusader. Krier would again pilot the iron bird in June of 1976 with the shuttle software installed. Finally, on 27 August 1976, a series of flights to test the software started. Gary Krier and Tom McMurtry shared

the duties of this test program. The pilot entered a code to shift the aircraft's computer program from the normal DFBW program to the ATL program.

The program was successful and led to the testing of the shuttle's backup flight system software in March and April 1977. McMurtry flew the first flight of this series on 18 March 1977. On this flight, he performed the highly demanding profile six times, all successful. The profile required the Crusader to climb to high altitude, retard the throttle to idle, and deploy the speed brake. Between 18 March and 15 April NASA 802 flew eight times to validate the software.

On 12 August 1977, Shuttle *Enterprise* was released from the 747 shuttle carrier aircraft and performed the first approach and landing test at Edwards.

EPILOGUE

XF8U-1 138899 sitting in a place of honor at the Seattle Museum of Flight. 1X went on display in 2016 after this stunning restoration was completed at Paine Field, northeast of Seattle. (Craig Wall)

The "end of the line" for military aircraft can take many forms. From disappearing into the smelters of the scrap metal dealers to becoming prized museum pieces, these aeronautical veterans find new homes in different and widely diverse venues. Some donate their valuable spare parts to keep newer aircraft flying while others support the programs of their own successors. Old soldiers may fade away, as the saying goes, but aircraft like the F-8 Crusader will always be champions, and celebrated as such for a long time to come.

The end for BuNo 147035 came in April 1972. The first F8U-2N was towed from the Vought plant to NAS Dallas, where it was

Outside the experimental hangar at Vought the 1X and 2X Crusaders sit in open storage. RF-8A 145607 has arrived for modernization and sits in the same line.

This 21 October 1961 accident helped illustrate the value of zero-zero (zero altitude, zero speed) ejection seats in the low-altitude, low-speed part of the flight envelope. Vought provided ejection seats for the Crusader until the Navy developed a relationship with Martin Baker that caused all the Crusaders to be refitted with MB ejection seats. CVA had developed low-altitude enhancements to their seats and was well capable of developing a zero-zero ejection seat before the change to Martin Baker seats was mandated by the Navy. (USN)

F8U-1 141361 on the airport operations ramp at Grand Prairie ready for a delivery flight. The speed brake is on display as it has drooped down to touch the pavement.

cannibalized for parts. The forward fuselage was returned to the structures test lab at Vought for catapult keel fatigue tests. 147035 had completed 713 test flights, accumulating a total of 882 flight hours supporting the Crusader program. In its final years of service it was utilized as an A-7 chase plane. 147035 dropped bombs from wing-mounted pylons to support the development of the F-8E and attack proposals of the F-8 design.

U.S. Navy and Marine Fighters Retire

The F-8J would serve the fleet until the final cruise by VF-191 and VF-194 in 1976. The remaining F-8H aircraft in the Naval Reserve squadrons would eventually be replaced by F-4 Phantoms in 1976. Marine Corps operations of the Crusader ended with VMFA-112 Cowboys converting to the F-4B/N in 1976. Their last example is now on display in Liberal, Kansas.

VF-32 F8U-1 on the deck of the USS Saratoga during the early deployments of the Crusader shows evidence of gun firing and the single Sidewinder rail of the -1 airplanes.

Project Bullet, now RF-8G 144608, arrives at Vought for rework prior to a visit by Senator John Glenn. The motto of VFP-63, "Eyes of the Fleet," is visible with the wing raised.

Preparing for launch, a VFP-62 RF-8G is hooked to the catapult. The smaller nose of the early Crusaders and photo birds is easily visible in this shot, along with what raising the wing does to expose more wing to the airflow.

This left the RF-8Gs and French Navy F-8E(FN)s to soldier on toward the 1980s. VFP-63 would finally cease Crusader operations in 1982 with the departure of their last examples to the Military Aircraft Storage and Disposition Center (MASDC). On 30 June 1982, the U.S. Navy's last active-duty photographic squadron VFP-63 was disestablished. VFP-63 was also the last active-duty user of any F-8 Crusader variant. The only remaining U.S. Navy Crusaders were flown by two reserve squadrons (VFP-206 and VFP-306) equipped with a handful of RF-8G aircraft, based at NAF Washington, D.C.

Last RF-8G Retired

LCDR Barry Gabler made the final landing of a Navy Crusader aboard the USS *America*. It occurred during a 16–17 Sep-

tember 1987 VFP-206 training period off the East Coast of the United States. VFP-206 would continue to operate the Crusader until the last RF-8G 146860 was retired by VFP-206 on 29 March 1987 to the Smithsonian Air and Space Museum. That aircraft flew 7,475.2 hours, including 400 hours of combat time in Southeast Asia.

PAF F-8H Retired

Philippine Air Force (PAF) F-8H Crusaders retired on 7 April 1988 after more than 10 years of service. Twelve aircraft remained in service with 7th TFS, Basa Air Base, at that time. Major Pacualito Ramos was the high time pilot with the PAF, having flown more than 2,000 hours.

The Crusader, by virtue of its short landing gear and tailhook location, would get light on the main gears during arrested landing and "stand" on the nose gear. On occasion the nose gear would fail, causing an accident. At least twice Vought performed engineering studies on the suitability of the F8U nose gear.

The nose stand landings were not limited to the fighter version of the Crusader; here photo bird 146889 of VFP-62 is light on the mains. (USN)

F8U-2 145574 assigned to VF-84 having a slight problem. The rocket pack is extended along with the speed brake while the aircraft is in the landing configuration, gear down and wing up. Looks like a speed brake change will be needed in the near future.

XF8U-1 138999 arriving back at CVA's Grand Prairie facility after completion of its 500th flight.

1X

1X has led an interesting life after retirement from CVA. 138899 flew from Grand Prairie to Dulles International Airport on 25 October 1960. It was presented to the Smithsonian Air Museum for display. Since that time, 1X has been moved to Seattle, Washington. Under the guidance of Craig Wall, 1X has been restored to her former glory and now sits fully restored inside the main gallery of the Museum of Flight.

Vought Chief Test Pilot John Konrad after the 500th flight of XF8U-1 138899.

Leaving Grand Prairie for the last time on 25 October 1960, XF8U-1 is headed for the Smithsonian Institution's Air and Space Museum in Washington, D.C., with Vought's John Konrad at the controls.

In some ways looking better than new, the 1X has been preserved and placed indoors where it can be admired for many years to come. (Craig Wall)

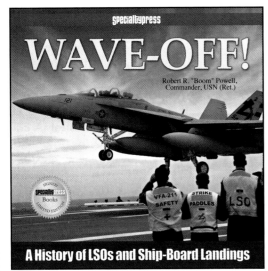
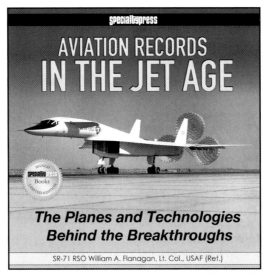

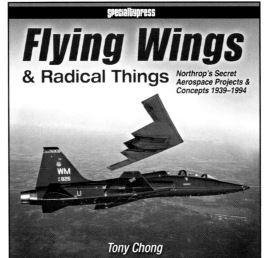
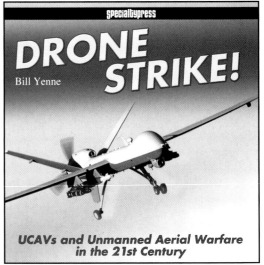

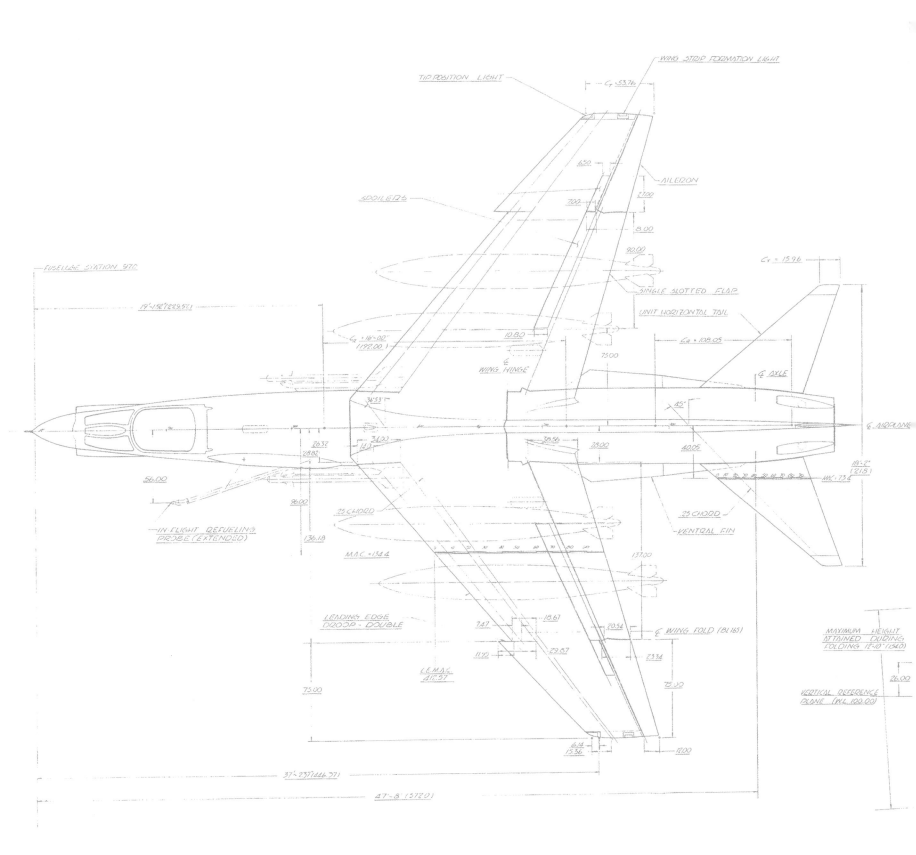